OTHER MAGE TITLES BY WILLEM FLOOR

VARIOUS IRANIAN STUDIES
Agriculture in Qajar Iran
Public Health in Qajar Iran
The History of Theater in Iran
A Social History of Sexual Relations in Iran
Guilds, Merchants, and Ulama in Nineteenth-Century Iran
Labor & Industry in Iran 1850-1941
The Rise and Fall of Nader Shah: Dutch East India Company Reports 1730-1747
Games Persians Play: A History of Games and Pastimes in Iran
Studies in the History of Medicine in Iran

THE PERSIAN GULF
A Political and Economic History of 5 Port Cities, 1500–1750
The Rise of the Gulf Arabs, The Politics of Trade on the Persian Littoral, 1747–1792
The Rise and Fall of Bandar-e Lengeh, The Arabian Coast, 1750–1930
Bandar Abbas: The Natural Trade Gateway of Southeast Iran
Links with the Hinterland: Bushehr, Borazjan, Kazerun, Banu Ka'b, & Bandar Abbas
The Hula Arabs of the Shibkuh Coast of Iran
Muscat – City, Society and Trade
Bushehr: City, Society & Trade, 1797–1947
Khark: The Island's Untold Story

TRANSLATIONS
A Man of Two Worlds: Pedros Bedik in Iran, 1670–1675
Pedros Bedik, translated with Colette Ouahes from the Latin

Astrakhan Anno 1770
Samuel Gottlieb Gmelin

Travels Through Northern Persia 1770–1774
Samuel Gottlieb Gmelin

Titles and Emoluments in Safavid Iran: A Third Manual of Safavid Administration
Mirza Naqi Nasiri

Exotic Attractions in Persia, 1684–1688
Engelbert Kaempfer, translated with Colette Ouahes from the Latin

TRANSLATIONS WITH HASAN JAVADI
The Heavenly Rose-Garden: A History of Shirvan & Daghestan
Abbas Qoli Aqa Bakikhanov

Travels in Iran and the Caucasus, 1652 and 1655
Evliya Chelebi

Awake: A Moslem Woman's Rare Memoir of Her Life with the Editor of Molla Nasreddin
Hamideh Khanum Javanshir

Mohammad Ali Mirza with two of his younger brothers;
Salar al-Dowleh is on the right.

Salar al-Dowleh

A Delusional Prince
&
Wannabe Shah

Willem Floor

MAGE PUBLISHERS

COPYRIGHT © 2018 WILLEM FLOOR

All rights reserved.
No part of this book may be reproduced
or retransmitted in any manner whatsoever,
except in the form of a review, without the
written permission of the publisher.

Library of Congress Cataloging-in-Publication Data
Available in detail at the Library of Congress

ISBN
978-1933823-96-6

Printed and Manufactured in the United States

MAGE PUBLISHERS
Washington DC
as@mage.com
Visit Mage Publishers online at
www.mage.com

Contents

INTRODUCTION IX
A RAPACIOUS GOVERNOR 1
HIS FIRST REBELLION (1904) 5
HIS SECOND REBELLION (1907) 6
    FLIRTS WITH REFORMERS TO BECOME HEIR-APPARENT 7
    REFUSES TO GIVE UP GOVERNORSHIP OF LORESTAN AND REBELS . . .10
    PLUNDERS THE NEHAVAND-HAMADAN REGION 13
    SHAH OFFERS HIS BROTHER LIFE AND PARDON 14
    SALAR AL-DOWLEH DEFEATED, INTERNED AND EXILED 18
HIS THIRD REBELLION (1910-12) 23
    SUPPORTS THE EX-SHAH'S BID TO REGAIN THE THRONE 23
    SALAR AL-DOWLEH TAKES SENNEH AND KERMANSHAH 25
    SALAR AL-DOWLEH MARCHES TOWARD TEHRAN 28
    MAKES A BID FOR THE THRONE HIMSELF 35
    DEFEATED AT BAGH-E SHAH 37
    DESPITE DEFEAT LOCAL SUPPORTERS HOLD THE INITIATIVE 38
    TAKES KERMANSHAH, AGAIN 42
    YAR MOHAMMAD KHAN EXPELS SALAR AL DOWLEH 47
    SALAR AL-DOWLEH RETAKES KERMANSHAH 50
    RUSSIA AND BRITAIN URGE SALAR AL-DOWLEH TO GIVE UP 52

  DEFEATS GOVERNMENT FORCE DESPITE GROWING QUARRELS AMONG HIS
    TRIBAL SUPPORTERS 57

  SALAR AL-DOWLEH DEFEATED; DEATH OF YEPRIM KHAN 59

  FREEDOM FIGHTERS IN GOVERNMENT SERVICE PARTLY DEFECT,
    PARTLY LEAVE 61

  SALAR AL-DOWLEH RETAKES KERMANSHAH AND LOSES IT AGAIN . . .64

  SALAR AL-DOWLEH AND YAR MOHAMMAD KHAN TRY TO
    RETAKE KERMANSHAH 69

SALAR AL-DOWLEH'S KHORASAN AND CASPIAN ADVENTURE (1912-13). 72

  FLEES TO ASTARABAD AND CALLS ON TURKMEN SUPPORT 72

  DEFEATED AT SHAHRUD, SEEKS TURKMEN SUPPORT AND
    DEAL WITH TEHRAN 74

  GOES ON LOOTING SPREE; ENDANGERS DEAL WITH TEHRAN 79

  SALAR AL-DOWLEH INVADES AND PLUNDERS MAZANDARAN 85

  MARCHES TO RASHT, DEFEATED AT TONKABON, FLEES TO KURDISTAN .88

MOVEMENTS IN KURDISTAN AND KERMANSHAH AND EXILE (JULY-SEPTEMBER 1913) 92

SALAR AL-DOWLEH'S ALLEGED ACTIVITIES DURING WW I 105

  GERMANY ACCEPTS THE HELP HE OFFERED 105

  RECALLED FROM KHANEQIN (FEBRUARY 1915); RUMORS ABOUT
    HIS RETURN 109

A FAILED SECOND CASPIAN ADVENTURE (END 1918) AND EXILE 114

SALAR AL-DOWLEH AND KHUZESTAN (1924) 119

INCURSION FROM IRAQ (MID-1925) 122

  INTRIGUE IN DAMASCUS AND FINANCIAL PROBLEMS 122

  SALAR AL-DOWLEH GOES TO KURDISTAN (APRIL 1925) 127

TRIES TO FOMENT UPRISING IN KHUZESTAN AND FAILS TO
REACH KERMANSHAH 131
FLEES, IS CAPTURED AND EXILED TO SYRIA 133

LAST INCURSION FROM IRAQ (MID-1926) 137
PREPARATION AND GOES UNDETECTED TO KURDISTAN (JUNE 1926) 137
MARCHES ON SENNEH AND IS DEFEATED 139
GENERAL BELIEF IN IRAN THAT SALAR AL-DOWLEH WAS
A BRITISH STOOGE 145
SALAR AL DOWLEH'S CAPTURE 149
CONTINUED SUSPICION ABOUT BRITISH INVOLVEMENT 151

WHERE TO SEND SALAR AL-DOWLEH? 153
RESIDENCE IN HAIFA (1926-34) 157
IRAN STOPS PAYMENT OF SALAR AL-DOWLEH'S
PENSION (JUNE 1933) 163
RESIDENCE IN ALEXANDRIA (1936-59) 169
ASSESSMENT 172

APPENDIX I 181
SALAR AL-DOWLEH'S WIVES AND CHILDREN 181
APPENDIX II 183
LETTERS SALAR AL-DOWLEH TO BRITISH KING AND BRITISH
MINISTER IN TEHRAN (20/06/1920) 183
APPENDIX III 185
SALAR AL-DOWLEH'S LETTER TO BRITISH CONSUL IN KERMANSHAH
26 MARCH 1911 185
APPENDIX IV 190
PETITION OF THE BASTIS TO BRITISH CONSUL, KERMANSHAH
26 SEPTEMBER 1912 190
ANNEX V 191

SALAR AL-DOWLEH'S DEBTS IN SWITZERLAND, 1925 191

APPENDIX VI 192

    SALAR AL-DOWLEH'S LETTER TO HIS WIFE HELEN,
    3 SEPTEMBER 1925 192

APPENDIX VII 194

    EXTRACTED FROM THE SHAFAGHI SORKH, 16 AUGUST 1926.. 194

APPENDIX VIII 197

    REPORT OF THE CONTENTS SALAR AL DOWLEH'S CAPTURED BAG,
    12 SEPTEMBER 1926 197

APPENDIX IX 199

    LETTER FROM AN EGYPTIAN AIR OFFICER TO
    SALAR AL-DOWLEH 20 OCTOBER 1926 199

APPENDIX X. 203

    SALAR AL-DOWLEH'S LETTER TO HIS SON MAJID
    8 NOVEMBER 1926. 203

ANNEX XI 204

    GOUVERNEUR-GENENERAL DU DISTRICT DU NORD, HAIFA
    3 NOVEMBER 1933. 204

ANNEX XII 207

    AL-AHRAM ARTICLE ABOUT SALAR AL-DOWLEH, 1936 207

BIBLIOGRAPHY 209

    ARCHIVES. 209

    NATIONAL ARCHIVES, KEW GARDENS, LONDON, UK. 209

    BRITISH LIBRARY/INDIA OFFICE, LONDON, UK. 210

    BOOKS AND ARTICLES 211

INDEX 216

INTRODUCTION

It was not my intention to write this study, but, in the course of my research for my forthcoming book *The History of Kermanshah*, I found many documents about activities of this rebel prince about which I had no knowledge. Because I thought, perhaps mistakenly, that others interested in the modern history of Iran might not be familiar with these events either I decided to write an article about this delusional prince. However, I had underestimated the volume of information available and therefore, before I knew it, I had written a book.

One may well question the importance and relevance of a study about this historical figure, after all this rebel prince did not have a positive impact on Iran's political discourse, its society and economy. In fact, rather the opposite was the case, for he may well have caused more damage to his country, its people, and for a longer period than his older brother, Mohammad Ali Shah. Salar al-Dowleh was able to be a serial rebel, because of the social divide and political cleavages that split Iranian society and which divisions the various political factions in Tehran had been unable to bring together. On the contrary, the reactionary forces were very strong and combative. They mainly consisted of conservative *olama*, big landowners, and tribal chiefs, in short, the old power elite who only stood to lose if the Constitutional Movement would be successful. Also, because the successive central governments in Tehran were unable to show the population at large that a constitutional government was indeed an improvement over an absolutist one, there were also still many among the ignorant masses who believed that this rebel prince, and others like him, would bring them cheap bread and less oppression. Unfortunately for them, Salar al-Dowleh only was out for himself and used all those that supported him to advance his own cause, i.e. to gain the throne of Iran and, if that was not possible, at least vast wealth. He was so one-tracked minded that even after the fall of the Qajar dynasty in 1925 he believed that he could rouse the masses against the Pahlavi upstart. This conviction of righteousness and entitlement was typical for the delusional prince from his youth until his last days, when he still addressed other people with the royal 'We.'

Thus, the phenomenon Salar al-Dowleh was but a reflection and product of these unsettled political times during which Iranian society tried to find its way toward a different and more democratic type of society. In that sense, the series of the rebellions started by this prince are as important as the debates by the various politicians in the *Majles*, because they all arose from the same unresolved dynastic, political, social, and economic conflicts in Iranian society. This is also clear from Salar al-Dowleh's 'career.' He was first courted by the freethinking Democrats, who wanted an alternative for Mohammad Ali Mirza as crown prince. They ditched him in 1907, when they changed their mind about then Mohammad Ali Shah, although Salar al-Dowleh now courted them to clear his road to the throne. After his nephew Ahmad Shah was enthroned in 1909 Salar al-Dowleh abandoned the progressive forces and tried to achieve his objective by embracing the reactionary forces in Iran. However, the tools he used in all his rebellions did not change, mainly poor tribal forces, who did not care about politics, but were out for plunder, as well as local bandits and reactionary landowners. After his final ouster from Iran in 1913, driven by financial need, Salar al-Dowleh again tried to play a role in Iran in 1914, 1918, 1924, 1925 and 1926. In none of these endeavors he was successful and he finally was exiled to Haifa (1927-1936), and, when his Iranian pension was stopped, he moved to Alexandria (1936-1959) where he died in obscurity, despite some efforts to be noticed again.

This is the first book-length study of the rebel prince, because so far only articles have been devoted to his life, be it that the majority of these articles focused on particular documents, a certain time period, or certain events, and rarely went beyond the events that took place in 1913. A few short articles give an overview of his entire life, but they are incomplete and sometimes erroneous. I have tried to read all published studies and documents as well as all unpublished documents to present you with as complete a picture as possible.

As it had not been my intention to write this book as I mentioned above, I noticed when I in fact started writing that I had overlooked certain documents in the British archives, as these were not in Kermanshah related files. I was so lucky that Nahid Assemi and Rowena Abdul Razak (London) were so kind to scan those missing documents in respectively, the India Office and the National Archives. Also, Mas`ud Rahmati (Bandar Abbas) was so kind to get me scans of articles in Iranian journals that I had no access to. I wish to thank all three of them for their kindness, for without their benevolent work I would not have been able to complete this study. Finally, I wish to thank Mr. Davood Ghajar-Mozaffari (California), Salar al-Dowleh's grandson, who provided me with information about his family and stories that his father told him, which are referenced in the text.

Top: Salar al-Dowleh standing behind his father Mozaffar al-Din Shah (on the right). Bottom: Salar al-Dowleh with his staff

A RAPACIOUS GOVERNOR

Abu'l-Fath Mirza Salar al-Dowleh (1881-1959), the third son of Mozaffar al-Din Shah (r. 1896-1907), was born on 1 November 1881 in Tabriz. His mother was Nur al-Dowleh, "a tribeswoman from Azerbaijan, quite plebeian and not particularly attractive."[1] The prince grew up and had his education in Tabriz at the *Madraseh-ye Mozaffari*, where for seven years he received a military education and had to march in the square every day. When Naser al-Din Shah (r. 1848-1896) passed through Tabriz in 1889, he made him an imperial guard and members of the Amiriyeh regiment (*fowj-e amiriyeh*). When in 1894, with his father, he came to Tehran to visit his grandfather, the latter bestowed upon him the title of Salar al-Dowleh.[2] In May 1897, Mozaffar al-Din Shah appointed his 15-year old son governor of Kermanshah. The prince-governor arrived in the city in June 1897. From the very beginning of his administration he showed himself to be totally unfit to be a governor. He had his servants kill an Ottoman merchant in the bazaar and dismissed Abdollah Khan Farrash-bashi from his function as *farrash-bashi* and *kalantar* of Kermanshah as well his brother Rahman Khan as *beglerbegi*, both experienced and wealthy members of a local elite family. These notables were not the only ones who were unhappy with the prince's behavior, so was his *pishkar* (chief executive) Hosam al-Molk who already in September 1897 resigned from his function. He was replaced by Zahir al-Molk Zanganeh.[3] Nevertheless, the official newspaper *Iran* drew a positive picture of Salar al-Dowleh as governor by

---

1. Taj al-Saltaneh 1361, p. 70.
2. Churchill 1909, p. 95; Bamdad 1347, vol. 1, p. 48; Afzal al-Molk 1361, p. 90; Ra'is-Niya 1382, p. 871.
3. Soltani 1381, vol. 4, pp. 468-69, 996; Afzal al-Molk 1361, p. 187.

reporting that every day at least one or two hours he in person was in the *divan-khaneh* to deal with government affairs.[1] However, the reality was somewhat different. In a short period, due to his immoral behavior as well as his exactions and oppression, Salar al-Dowleh had become a generally hated man. It was said that not only his rule was very oppressive, but also that no beautiful woman or girl was safe from his lust.[2] He forced holders of crown lands (*khaleseh-ye enteqali*) to sell them to him,[3] while "His exactions were so heavy that he was removed in response to the appeals made by the victims."[4] There were many meetings of those who had him removed, prominent among them was the Imam Jom`eh. On his return from Kermanshah, Eyn al-Saltaneh observed a change in the prince's behavior. Whereas before he had been friendly and polite, thereafter he was very arrogant and self-conceited. He appeared to have had a strong libido, because it was said that on his return to Tehran he employed two servants who at night accompanied him to the brothels. He had become very thin and ugly. Zell ol-Soltan, his uncle, whose daughter he was supposed to marry, was worried about this.[5]

Although his father had dismissed him after six months, because of mismanagement of his governorship, it did not stop him from appointing his son governor of Khamseh (Zanjan) (1899-1901) the following year, where Salar al-Dowleh also behaved in an unjust and oppressive manner, including the illegal and forced acquisition of prime land and properties.[6] Hajj Sayyah described one of the prince's methods to acquire money as follows:

---

1. *Ruznameh-ye Iran* 1375, vol. 5, p. 3702 (no. 920; 03/10/1897). The personal daily presence of the governor in the *divan-khaneh* or in the *talar-e hokumat* (from morning till evening) dealing with government affairs as well as that of his deputy and administrative staff, in particular the *mostowfis*, thereafter became a refrain in the reports from Kermanshah in *Ruznameh-ye Iran* 1375, vol. 5, pp. 3787 (no. 942; 31/08/1898), 3955 (no. 983; 14/11/1900), 3988 (no. 991; 20/03/1901), 3999 (no. 994; 20/05/1901), 4036 (no. 1003; 24/10/1901), 4047 (no. 1006; 17/12/1901), 4084 (no. 1105; 28/06/1902), 4108 (no. 1021; 11/10/1902). It also occurred a few times in the newspaper before that time, e.g., *Ruznameh-ye Iran* 1375, vol. 4, p. 2852 (no. 708; 04/02/1890)

2. Eyn al-Saltaneh 1376, vol. 2, p. 1231.

3. Afzal al-Molk 1361, p. 187.

4. Administration Report 1905-06, p. 46; Afzal al-Molk 1361, pp. 90, 135, 177 (return to Tehran); Sheybani 1366, p. 333.

5. Eyn al-Saltaneh 1376, vol. 2, pp. 1231-32 (whether because of this or not, the two did not marry).

6. Afzal al-Molk 1361, pp. 297; Sheybani 1366, p. 348.

Salar al-Dowleh's income from bread in Zanjan was not
less than the government of Tehran's bread income.
Governors, wherever they go, make the corrupt and the
criminals of that place their collaborators and oppress
the people. In Tehran it became known that Mirza Abu'l-
Fazl Hajji Moshir al-Mamalek Zanjani had become the
vizier and financial administrator of Salar al-Dowleh
and everybody knew that Hajji Ashraf al-Molk, who
was among the leading propertied and influential men,
kept much money in his house, and that one day they
had given money to two or three killers, who when he
returned home from government house was shot close
to his house. The next evening Salar al-Dowleh and that
same Moshir al-Mamalek under the guise of sealing
the house went there and during the day took away
all his treasury. His wife with a few children came to
Tehran and appealed to everyone, although in Tehran,
nay throughout the general public knew of this affair,
but they were not successful [in getting justice]. Salar
al-Dowleh's rule over Khamseh did not last long and
Mozaffar al-Din dismissed him.[7]

Despite the financial gain Salar al-Dowleh was not satisfied with his
small governorate and when he learned that Eyn al-Dowleh, governor
of Khuzestan, Lorestan, Borujerd and Bakhtiyari was appointed governor
of Tehran he begged his father to appoint him in his place. His son's
previous bad record did not prevent Mozaffar al-Din Shah to give in to
his son's plea and awarded him with this potentially more remunerative
appointment. From 1901-04, he was governor of Khuzestan, Lorestan,
Borujerd and Bakhtiyari and during that period, like in Zanjan, the prince
very eagerly bought crown lands.[8] In 1904, Salar al-Dowleh was dismissed from his governorship, because he had created all kind of

---

7. Hajj Sayyah p. 510; see also Eyn al-Saltaneh 1376, vol. 2, p. 1494 (the prince had taken 100,000 tumans; the Shah was so mad at him that Salar al-Dowleh thought about fleeing; finally 30 to 40,000 tumans were taken from him and given to the heirs).

8. Sepehr 1368, part 2, p. 21; Sheybani 1366, p. 376; Bamdad 1347, vo. 1, p. 48. For his activities in Khuzestan, see Nezam al-Saltaneh Mafi 1361, vol. 2, pp . 265-66,

problems, in particular with the Bakhtiyaris and the Delfan Lors. With the latter he got involved into an armed conflict in which 800 of the prince's men died, although the two sides later settled their differences by Salar al-Dowleh marrying Nazar Ali Khan Amra'i, the Delfan chief's daughter, Ziba Khanom, Salar al-Dowleh also had killed one of the leading notables of Khuzestan, oppressed many families and even raped unwed women. I leave aside here the problems that he created with the tribes in Lorestan, which led to much unnecessary bloodshed. At that time Eyn al-Dowleh had become Prime Minister and, a novelty in itself, he summoned the governors to Tehran to pay their taxes. With great difficulty Salar al-Dowleh was induced to come to Tehran in April 1904, where he complained to his father. When Eyn al-Dowleh told the Shah the particulars about Salar al-Dowleh's behavior, he became so angry that he beat his son with his own hands with a wooden stick.[9]

272-73, 305, 310, 341; Lorimer 1915, vol. 1, p. 1739. On the sale of crown lands, see Floor 1998, pp. 340-45.

9. Sepehr 1368, part 2, pp. 21, 47-48, 67-69; Bamdad 1347, vol. 1, p. 48; Nezam al-Saltaneh Mafi 1361, vol. 2, pp. 272-73, 305, 310, 341; vol. 3, p. 586; Bakhtiyari 1362, p. 258; Churchill 1909, p. 95 (in Arabistan he married the daughter of a local chief); Mo'jezi 1380, vol. 1, p. 350; Litten 1925, p. 229 (daughter of an Arab chief); Lorimer 1915, vol. 1, p. 1739; Sheybani 1366, pp. 347, 376; Mogith al-Saltaneh 1362, pp. 19, 23, 26-27, 55, 63, 72, 85, 106, 117. Sartip Kalantar Asad Khan, a rich man and a leading notable of Dezful, was tortured and mulcted by Salar al-Dowleh of 50,000 *tumans*. IOR/L/PS/20/227, 'Biographical Notices of Persian Statesmen and Notables, September 1909,' p. 11.

HIS FIRST REBELLION (1904)

That same evening, Salar al-Dowleh fled from Tehran to Khorramabad (Lorestan), cut the telegraph lines and rebelled, i.e. it was only a mini-rebellion, a kind of rehearsal for his later exploits. He was supported by a variety of Lor tribesmen. Mozaffar al-Din Shah sent some courtiers to induce his son come back, but, after he threatened to shoot them, they returned to Tehran. The Shah then sent prince Movaththaq al-Dowleh, the khvansalar (supervisor of the royal kitchen) to bring Salar al-Dowleh back. The Vali of Posht-e Kuh and the governor of Borujerd and Lorestan were ordered to see to it that Salar al-Dowleh was arrested, if they did not want to loose their head. This had the desired effect and Movaththaq al-Dowleh took the prince with him to Tehran.[10]

---

10. Sepehr 1368, part 2, pp. 21, 67, 69; Nezam al-Saltaneh 1379, p. 88; Churchil 1909, p. 95; Bamdad 1347, vol. 1, p. 48.

HIS SECOND REBELLION (1907)

For a while the prince received no new appointment. It was only on 1 April 1905, that Salar al-Dowleh became governor of Kurdistan, Hamadan, Garrus, Malayer, Tuyserkan, Khvansar and Golpeygan.[11] Apparently, Salar al-Dowleh had to go out of his way to acquire this appointment, because he had to take refuge at the door of the royal women's quarters, before his father was willing to grant him this governorship.[12] In Kurdistan he showed that he had not changed one bit and remained as oppressive, greedy and grasping as in his preceding governorships. On the day of his arrival, 5 June 1905, the leading citizens and the craftsmen of Senneh welcomed him. When he arrived at the welcoming party of craftsmen, while sitting in his coach, he ordered them to prostrate themselves before him and kiss the ground and when they did he laughed at them. When he arrived at Government House, where a group of olama was waiting to welcome him, he, without even sitting down, told them: "I am the absolute ruler (*malek al-reqab*). The Shah, my dad, has granted Kurdistan and Garrus to me. I have total control over the life and property of the people of Kurdistan. Whether I kill everyone or grant mercy to everyone nobody will question me." He

---

11. Nezam al-Saltaneh Mafi 1361, vol. 2 p. 376; Mogith al-Saltaneh 1362, pp. 87 (March 1905/Moharram 1323); Mardukh 1351, p. 232; Sepehr 1368, part 2, p. 69 gives the date as 1904 (1322 Q) and mistakenly writes that Salar al-Dowleh was the Shah's brother and only was appointed governor of Hamadan. A year later Salar al-Dowleh was appointed governor of Kurdistan and Garrus and was granted the revenues of their gaming-houses as income. Idem, p. 200.

12. Sepehr 1368, part 2, p. 140. His predecessor, Naser al-Molk, prior to leaving Kurdistan, told people "to protect themselves against the fire of his [Salar al-Dowleh's] desires." Mardukh 1351, p. 232.

then dismissed the welcoming party.¹³ After mid-September 1905, he demanded money from the rich in Senneh and beheaded a few, allegedly also Moshir al-Divan of the Vaziri family, the most important man in the province. He was the hereditary vizier of Kurdistan and Salar al-Dowleh replaced him with his own vizier, Nasir al-Molk Shirazi. He also executed the *farrash-bashi* of the previous governor, refusing 30,000 *tumans* to save his life; the man had been in function for 20 years and had amassed much wealth.¹⁴

FLIRTS WITH REFORMERS TO BECOME HEIR-APPARENT

At that time the political situation in Tehran had become tense and uncertain, due to the events that led to the granting of the Constitution. Moreover, Prime Minister Eyn al-Dowleh wanted the Shah to choose another of his sons as heir rather than Mohammad Ali Mirza and one of the candidates he considered was Salar al-Dowleh. The latter saw this as an opportunity to promote his candidacy by passing himself off as somebody who supported the Constitutional movement and get the support of the reformers. He tried to do so by giving money to help pay for the cost of the various sit-ins, asylums and what not of the reform movement. He, together with other princes and notables, secretly sent the enormous sum of allegedly 25,000 *tumans* to Behbahani and Tabataba'i, two important religious leaders of the reform movement, when in February 1905 they went in protest to Shah Abdol-Azim. Salar al-Dowleh's contribution was 400 *tumans*, which he sent via Malek al-Motakallemin, one of the stalwarts of the reform movement.¹⁵ The Constitutionalists had no faith in Mohammad Ali Mirza either and to weaken his position they thought to prop up Salar al-Dowleh as a substitute. They knew he was very ambitious, and since at that time he was governor of Kurdistan and Garrus he would be able to mobilize a large

---

13. Mardukh 1351, p. 233.
14. Administration Report 1905-06, p. 46; Political Diaries vol. 1, pp. 179, 195. According to Sepehr 1368, part 2, p. 286, he was said to have forced Moshir al-Mamalek, the vizier of Kurdistan, alone to pay 70,000 *tumans*, which suggests that he did not execute him; see also Mardukh 1351, pp. 233-34 (60,000 *tumans*; with other examples of his misbehavior).
15. Sharif Kashani 1362, vol. 1, p. 39; Nazem al-Eslam Kermani 1346, vol. 3, p. 104; Kasravi 1319, vol. 1, pp. 90-91, 121; vol. 2. pp. 89, 117; vol. 3, p. 25; Safa'i 1344, vol. 1, pp. 121, 126.

tribal force to defend the Constitution, its reform and reformers. Therefore, the Constitutionalists sent Malek al-Motakallemin to Kurdistan to invite him to join their cause, and offer him the throne when their movement was successful. Malek al-Motakallemin had been chosen as emissary, because he knew Salar al-Dowleh. Malek al-Motakallemin had become acquainted with the prince during his forced stay in Tehran (May 1904-April 1905) through his friend Nasir al-Molk Shirazi, Salar al-Dowleh's *pishkar* or chief executive. Malek al-Motakallamin returned to Tehran from Kurdistan with Salar al-Dowleh's agreement that after the preliminaries had been arranged in Tehran, the prince would mobilize the tribes in W. Iran and march on Tehran.[16] Malek al-Motakallemin went all the way to prop up his candidate for the throne, when praising in the newspaper *Tarbiyat* Salar al-Dowleh's alleged efforts to establish security on the roads, curtail criminal behavior and murder, modernizing the provincial army, establishing guard-posts (*qaravol-khanehha*) in the city as well as his personal interest to revive the court of justice (*adliyeh*) and the commercial court, where arbitrariness had been the rule for years, where justice was rendered to the people, to improve the sanitation of Sanandaj, to ban gambling dens, the use of opium, and stick dancing (*raqs-e chubi*), where Kurdish men and women, without *hejab*, were holding hands.[17] Needless to say that none of these lofty intentions were ever realized during the prince's administration. His only concrete contribution to Kurdistan was the building of the *Madraseh-ye Salariyeh*, a school for orphans.[18] The prince was so elated by this invitation from the Constitutionalists that after Malek al-Motakallemin's departure to Tehran he already believed himself the next Shah of Iran. According to his *pishkar* for his private affairs, Sadiq Akram, sometimes, in the privacy of his home, Salar al-Dowleh dressed up in a royal dress that he had made for him and put on the royal *jiqeh*. Only his close confidents would be present and he would tell them about his plans for his future kingship, constitutional government and reform laws.[19]

---

16. Malekzadeh 1329, vol. 2, pp. 32-33; Enayat 1340, p. 313; Farmanfama'iyan 1382, vol. 1, p. 240. Nazem al-Eslam Kermani was nauseated by the development of the relationship with Salar al-Dowleh. Nazem al-Eslam Kermani 1346, vol. 1, pp. 141, 222, 259; vol. 2, pp. 48, 198, 206; Kasravi 1319, vol. 1, p. 91; vol. 2 , p. 117; vol. 3, p. 25.

17. *Ruznameh-ye Taribiyat*, vol. 3, no. 372 (30/06/1323), pp. 1889-90.

18. Sepehr 1368, pt. 2, p. 298.

19. Malekzadeh 1328, vol. 2, p. 33; Enayat 1340, p. 313; Ehtesham al-Saltaneh 1366, p. 607.

According to Malekzadeh, shortly thereafter Salar al-Dowleh mobilized Kurdish tribes and raised the flag of rebellion. However, he was too hasty and was defeated by government troops, taken to Tehran and imprisoned in Eshratabad palace. From there he maintained contacts with the Constitutionalists, and when the protests started he made it known that he supported the Constitutional movement and encouraged his friends to do the same.[20] However, it seems that Malekzadeh confused some of the 1906 events with those of 1907 (see below). What really happened was that, because of Salar al-Dowleh's unjust rule and exactions in Kurdistan, people demanded his dismissal and, as a result, on 9 December 1905 he was summoned to Tehran, where he spent some time being unhappy with his lot.[21] But not for long, because in early 1906, Farmanfarma resigned as governor of Lorestan and Salar al-Dowleh was appointed to that function.[22] Although the people of Borujerd had offered to pay Mozaffar al-Din Shah 30,000 *tumans* per year, if he would appoint somebody else than Salar al-Dowleh as governor, the Shah declined the offer.[23]

In Tehran, Malek al-Motakallemin represented Salar al-Dowleh's political interests, which the latter continued to boost through his largesse to the Constitutionalists. According to Dowlatabadi, at the end of the *bast* in Shah Abdol-Azim in January 1906, money was running out, but the *bastis* needed to stay a few days longer to get Mozaffar al-Din Shah agree to their demands. The expense to hold out for two more days was at least 500 *tumans*, which they did not have and thus, the *bastis* would have to leave and without a positive result. When Dowlatabadi discussed this with Malek al-Motakallemin, the latter pulled a 500 *tuman* bank note from his pocket and said "that he recently had received this from Salar al-Dowleh for such a purpose."[24] According to Malekzadeh, when the Constitutionalists were taking *bast* in the British Legation in July 1906, Malek al-Motakallemin was appointed to collect money for their upkeep, but he received rather little from the rich and wealthy in

---

20. Malekzadeh 1328, vol. 2, pp. 33-34.
21. Sepehr 1368, part 2, p. 286. He left Kurdistan on 19 December 1905. Mardukh 1351, p. 235.
22. Administration Report 1905-06, p. 40; Administration Report 1906-07, p. 39; Mogith al-Saltaneh 1362, p. 119.
23. Mo'aser 1352, vol. 1, p. 37.
24. Dowlatabadi 1336, vol. 2, p. 31; Kasravi 1319, vol. 3, p. 25.

Tehran. Therefore, he sent a message to Salar al-Dowleh about their need, who immediately sent 8,000 tumans via Sadiq Akram.[25] Unfortunately for Salar al-Dowleh, Eyn al-Dowleh dropped his plan to change the royal heir.[26]

REFUSES TO GIVE UP GOVERNORSHIP OF LORESTAN AND REBELS

In March 1907, Salar al-Dowleh refused to give up his post to Sardar Mokarram, who was appointed as the governor of Lorestan, and rebelled.[27] This was not a sudden decision, because the prince had been considering such a move for months. Already in November 1906, when his father was sick and his brother had come to Tehran, Salar al-Dowleh considered marching on Tehran with his Lors.[28] This was possible, because of his good relations with various Lor chiefs, so that when Salar al-Dowleh rebelled he indeed "was able to collect a force of Lurs who were ready to serve him, provided there was plenty of plundering and little fighting."[29] For in practice his rebellion meant that his tribal force plundered the area around Hamadan and Nehavand.[30] He mainly relied on the support of his new father-in-law and former enemy, the powerful Lor chief, Nazar Ali Khan Amra'i. Only a few months earlier he and the Vali of Posht-e Kuh had been fighting Nazar Ali Khan. Given this relationship, Salar al-Dowleh made his headquarters in Tarhan, the center of the Delfan tribe's power.[31]

Because of the use of the generic term Lors to identify a significant part of Salar al-Dowleh's supporters the impression is created as if all Lor tribes supported him, which they did not. In fact, his governorship of Lorestan was characterized by opposition of some Lor tribes to the prince. These tribes included the Beyrawands, the Judekis, the Sagwands

---

25. Malekzadeh 1329, vol. 2, pp. 72-73.
26. Kasravi 1319, vol. 2, p. 117.
27. Administration Report 1906-07, pp. 32-33, 39-40.
28. Mo'aser 1352, vol. 1, p. 151.
29. Sykes 1969, vol. 2, p. 430; Mafi 1363, vol. 1, p. 301.
30. Nezam al-Saltaneh Mafi 1361, vol. 2, pp. 219-20, 437, 476; Mogith al-Saltaneh 1362, p. 192; Nazem al-Eslam Kermani 1346, vol. 3, p. 37; Mohit Mafi 1363, vol. 1, p. 302.
31. On the socio-economic and political role Tarhan played during the last 30 years of Qajar rule, see Adinehvand 1396.

and the Mumiwands.[32] The allegiance of these tribes was flexible and one time enemies might become allies at a later stage. The case of Nazar Ali Khan Amra'i is a case in point, who at first fought with Salar al-Dowleh, but during his rebellion became his chief supporter. Amir Afkham, the governor of Kermanshah since March 1906, had sent two mountain guns to Salar al-Dowleh to use against those Lors, which guns, in 1907, during his rebellion, he used to attack government forces at Nehavand, which, ironically, were led by the same Amir Afkham. Late in the fall of 1906, the Vali of Posht-e Kuh joined Salar al-Dowleh with an armed force to subdue the rebellious Beyrawands. The joint force operated east of Khorramabad for some time, without either side gaining the upper hand. Of course, the various military activities also involved plunder. For example, Salar al-Dowleh looted 5,000 *tumans* from the Judeki tribe. In the beginning of 1907, the Vali withdrew his force.[33]

Salar al-Dowleh's rebellion resulted in clashes with government troops. Mohammad Ali Shah asked his brother to come to Tehran, but he replied that his family was in Lorestan and, moreover, he had no house in Tehran. The Shah then offered him Eshratabad palace as his residence and ordered him to come to Tehran.[34] As of that time, Salar al-Dowleh called himself Abu'l-Fath Shah Qajar and published a statement proclaiming his adherence to the Constitution. He also wrote to his supporters in Kermanshah, in particular to *Mojtahed* Aqa Mohammad Mehdi. However, the Constitutionalists in the *Majles* had second thoughts about their support for the prince, in view of his reckless and unpredictable behavior. They abandoned their Salar al-Dowleh project, because they thought that by opposing him Mohammad Ali Shah (r. 1906-1909) would be more beholden to their side and thus, they issued a statement denouncing Salar al-Dowleh's actions as rebellious. However, rather than demanding that Mohammad Ali Shah meet some of their demands, they uncritically supported him, thus strengthening his position, while unwittingly weakening their own.[35] Both the Shah and the Constitutionalists were unprepared to deal with the rebellion,

---

32. Mo'tamadi 1347, p. 218, doc. 16; IOR/L/MIL/17/15/10/5, Military Report on (SW) Persia, vol. 5, Luristan, p. 29.

33. Administration Report 1905-06, p. 40; Idem 1906-07, pp. 32-33, 39-40; Nazem al-Eslam Kermani 1346, vol. 2, p. 68; IOR/L/MIL/17/15/10/5, Military Report on (SW) Persia, vol. 5, Luristan, p. 29.

34. Mogith al-Saltaneh 1362, pp. 175, 182; Hamadani 1354, p. 275.

35. Malekzadeh 1328, vol. 3, p. 33.

initially lacking sufficient force and unity. The British estimated Salar al-Dowleh's force at 15,000 to 25,000 men.[36] A number that was much too high. According to Browne: "He had been prancing round Hamadan with a few hundred Lurs, threatening to march on Tehran and depose his brother. At last he had to be taken seriously, and an army was sent out to meet him."[37]

At the beginning of May 1907, Salar al-Dowleh's troops were marching toward Nehavand. Salar al-Dowleh wrote to prince Pasha Khan, the deputy-governor of Nehavand that he only wanted to free people from oppression and gave his word that everyone in Nehavand and environs would be safe. If one dinar was taken he would give two as compensation.[38] However, the behavior of Salar al-Dowleh's troops belied his words, because they plundered in particular the properties of Zafar al-Soltan and also killed many people. Salar al-Dowleh also had ordered the deputy-governor of Nehavand to send flour, which he did immediately.[39] The plundering was inevitable, because Salar al-Dowleh's troops were badly equipped and provisioned. To give his actions a sheen of respectability and normalcy he asked or ordered local governors and landowners to send him supplies. In one letter, he explicitly wrote that, if 50-60 *kharvars* of flour were not sent his army had to collect the flour itself, which his troops indeed did.[40] On 10 June 1907, Salar al-Dowleh wrote to Khodadad Khan, presumably a local landlord and/or deputy-governor, that some Lors had left the army camp without permission and had started plundering. He promised that they would be punished, although this foray had happened because they were hungry and had no food. "Each day five *kharvars* of flour has to be sent immediately so that the army is not hungry and goes plundering.[41] He also promised Pasha Khan, the deputy-governor of Nehavand that he would send him money for the flour that he had supplied, but it is doubtful that this ever happened, as Salar al-Dowleh wrote that at that time he was unable to

---

36. Mo'tamadi 1347, p. 204; Mogith al-Saltaneh 1362, p. 209; Mafi 1363, vol. 1, pp. 301-02; IOR/L/PS/20/211, 'Summary of Principal Events in 1907', p. 64.
37. Browne 1966, p. 142.
38. Mo'tamadi 1347, pp. 219-20, docs. 17-18.
39. Mo'tamadi 1347, pp. 208-10, doc. 3.
40. Mo'tamadi 1347, pp. 220-21, docs. 19-22.
41. Mo'tamadi 1347, p. 222, doc. 23.

do so as his army was on the move. Nevertheless, he asked for more flour for his own household.[42]

PLUNDERS THE NEHAVAND-HAMADAN REGION

Tehran gave orders to its regional governors to oppose Salar al-Dowleh, e.g. on 17 May to Mirza Abu'l-Qasem Khan, the governor of Thalatheh-Malayer.[43] On 22 May 1907, Salar al-Dowleh wrote to Amir Afkham, the governor of Kermanshah to send him 30,000 *tumans* for his own and his army's expenditures. Amir Afkham replied with excuses. Also, news reached Hamadan that the prince would come to Nehavand on 25 May and to Hamadan on 28 May. This news caused consternation, because it was harvest time and the rebel troops would trample the crops and thus, leave the poor peasants with the prospect of no grain and thus, hunger, leaving aside the destruction of other property. Moreover, the prince had again written to Amir Afkham ordering him to send 20,000 *tumans*, in which case he would not come to Hamadan. The Amir replied that he would give him 25,000 *tumans* if he would come to Hamadan. Meanwhile, Tehran had ordered Amir Afkham to mobilize 5,000 *savars*/horsemen from Khamseh province, who, together with 10,000 soldiers from Tehran and Hamadan, would join troops from Kermanshah and Hamadan to oppose Salar al-Dowleh. As a result, Amir Afkham went to La`lchin, one of Hamadan's villages, to raise troops. On 25 May, Khodabandlu *savars* already arrived in Hamadan, whom Zahir al-Dowleh, governor of Hamadan send to Nehavand, fearing that they would cause unrest and destruction to his city.[44] On 22 May 1907, Tehran repeated the order to the governor of Thalatheh-Malayer to oppose Salar al-Dowleh and provided additional information that troops from Tehran and Hamadan would come to his assistance. This clearly referred to Tehran's order to Amir Afkham. On 23 May, the governor of Thalatheh-Malayer informed Tehran that he had raised almost 3,000 troops (horse and foot). Further, that they had built barricades at Nehavand to prevent Salar al-Dowleh's force to take the town.[45] However, there was a problem

---

42. Mo'tamadi 1347, p. 224, doc. 27.
43. Mo'tamadi 1347, p. 207, doc. 1.
44. Mo'tamadi 1347, pp. 204-05.
45. Mo'tamadi 1347, p. 208, doc. 2.

with these troops; they had neither arms nor ammunition and the governor therefore, asked for both rifles and ammunition to be sent.[46] On 24 May, Zafar al-Soltan arrived with 50 men to defend his property, who erected additional barricades. He also asked Tehran for ammunition.[47] On 29 May, Tehran wired that ammunition and rifles were being sent to Hamadan and from there would be forwarded to Nehavand.[48] On 31 May, Tehran asked for news and confirmed that ammunition and arms had been sent.[49] The governor of Thalatheh-Malayer replied that at least 3,000 men were defending Nehavand and environs. Also, 350 *savars* of the Mumiwands had defected from Nazar Ali Khan Amra'i's force and had joined the Nehavand defending force and guarded 30 barricades. He expected further tribal support of Sid Mehdi Khan, chief of the Delfan tribe, which showed that all was not well among Salar al-Dowleh's Lor supporters and that financial inducements and old feuds led to these defections.[50] By that time, Salar al-Dowleh's troops had plundered allegedly some 100,000 *tumans* in value from the properties of Zafar al-Soltan and from the Borujerd and Thalatheh governorates some two *korur* (one million) *tumans* in value. Salar al-Dowleh gathered some 2 million pounds in arms and ammunition as well as the government arsenal in Khorramabad, according to the notes of his own servant. As a result, "the people, men and women, here are crying out."[51]

SHAH OFFERS HIS BROTHER LIFE AND PARDON

Although Salar al-Dowleh wanted to claim the throne, he apparently felt uncertain about his chances to win on the battlefield, because neither

---

46. Mo'tamadi 1347, pp. 210-11, doc. 4.
47. Mo'tamadi 1347, pp. 211-12, doc. 6.
48. Mo'tamadi 1347, pp. 212-13, doc. 8.
49. Mo'tamadi 1347, p. 213, doc. 9.
50. Mo'tamadi 1347, pp. 213-14, doc. 10. The honorific *Sid* (سید) is given to a man whose mother is a sayyedeh. On the role of sayyeds in Qajar society, see Willem Floor, "Sayyeds in Qajar Iran, according to European sources." *Studia Iranica* 45/2 (2016), pp. 245-73.
51. Mo'tamadi 1347, p. 218, doc. 16. On 7 June Tehran asked whether Zafar al-Soltan had sent flour to Salar al-Dowleh, which he indeed had done. Mo'tamadi 1347, pp. 215, docs. 12, 13. In fact, Salar al-Dowleh had a secret correspondence with Zafar al-Soltan, whom he gave assurances that all would be well, that he needed good servants like him, and that he had to send [more] provisions quickly. Mo'tamadi 1347, pp. 222-23, docs. 24, 26.

the tribes of Kermanshah nor the Vali of Posht-e Kuh had joined him. However, in the opinion of Haworth, the British consul in Kermanshah the government troops at Kermanshah and Hamadan were unable to do much against him. "The only ones that can oppose him are the Kalhor and people of that ilk," he wrote on 30 June 1907. But, he added, they may as likely join Salar al-Dowleh, as they indeed did in 1911.[52] This perceived military weakness is probably why Salar al-Dowleh approached the British consul on 16 May 1907 asking him to mediate between him and his brother. The consul wrote to his Legation in Tehran, which passed on the message to the Iranian government. In reply, Mohammad Ali Shah promised his brother's safety and a pardon. This lenient attitude was partly induced by the apprehension among the government as well as the population at large about the outcome of the rebellion. For example, the prince's rebellion had caused so much anxiety and fear that people in Kermanshah were more worried about Salar al-Dowleh's activities than about domestic matters, according to the British consul. Nevertheless, because of his opposition to the government Salar al-Dowleh enjoyed some popularity among the 'popular party' in Kermanshah. As per his instructions the British consul let Salar al-Dowleh know that the Shah assured his pardon and life, if he submitted. He sent the Consular Mirza to Salar al-Dowleh's camp. On 30 May 1907, the Consular Mirza returned with Salar al-Dowleh's reaction. The prince did not actually respond to the consul's letter, but only made his demands known and said unless his demands were accepted he was not responsible for the consequences. He wrote that he did not want to return to Tehran, because he did not trust the Prime Minister, who just would serve him a cup of coffee or put his eyes out.[53] He requested the British King-Emperor to intercede on his behalf so that he might continue as governor of Luristan, Arabistan, Borujerd and Nehavand, to whose chiefs he was related by marriage. He would pay taxes and keep law and order. The prince told the Mirza that "he'd rather die fighting than go to Tehran where he would be eliminated with a cup of coffee." He showed him letters promising support from various parts of the country, among which from Tabriz with a dozen seals, because

---

52. FO 248/907, Haworth to Legation, 30/06/1907. For the changing policy of the Vali in his support or lack thereof to Salar al-Dowleh, see Chamanara 1384, pp. 95-98.

53. This refers to the alleged custom among Qajar royals to serve poisoned coffee (Qajar coffee) to kill political opponents.

the Tabrizis were afraid Amin al-Soltan, the Prime Minister, proposed taking away the Constitution; therefore they would lay the province at his feet, if he would come. He would not attack Kermanshah, because the consuls and the Imperial Bank of Persia (IBP) were there. He would plunder the area around Dowlatabad and land belonging to Seyf al-Dowleh and cut all telegraph lines. At the Consulate's Mirza's request, he promised not to cut Kermanshah's lines with Tehran and Bushehr. He would go to Nehavand, where people would pay revenues, as his force could not be supported in Lorestan, which, as long as he lived, he would not give up. A day after the Mirza met Salar al-Dowleh, a letter from the Russian consul arrived promising that the Rusian government would do its best to help him. The prince wrote a short reply saying that he trusted Great Britain as it had brought about the Constitution. He gave a similar reply to Amir Afkham and Zahir al-Dowleh, stating that he would only treat with the British. Da'ud Khan Kalhor had written the prince that he would not fight against Mohammad Ali Shah, although the general opinion in Kermanshah was that he would fight for Salar al-Dowleh.[54]

On 6 June 1907, Captain Haworth received a letter addressed to Aqa Mohammad Mehdi, who at that time had taken refuge in the British consulate, after soldiers and a mob had sacked the bazaar of Kermanshah and had attacked members of the 'Popular Party' on 2 June. The letter had been sent by Salar a-Dowleh, in which the prince asked whether the *mojtahed* had heard that one of the *Majles* members in Tehran had been killed by the opposition and why he did nothing. Haworth had received the letter by mistake, because it was in a folder with another letter that he thought was for him, brought by Salar al-Dowleh's messenger. In this letter Salar al-Dowleh asked Aqa Mohammad Mehdi to raise the religious banner and declare jihad, for without the use of force the people would not get their rights. Every able man should get a sword and don a white *kafan* of the jihad. If the Mullah did not do this then he would be worse than a Christian, a Jew, and an idolater. Salar al-Dowleh further announced that Kermanshah would be the capital of his

---

54. FO 249/907, Diarry for the month of June 1907; Administration Report 1907-08, p. 52; Political Diaries vol. 2, pp. 199, 209-10; IOR/L/PS/20/260/2, Persia no.1 (1909) Correspondence respecting the affairs of Persia, December 1906 to November 1908,' Spring-Rice to Grey 18/06/1907, p. 30 (no. 27); FO 248/907, Tel. Haworth to Tehran, 20/06/1907; Mo'tamadi 1347, pp. 222-23, doc. 24 (as long as he lived, would not give up Lorestan, Arabistan, Borujerd and Nehavand). Safa'i 1346, p. 169 (Salar al-Dowleh letter to Amin al-Soltan); Mo'tamadi 1347, p. 204, nos. 3-4.

kingdom. Finally, he wrote that he trusted that the British government would set matters straight for him otherwise he would start hostilities on the 22nd of the Iranian month, presumably 22 Khordad 1286 or 13 June 1907.[55] This appeal to Mullah Mohammad Mehdi was not haphazard, for he was the leader of the 'Popular Party' and the leading mojtahed of Kermanshah. According to Grothe, the rank-and-file of this party believed Salar al-Dowleh to be "the affable, generous royal prince, who would rap the rich and big thieves on their knuckles" and they cheered him on. People who had met him in Kangavar described him as: "an idealist, a theoretician, who lacked the knack for organization, for practical and targeted acting. In his conversations he praised Napoleon, whom he lyrically adored and whose works, he knew French well, he eagerly had studied. Also, he loved to study military technical works, above all artillery related works."[56]

On 12 June 1907, the British consul received via his Minister a letter from Prime Minister Amin al-Soltan and the Majles to Aqa Mohammad Mehdi promising Salar al-Dowleh safety and a full enquiry in Tehran or Hamadan. He had to tell Aqa Mohammad Mehdi to accept this and leave the Consulate. The prince asked two days to think; he wanted the inquiry to take place in Kermanshah and he hoped that his messengers would reach Tehran in that time to get this tabled. Indeed it worked, for Zahir al-Dowleh, the governor of Hamadan, was instructed to go to Kermanshah and investigate the matter. Salar al-Dowleh sent a second letter acknowledging that Zahir al-Dowleh and Amir Afkham had been appointed to meet him, but that he only wanted to deal with the British. He believed that the Shah and the Prime Minister were slaves of the Russians and "apparently does not believe that Great Britain and Russia are in complete agreement. I think if he gets suspicious of the English he will fight." According to Zahir al-Dowleh, when he visited Salar al-Dowleh's camp, he found he had only 1,100 men with him, one-quarter of whom were without arms, "while some had not even clothing." Salar al-Dowleh had been bluffing that he had 10,000 men and his

---

55. FO 248/907, Haworth to Legation, 06/06/1907; Stead 1908, p. 18; Administration Report 1907-08, p. 54; Political Diaries vol. 2, pp. 253-54. Haworth took Salar al-Dowleh's threat seriously and on 7 June asked troops to be sent to protect Christians, in case Salar al-Dowleh declared jihad. FO 248/907, Haworth to Legation 07/06/1907. The Russian consul Petroff also received a letter from Salar al-Dowleh, but he did not tell Haworth what was in it. FO 248/907, Haworth to Legation 30/06/1907.

56. Grothe 1910, pp. 85-87.

intention was just to get a better deal and governorship. He believed himself to be a Napoleon and a Nader Shah, reason why he believed people joined him. "The mistake he made was in imagining he had that which he has not- a character which by its own force surmounts all difficulties."[57]

SALAR AL-DOWLEH DEFEATED, INTERNED AND EXILED

Nevertheless, an earlier government force had been defeated by Salar al-Dowleh, although he had suffered losses. Fortunately, Mohammad Ali Shah was able to mobilize the Kalhor tribe under Da'ud Khan, whom he reinforced with a government force with two cannons.[58] Things had already taken a turn for the worse for Salar al-Dowleh when a caravan with allegedly 40,000 or even 80,000 tumans for him was plundered by the Kerendis. As a result, he spent one month inactively near Nehavand, which had a negative effect on the fighting spirit of his troops. When Nazar Ali Khan's men heard that their camps in Lorestan were threatened they panicked and group after group left to defend their lands. Also, the Vali of Posht-e Kuh threatened them from the west, at the Posht-e Kuh border at Qarasu river, and the Bakhtiyaris from the south of Khorramabad.[59] On 8 or 9 June there was a battle between Salar al-Dowleh and Amir Afkham's troops at Nehavand. His artillery chief did not hit anything, having been told if he did he would be beheaded later. Salar al-Dowleh, who was caught unaware by the skirmish ran to the fight, shot the artillery chief and aimed himself two shots that hit Nehavand's walls. When Da'ud Khan Kalhor arrived with 1,500 men, Salar al-Dowleh and his Lors, commanded by his father-in-law Nazar Ali Khan, Fath Lashkar withdrew to Khorramabad.[60] Despite Mirza Abu'l-Qasem Khan's insistence, the Kalhor chief refused to pursue the

---

57. Administration Report 1908, p. 57; Political Diaries vol. 2, pp. 299, 315-16; FO 248/907, Diary ending 31 July 1907. Salar al-Dowleh did not want this visit, for he wrote to Zafar al-Soltan to see to it that Zahir al-Dowleh and Hosam al-Molk remained in Nehavand; there was no need for them to come, and he would come and meet them himself. Mo'tamadi 1347, p. 205, 223, doc. 26; Mirza Saleh 1384, pp. 257, 262.
58. Mafi 1363, vol. 1, pp. 317-18, 320.
59. Grothe 1910, p. 86.
60. Mafi 1363, vol. 1, pp. 319-20, 348-49; Adhari 1378, p. 46; Kasravi 1320, vol. 2, p. 119; Administration Report 1908, p. 55-56; Stead 1908, p. 18.

Lors, who unhindered returned home.⁶¹ The news of Salar al-Dowleh's defeat was greeted with joy and in Nehavand a general illumination (*cheraghani*) was organized. It also induced various poets to write victory odes (*fathnamehs*) such as the *Salarnameh* by Afsah al-Sho`ara. Mirza Asadollah b. Shaykh Ali Akbar wrote a *mathnavi* of 341 verses extolling the role of Mirza Abu'l-Qasem Khan, the governor of the Thalatheh province, while a local poet wrote a *qasideh* of 30 verses commemorating the victorious event.⁶²

Because of his sudden movements, the British consul's letter had not reached Salar al-Dowleh. Therefore, on 13 June 1907 another letter was sent offering him a pardon. Because of all the fighting the province was unsettled and many robberies were taking place, including in the city. After his defeat Salar al-Dowleh, who had been abandoned by his Lor supporters, accompanied by one servant fled to Kermanshah and, totally unexpected, on 18 June took refuge at the British Consulate. Haworth thought that the prince had accepted the pardon, but it soon became clear that he had not received either of the two letters sent to him. Salar al-Dowleh only asked for safety of himself, his family and property as well as that of Nazar Ali Khan. The prince further told the consul that the battle was not his fault and that his letters to Amir Afkham proved that. He was expecting the arrival of the two consuls that day or the next and was actually asleep when the battle began. He also made a new demand (being allowed to leave the country to a British possession), which the consul forwarded to Tehran. The *Majles* decided that Salar al-Dowleh should be handed to the Iranian government and on 22 June at night (to safe his face) Haworth transferred him to Zahir al-Dowleh, after he had received assurances as to the prince's safety.⁶³

On 1 July 1907, Salar al-Dowleh was taken under guard to Tehran, accompanied by Seyf al-Dowleh, the ex-governor of Kermanshah.⁶⁴ He arrived there on 15 July 1907, where he first sought refuge in the house

---

61. Mo`tamadi 1347, p. 218, doc. 16.

62. Mo`tamadi 1347, p. 207.

63. Administration Report 1908, pp. 55-56; FO 248/907, Tel. Haworth to Tehran, 19/06/1907 and Idem, 12/07/1907; Stead 1908, p. 18; Mo`tamadi 1347, p. 18; Litten 1925, p. 229. From the Consulate the prince wrote a letter to the British king asking for protection for him and his family (see Appendix II). Safa'i 1348, p. 180; Mirza Saleh 1384, p. 278.

64. Administration Report 1908, p. 57; Political Diaries vol. 2, pp. 299, 315-16. For Mohammad Ali Shah's instructions, see Safa'i 1348, p. 129.

Amin al-Soltan Sadr al-A`zam. Then his mother Nur al-Dowleh went to Ayatollah Behbahani and his son Mohammad Reza Mirza to Ayatollah Tabataba'i to ask them to intercede with Mohammad Ali Shah to spare the life of respectively, her son and his father. The Shah decided to place his brother under arrest in `Eshratabad, to which palace he was transferred, on 18 August 1907.[65]

Not everybody was happy with what they considered a slap on the hand that Salar al-Dowleh received as punishment for the considerable destruction of life and property that he had caused. In the Majles several deputies demanded his execution, more spoke out against the house arrest. One of them, Aqa Sayyed Hoseyn, said:

> After all this we only offer him hospitality in Tehran? ... One of whose biggest faults is that he killed and plundered all around. He destroyed more than 20 villages. Nobody said anything. This was done based on what, what happed that he received a pardon, why was he pardoned and who did so? If the meaning of the Constitution is that one remains in prison and another with all these crimes is pardoned.[66]

Some Majles deputies also criticized the role of the British Legation in this affair. However, the British did not disagree with Aqa Sayyed Hoseyn's point of view. In fact, in June 1907, Cecil Spring-Rice, the British Minister in Tehran wrote to Grey, the Foreign Secretary that: "We are now in the position of having to protect a man who has been in open rebellion and has caused a considerable number of deaths. I think the time has come to ask the Government and Assembly to lay down some regulations as to the rights and duties connected with bast."[67] However, the Iranian government did not change or restrict the use of the custom of bast, simply because many of those who criticized the British for

---

65. Mafi 1363, pp. 317-18; Adhari 1378, p. 151; Hamadani 1354, p. 277; Grothe 1910, p. 87 (in a royal castle in the Elburz); see also Kasravi 1320, vol. 2, p. 120, according to whom Salar al-Dowleh was kept in arrest in Park-e Atabeg; In June 1908 he was kept in arrest in the Bagh-e Shah. Bashiri 1367, vol. 1, p. 258. Oral communication by Davood Ghajar-Mozaffari (04 August 2017). Sometimes, the prince was allowed to come to court to attend at official events, see, e.g., Eyn al-Saltaneh 1377, vol. 3, p. 1908.

66. Mirza Saleh 1384, p. 243.

67. FO 800/70, Spring-Rice to Grey, 22/06/1907.

having honored this Iranian custom in the past, during the coup d'etat of 1908 gladly made use of the refuge that the British Legation and its Consulates reluctantly offered. There were also those, like Azad al-Soltan, Salar al-Dowleh's younger brother, who in mid-March 1909, told the British consul in Kermanshah that he had behaved badly by handing over Salar al-Dowleh after he had sought British protection.[68]

According to Salar al-Dowleh's grandson, the officer in charge of his guards at 'Eshratabad was Reza Khan. Here the rebel-prince remained despite the fact that in January 1908 Mohammad Ali Shah formally pardoned his brother. The prince used his time to conspire against his brother, even going so far as to incite the Lors to rebel, while people like Malek al-Motakallemin considered him a royal substitute for his brother and worked to that end. According to Eyn al-Saltaneh, on 8 March 1908, the prince escaped from his house arrest, but seven days thereafter he was seized and returned to 'Eshratabad. Salar al-Dowleh then lodged a complaint with the *Majles* in which he portrayed himself as a victim and defender of the Constitution. However, the deputies were not impressed and felt that he should be executed.[69] After some time the prince was able to escape again and this time he fled to the Russian embassy. Salar al-Dowleh also asked the British for asylum, but Marling advised him against it. The Russian government promised the Iranian government that he would be kept on Russian soil, viz. in Warsaw, under police guard. In July 1908, after Mohammad Ali Shah's coup d'etat, Salar al-Dowleh was expelled to Europe. Eyn al-Saltaneh recorded that after some time in Russia, the prince was able to flee and went to France.[70] In mid-1909, Salar al-Dowleh was in St. Petersburgh receiving £1,200/year from the Russian government.[71]

---

68. Political Diaries, vol. 3, p. 568. In July 1907, Salar al-Dowleh received 150,000 *tumans* as part of the loan given by Great Britain and Russia to the government of Iran. Nezam al-Saltaneh Mafi 1361, vol. 2, p. 400.

69. Eyn al-Saltaneh 1377, vol. 3, pp. 1976, 1994; Mirza Saleh 1384, p. 624.

70. Churchill 1909, p. 95; Bamdad 1347, vol. 1, pp. 48-49; Browne 1966, p. 141; Administration Report 1908, pp. 54-56; Nezam al-Saltaneh Mafi 1361, vol. 2, pp. 441, 445, 447 (his family was still in Khorramabad at that time), 474; Hamadani, pp. 275-77; Sharif Kashani 1362, vol. 1, p. 150; Mogith al-Saltaneh 1362, pp. 207, 214, 243; Adhari 1378, p. 15; Eyn al-Saltaneh 1377, vol. 3, pp. 2211, 2354 (unknown where he is; the Russians also don't know); Idem, vol. 5, p. 3495; Adhari 1378, pp. 50-51; Mo'aser 1352, pp. 1006-07.

71. Political Diaries, vol. 3, p. 568.

Thus, since July 1908, Salar al-Dowleh spent his time in exile in W. Europe, where he was in contact with reformers who also were in exile. He traveled to Istanbul to meet with reformists such as members of the *Anjoman-e Sa`adat* asking for financial and other support to go to Iran and rise up against Mohammad Ali Shah. He promised that once he was on the throne he would be true to the Constitution. Salar al-Dowleh also contacted the Ottoman government with the same proposal, but neither interlocutor agreed to help him and he returned empty-handed to Europe.[72] On 16 July 1909, Mohammad Ali Shah was deposed and fled and went to live in exile in Odessa. Salar al-Dowleh had hoped that the Constitutionalists would offer him the throne or at least the post of Regent after the restoration of the *Majles* and the Constitution in July 1909, but they did neither. They put his nephew Ahmad Mirza on the throne and made Azud al-Dowleh his Regent. This disappointing result caused Salar al-Dowleh to abandon the cause of Constitutionalism and to embrace that of Royal Despotism.[73]

Strapped for funds and abandoned, Salar al-Dowleh tried to drum up money and support anywhere. He joined the Freemasons in Paris to get funds, and, with the help of Armenians went to Geneva to get funds. According to the *New York Herald*, he played with the idea to go the USA and marry a rich heiress and then to make a new bid for the throne. In mid-July 1910 the government in Tehran alerted all governors of border provinces to be on the lookout for Salar al-Dowleh. Indeed, in August 1910, he tried to return to Iran via Russia, but on arrival at Enzeli he was detained; he had to borrow money for his daily expenses and was sent back to Europe. In February 1911, Salar al-Dowleh even had his son Mohammad Reza ask for a reduction of his taxes due on a crown domain owned by him.[74] The government of Iran, aware of Salar al-Dowleh's financial troubles, earlier had asked the Russian Legation that Russia would not support him in case the prince tried to return. The Legation replied that it would not do so, but, given his indebtedness to the Russian Loan and Credit Bank it had an interest to preserve his property.[75]

---

72. Malekzadeh 1328, vol. 5, p. 1017; see also Adhari 1378, docs. 5 and 7.
73. Enayat 1340, p. 314; Malekzadeh 1328, vol. 2, p. 34.
74. Adhari 1378, docs. 10-12, 15-19; Afshar 1362, vol. 4, pp. 302-03, 310; Eyn al-Saltaneh 1377, vol. 5, p. 3495.
75. Bashiri 1367, vol. 4, pp. 155-56 (10/06/1910); Ra'in 1347, vol. 1, p. 648, vol. 2, p. 345. The Russian Bank had already pressed Salar al-Dowleh since April 1904 for payment and in 1910 and 1911 tried to protect its financial interests, see Mozaffar

HIS THIRD REBELLION (1910-12)

SUPPORTS THE EX-SHAH'S BID TO REGAIN THE THRONE

Meanwhile, Mohammad Ali Mirza made plans to regain the throne. In November 1910, with the Tsar's permission, the ex-Shah traveled from Odessa to Vienna, accompanied by Sho`a` al-Saltaneh, his second brother, to meet with his third brother Salar al-Dowleh to finalize the plan for his return to power. The ex-Shah, together with Sho`a` al-Saltaneh, would raise tribesmen around Astarabad, while from Ottoman territory, Salar al-Dowleh would raise Kurdish support and invade Iran. In Vienna, they discussed their plan with Hartwig, the former Russian minister in Tehran, who repeated the official Russian position that although Russia could not support them, it would do nothing against them.[76] According to Mardukh, already that same winter of 1910/11 Salar al-Dowleh came to Kurdistan. He was too late to meet with the prince, but Shaykh Hosam al-Din, who had, informed him about the planned two-pronged invasion and that the Jaf chiefs had already pledged their support to Salar al-Dowleh. It was agreed that Mardukh and the Jafs would move to take Kurdistan in early spring.[77]

Shahedi, *Tarikh-e Bank-e Esteqrazi-ye Rusi dar Iran*. Tehran: Vezarat-e Omur-e Khareji, 1381, pp. 309, 701, 716.

76. Kazemzadeh 1968, pp. 598-600; Adhari 1378, p. 75; Malekzadeh 1328, vol. 6, pp. 267-73. Arshad al-Dowleh mistakenly mentioned that they met in Odessa. Moore 1914, p. 33.

77. Mardukh part 2, p. 277.

On 18 July 1911, news was received that Mohammad Ali with some followers and plenty of arms supplied by the government of Russia had landed at Gumush Tepeh and marched to Astarabad to retake the throne. Salar al-Dowleh came from Baghdad in disguise, went to Sanandaj, convinced some tribal Khans unhappy with Tehran policy to join him and made it his temporary base of operations. Bahador al-Saltaneh Kordestani reported the prince's arrival and activities and asked for forces to be sent to oppose him.[78] There was also suspicion and some evidence that Salar al-Dowleh had received some support from the Ottoman government.[79] On 5 June 1911, from Tabriz, Nezam al-Dowleh wrote that Kurdish tribes in Ottoman territory were also involved. With 5,000 Kurds, Salar al-Dowleh was said to have arrived in Miyandoab; he was expected to arrive shortly in Maragheh to march with Shoja` al-Dowleh, the reactionary royalist governor of Maragheh, to Tabriz.[80] Already in July 1911, it was rumored that Salar al-Dowleh had taken Tabriz, "promising the people that if they would seat him on the throne, he would abolish all taxes except those necessary to supply his personal expenses."[81]

However, Salar al-Dowleh was in Kurdistan. In June 1911, he was said to have some 4,000 men in Kurdistan, where he acted totally independent.[82] At the end of June 1911, Salar al-Dowleh was in the house of Mahmud Pasha Jaf to raise troops. On 29 June he sent five letters to Moshir Divan, Asaf Divan, Hajj Mo`tamad, Vakil al-Molk and Habib Tajer informing them that with 6,000 Jafs, Mokris, Sardashtis, Sowjbulaghis, Avromans and others he was marching to Kurdistan to take vengeance on the Constitutionalists and renew respect for the olama. He gave orders that all partisans of the Constitution had to be arrested, who, after his arrival, would be punished. Also, to get the support of the Kurdish chiefs on whom he would bestow the titles of

---

78. Adhari 1378, docs. 13, 14, 20.

79. Adhari 1378, p. 18, docs. 21-22, 25.

80. Ettehadiyeh and Sa`vandiyan 1366, pp. 68, 73-74; Eyn al-Saltaneh 1377, vol. 5, p. 3452; Hamadani 1354, p. 372. Salar al-Dowleh was still believed to be in Azerbaijan in October, Idem, p. 101. In June 1911, he indeed had been in Miyan Do-Ab, Sowjbolagh and Mokri where he had discussions with local leaders, who declined to support him, after which he returned to Kurdistan. Adhari 1378, docs. 25-28.

81. Shuster 1968, p. 61.

82. Mo`ayyer al- Mamalek 1361, pp. 25, 32, 37; Eyn al-Saltaneh 1377, vol. 5, p. 3433 (merchants telegraphed not to ship goods to Azerbaijan as they were all seized).

al-Dowleh, al-Saltaneh and Sardar. He wrote that he supported the Constitution and the rights of the olama and Islam. He further wrote letters to Tehran, Kermanshah, Hamadan, Borujerd, Qazvin, Zanjan, Garrus, Soltanabad etc. The olama of Kurdistan supported him in his bid for the throne.[83] In July 1911 government forces were unable to deal with him in the Hamadan area, or rather his supporters, as he was not there yet.[84]

SALAR AL-DOWLEH TAKES SENNEH AND KERMANSHAH.

On 17 July 1911, Salar al-Dowleh took Senneh and environs and was expected to take Kermanshah thereafter. He proclaimed Mohammad Ali as Shah, himself the latter's crown prince (vali-ye `ahd) and telegraphed orders to the Majles to invite Mohammad Ali to return. The Prime Minister, Sardar As`ad immediately promised to make tribesmen available to oppose him.[85] The prince took Garrus and Kurdistan and in the name of the ex-Shah an illumination (cheraghani) was organized. The government in Tehran was paralyzed and it took one week before orders were given to take action against the rebel prince. Tehran appointed Sardar Jang and Sardar Zafar commanders of the Bakhtiyari troops who had to defeat Salar al-Dowleh, while they were also given the governorships of Kermanshah, Hamadan, Kurdistan, and Lorestan.[86] In this connection it is interesting to note that Eyn al-Saltaneh wrote in his Diary that many, including the prince's followers, expected that after taking Tehran war would break out between the two brothers, because Salar al-Dowleh was hell-bent on becoming Shah.[87]

---

83. Mardukh part 2, pp. 278-80, 289; Adhari 1370, doc. 25; Mostowfi 1324, vol. 2, p. 353; Soltani 1381, pp. 557-58.
84. Shuster 1968, p. 79, 86; on the status of the Bakhtiyari force to oppose him, see Mo`ayyer al- Mamalek 1361, p. 60, 74 (Kalhors joined). The situation in Hamadan itself was uncertain and there were riots. Adhari 1378, docs. 32-33.
85. Hamadani 1354, p. 374; IOR/L/PS/20/261/4, 'Persia. No 3 (1912). Further correspondence respecting the affairs of Persia', Barclay to Grey 17/07/1911, p. 94, (nos. 186, 187, 189); Eyn al-Saltaneh 1377, vol. 5, p. 3495. Nobody opposed the prince's entry into Senneh; in fact, he was welcomed out of fear, while rich people had already fled to save their money. Adhari 1378, doc. 31.
86. Dowlatabadi 1362, pp. 122, 126 (on 2 July 1911).
87. Eyn al-Saltaneh 1377, vol. 5, pp. 3511-12; Idem, vol. 7, p. 5599.

Salar al-Dowleh further wrote to Da'ud Khan Kalhor to join him in taking Kermanshah.[88] He also wrote to sympathizers in the city, such as the Mo`inis, viz. Akbar Khan Mo`aven-e Lashkar, Shaykh Ali Asghar, Hasan Khan Mo`aven al-Molk as well as the Hajjizadeh clan headed by Farrokh Khan Ilkhani, Hajj Hasan Kalantar, Aqa Qoli Farrash-bashi his nephew, Mo`tazed al-Mamalek, Hajj Sharif Khan Mo`tamadi and his adherents and many of the leading olama, such us Aqa Rahim Mojtahed and Aqa Mahmud, brother of Hajj Aqa Janbazi, who declared themselves for his cause. The prince also made it clear to his supporters in Kermanshah that the court of justice (*adliyeh*), the police office (*nazmiyeh*) and the telephone office had to be plundered. The prince's leading supporters met and arranged that on 11 July 1911 some ruffians and rowdies (*lutis* and *owbash*) attacked and looted these three institutions. They burnt the documents concerning taxes on salt, opium (*taryak banderol*) and gum tragacanth (*katira*). Two days before the attack governor Rokn al-Dowleh had gone to Tehran, ostensibly to prepare the defense against Salar al-Dowleh, thus leaving the field open and free to him. According to Farid al-Molk, because there was no police any longer the authorities sent the traditional executors of law and order (*gazmeh*, *a`tas* and *qaravols*) into the various city quarters.[89]

On 21 July 1911, McDouall reported that Salar al-Dowleh had wired Amir al-Mamalek, who locally was respected by all parties, that he placed Kermanshah under his control with orders to respect and protect the Consulates, keep order in the city, and convey the local authorities to Tehran, and to collect food and fodder for 7,000 horse and 10,000 foot, who left on 19 and 20 July. Several officials were threatened by the crowd and fled to the British Consulate; McDouall arranged that Amir al-Mamalek arranged their safe departure.[90] Salar al-Dowleh left Kurdistan on 24 July 1911, but before he left he sent telegrams to the acting and deputy governors to continue their duties. Meanwhile, groups from each tribe were joining Da'ud Khan Kalhor, who since 23 July was camped at

---

88. Hamadani 1354, p. 375.

89. Soltani 1386, pp. 175-77; Hamadani 1354, p. 373; Eyn al-Saltaneh 1377, vol. 5, p. 3458 (Nazar Ali Khan was plundering near Mahidasht and said he would come shortly to the city; the *adliyeh* was closed and the entire city was in uproar). According to Mardukh, he made chiefs swear on a small Qoran that he wore in his pocket. Mardukh, p. 280. On the *gazmeh* etc, see Floor 1973.

90. IOR/L/PS/20/261/4, 'Persia. No 3 (1912). Further correspondence respecting the affairs of Persia.', p. 99 (no. 207); Hamadani 1354, p. 374.

Qal`eh-ye Delgosha, 1.5 km outside Kermanshah, to support the prince.[91] On 30 July 1911, Salar al-Dowleh entered Kermanshah with 2,000 men, reinforced by 4,000 local levies, and on the next day received representatives of all classes of the population. All Tehran appointed officials had already left town which made any resistance unlikely. Those who had taken asylum in the British Consulate had left on 29 July with a safe-conduct from Da'ud Khan Kalhor. One of his main supporters, Aqa Mahmud the *mojtahed* was often in the prince's presence, who stayed in the city until 24 August.[92] Salar al-Dowleh asked Molitor, the Belgian official in charge of the Kermanshah Customs administration, to hand him the Customs revenues (representing some 60,000 *tumans*/month), who refused and referred the prince to Tehran. However, on 17 August he took more than 23,000 *tumans* from the Customs office. At that time, the Kalhor and Sanjabi chiefs were in Kermanshah as well as the Vali of Posht-e Kuh. Salar al-Dowleh ordered the merchants not to pay customs duties anymore. He also ordered Da'ud Khan Kalhor to seal the state arsenal and granary.[93] Neither the Customs revenues nor the wealth of the city's population were beyond his grasping hands, in particular the wealth of those who supported the Constitution. The prince had them tortured and forcibly exacted much money from them and others, while some were even killed. The homes and property of those who had fled, such as of Mo`tazed al-Dowleh, were plundered, sacked and sometimes even destroyed. The property plundered included their villages and flocks, while all gardens and trees were cut down, causing much misery to the poor peasants. Salar al-Dowleh's hatred for some of his enemies was such that, although they had fled, such as Mo`tazed al-Dowleh, he had the latter's brother shot and then killed in his presence.[94] In an

---

91. IOR/L/PS/20/261/4, 'Persia. No 3 (1912). Further correspondence respecting the affairs of Persia', Barclay to Grey 17/07/1911, p. 94 (no. 186); Idem, Barclay to Grey, 26/07/1911, p. 106 (no. 220)

92. IOR/L/PS/20/261/4, 'Persia. No 3 (1912). Further correspondence respecting the affairs of Persia', p. 151 (no. 319); IOR/L/PS/20/261/4, 'Persia. No 3 (1912). Further correspondence respecting the affairs of Persia', Barclay to Grey 01/08/1911, p. 118 (no. 247); Hamadani 1354, p. 374 (ass. governor and police chief took refuge), 376 (Salar entered on 4 Sha`ban or 11 August which is wrong), 377, 379; Hashimi 1389, p. 605; Eyn al-Saltaneh 1377, vol. 5, p. 3488 (the prince burnt the *adliyeh* and *nazmiyeh* offices; he hung and imprisoned some people).

93. Destree 1976, pp. 210-11; Adhari 1378, pp. 21-22 (docs. 35-36); Hamadani 1354, p. 376; Adhari 1378, docs. 35-36, 48-49; Kasravi 1350, p.188 (2 Mordad or 25 July).

94. Soltani 1386, p. 183; Vaziri 1352, pp. 49-50; Shuster 1968, p. 115; Mo`ayyer al-Mamalek 1361, p. 53, 73; Adhari 1378, p. 21; IOR/L/PS/20/261/4, 'Persia. No 3

undated telegram (probably end July-early August 1911) to Mo'azed al-Saltaneh, the Minister of Post and Telegraph, Salar al-Dowleh boasted of his large force led by Sardar Mozaffar, chief of the Kalhors, Amir Jang Vali of Posht-e Kuh and Sardar Akram Nazar Ali Khan, the latter two from Lorestan, who were marching to defend the ex-Shah's rights. Further that the Qalawands, a section of the Dirakwands, had dislodged the rebellious Bakhtiyaris in Arabistan, and that Mohammad Khan Asanlu of Zanjan with 50 *savars* had taken that town in his name.[95] On 13 August 1911 Hamadan invited the prince to come to their city, where on 24 August, led by Abbas Khan Chenari, his troops arrived.[96]

SALAR AL-DOWLEH MARCHES TOWARD TEHRAN

On 8 August 1911, Mohammad Ali Mirza, the ex-Shah sent Salar al-Dowleh a telegram asking him to hurry to Tehran, where there were only 3,000 Bakhtiyaris as defensive force; a delay might cause the ex-Shah a major problem.[97] After having filled his coffers with his ill-gotten gains, on 23 August 1911, Salar al-Dowleh accompanied by Da'ud Khan and a mix of Kalhor, Sanjabi and Jaf tribesmen (ca. 10,000 men) and 16 guns left Kermanshah into the direction of Malayer. He issued instructions and appointed a committee to look into the affairs of the people of Kermanshah and further named his younger brother Abdol-Fazl Mirza 'Azad al-Soltan governor of Kermanshah, with Mohtasham al-Dowleh as his vice-governor; Farid al-Molk was appointed *kargozar*. Before he left he sent a telegram to the *Majles*. Amir Mofakhkham Bakhtiyari, a strong supporter of the ex-Shah, who had been governor of Lorestan for some months, was ordered to oppose Salar al-Dowleh. Amir Mofakhkham left Borujerd with 2,000 men. His cousin, Sardar Zafar, who, in the beginning of August 1911, had left Tehran to Soltanabad, was to join him. However, there were doubts about the

---

(1912). Further correspondence respecting the affairs of Persia.' Barclay to Grey 12/08/1911, p.129 (no. 274).

95. Afshar 1367, pp. 2005-06, doc. 1.

96. Hamadani 1354, p. 376; Eyn al-Saltaneh 1377, vol. 5, p. 3493; Mardukh, p. 282.

97. Adhari 1378, p. 22; Mardukh, pp. 283-84 (has 5 August/9 Sha'ban as well as Salar al-Dowleh's reply and other telegrams from the ex-Shah); Kasravi 1350, pp. 189-90. There were people, such as grain owners in Taleqan, who actually liked the idea that the prince would take Tehran, because they expected the price of wheat to go up, allowing them to make more profit. Eyn al-Saltaneh 1377, vol. 5, p. 3526.

loyalty to the central government of both Sardar Zafar and Amir Mofakhkam; the latter was near Malayer by that time.[98]

After Amir Mofakhkham's departure from Borujerd, the Lors declared for the prince and joined his force, who appointed his father-in-law, Nazar Ali Khan, governor of that town. Given that situation, and the uncertainty whether Amir Mofakhkham would oppose or join Salar al-Dowleh, the defensive position of the central government in Tehran looked weak. The more so, because if Amir Mofakhkham would join him only Sardar Zafar with 500 men at Soltanabad would be between him and Tehran. From Kermanshah, Salar al-Dowleh first went to Dowlatabad and neared the position of Amir Mofakhkham. Hamadan was already in the hands of his adherents. On 12 August a group of notables had come to Kermanshah to discuss with the prince the mechanics of his taking over of the city, which his vanguard entered on 16 August. On 20 August 1911, according to Shuster, Salar al-Dowleh was said to be at Hamadan with 10,000 men and 16 cannons, which was erroneous. The ex-Shah was well informed, because indeed government forces in Tehran only numbered 3,000 men. As a result, panic broke out among the governing class in Tehran. The more so, because other sources reported even much higher numbers of the prince's troops. On 31 August 1911, Barclay reported that Salar al-Dowleh with 10,000 men intended to march to Qazvin after having taken Hamadan. Eyn al-Saltaneh remarked that the prince's soldiers "do not know any language, no Turkish, no Persian, not any other language (they are Sowjbulgahi Kurds)."[99] However, apparently Salar al-Dowleh skirted Hamadan and went to Nehavand, where his troops ravaged the villages in the city's

---

98. IOR/L/PS/20/261/4, 'Persia. No 3 (1912). Further correspondence respecting the affairs of Persia,' p. 167 (no. 366), 168 (no. 367); IOR/L/PS/20/223, 'Who's who in Persia. Calcutta: General Staff, India, 1916', p. 55; Malekzadeh 1328, vol. 6, p. 292; Dowlatabadi 1362, p. 128; Eyn al-Saltaneh 1377, vol. 5, p. 3488; Vaziri 1352, p. 57; Soltani 1381, vol. 4, pp. 562-63; Kasravi 1350, p. 189.

99. IOR/L/PS/20/261/4, 'Persia. No 3 (1912). Further correspondence respecting the affairs of Persia,' p. 167 (no. 366), 168 (no. 367); IOR/L/PS/20/261/4, 'Persia. No 3 (1912). Further correspondence respecting the affairs of Persia.', p. 152 (no. 322, 325); Hamadani 1354, pp. 378-79; Shuster 1968, p. 121; Mo`ayyer al- Mamalek 1361, p. 86, 91 (threatening telegram), 98-99; Jurabchi 1363, pp. 66 (40,000 men), 76 (30,000; Kalhors were said to have joined him); Malekzadeh 1328, vol. 7, p. 292; Dowlatabadi 1362, p. 133; Hashimi 1389, pp. 606 (doc. 9). Eyn al-Saltaneh 1377, vol. 5, p. 3494 (the prince threw a baker into his oven and the bread price dropped to 2 *shahis/man*, which made him popular with the people of Hamadan. He also arrested several people in that city). Some of the plunder of Hamadan was later sold in Tehran, for some items, see Eyn al-Saltaneh 1377, vol. 5, pp. 3571, 3574.

environs.[100] Earlier in August 1911/Sha`ban 1329, the *Majles* ordered Salar al-Dowleh to be arrested and promised to pay 25,000 *tumans* for him, dead or alive.[101] In reaction Salar al-Dowleh sent an angry telegram to the *Majles* telling the delegates that the ex-Shah and he were coming to Tehran to teach them a lesson.[102] Although Salar al-Dowleh sent a defiant reaction he was quite taken aback by this proclamation and he became ashen-faced. He wrote the telegraph operator that if this news would be spread he would hold him severely responsible for that.[103]

> To the honourable Majlis.
>
> From Kurdistan I telegraphed to you but you have sent no reply. In place of understanding that telegram and examining the state of the country and curing the diseases you have caused, you made plans to assassinate me and gave bribes to kill me, I myself have come to this country to be killed and you do not understand that honest and Godfearing Persians will not forget the 130 years of the Kajar kindness and especially in regard to the sons of the late Muzaffer-ed-Din Shah they will have no evil intentions. Therefore the Persians are my brothers and the children of the Shah who is the shadow and elect of God, and we will not act against each other, I think. This permission (to kill me) you have given to those of your own kind, it does not matter that the prayers of fifteen million Persians were and are our protection. Would my death cure the ills of the country? Your duty as God-fearing people is to put aside personal quarrels and seeking your own interests and devise something for the benefit of the country and its unfortunate subjects. As in the first Majlis they did not attend to the wishes and advice of Mohamed Ali Shah the deputies of that time acted in their own interests and were caught in

---

100. Hamadani 1354, pp. 380, 383.
101. Bamdad 1347, vol. 1, p. 48; Ettehadiyeh and Sa`vandiyan 1366, p. 88; Dowlatabadi 1362, p. 130; for the text see Shuster 1968, p. 88.
102. Adhari 1378, p. 20.
103. Mardukh, p. 282.

difficulties and for two years all Persia was in trouble and many killed and houses destroyed till finally Mohamed Ali Shah abdicated. After his abdication it was thought that all defects would be removed; but today not only Europe, Asia, and America are witness, perhaps even the African savages will not deny that affairs are a hundred times worse than before. Now I write directly some Bakhtiari sowars and some Tehran riff-raff will now restore order in Persia. For the last three months 2000 Bakhtiari sowars have failed to reduce a section of the Bairawand tribe and finally have fled to Burujird. Further the Bakhtiari themselves know that if they took Tehran it was because we were all discontented with Mohamed Ali Shah otherwise Persia would not have accepted such a thing. Gentlemen, Deputies by God you are responsible and will be for bloodshed, at the end what will be the result. In these days Mohamed Ali Shah will arrive in Tehran. I too, believe it or not, will come with 30,000 men all the way from the gates of Kermanshah to Nobaran troops are on the march. In Azerbaijan the Shah seven and in Garrus Shuja-ed-Dowleh with 3,000 sowars and as many foot, it has been ordered that they go to Tehran via Zinjan. Consider up to Tehran what destruction this crowd and sowars will cause and what will happen to the people. Grieve for the sake of the people whom you sacrifice to your interests, which by God will not profit you. Do not listen to the nonsense of the evil disposed, plan how to extricate Persia from this state of ruin, let the country have one shah one Majlis and a sound organization. Your conduct has no profit, affairs grow worse day by day till ten days if this last it will come to an end. The lord of the country will come to his throne and will give a proper organization to the State and the Majlis. It is good if this should happen through yourselves. This force which for ten days is on the march till now were in their own homes, what good or bad is part. I have not got Persia, or Customs or Bank to continually pay expenses. The expenses of this army will fall on the people. Why are you willing that these poor

people should suffer? If you wish come to the telegraph
office and I will come and talk to you and then with one
or two thousand sowars I will go to Mohamed Ali Shah
and arrange matters satisfactorily. The Shah has sworn to
show paternal kindness to all Persians after he comes to
the capital he will carry this out. If you do not reply you
do not accept me, you think you send some one to kill me
or appoint Shuja-es-Saltaneh or Sardar Muhiy to fight.
God knows this only your play and the ruin of Persia
because you fight against the designs of God. What I
write is with my whole heart, if you put aside enmity
all of you will acknowledge the justice of what I say.
Therefore, I send this telegram to try you and have send a
copy to the Consulate at Kermanshah, if no reply received
by this afternoon I march tomorrow morning. Now the
choice is with you. My wish is that the newspapers of the
world should see this telegram and know that I am not
a cause of bloodshed but that you are. I have also sent a
copy to the Mullas of Kerbela.

Salar-ed-Dowleh Kajar.[104]

Translation of a letter from Salar ed Dowleh Kajar to [Mr. Molitor], the Provincial Director of Customs Kermanshah. [Dated Kermanshah 26 August 1911.]

From the day that we occupied the province of
Kermanshah continued complaints have been received
from foreigners, from the Ottoman Consul, from
passengers, and merchants, of the road guards and
officials and bad characters on the road from the
Khaniqin border to Kangavar. Every day we enquired into
this. One thing became clear that Mu`tazid-ed-Dowleh

---

104. FO 248/1031, Enclosure in McDouall to Tehran, no. 82 of 24/08/1911. For the Persian text, see Adhari, p. 19; Malekzadeh 1328, vol. 7, p. 164. For the reply by the *Majles*, see Kasravi 1350, p. 191.

without the knowledge of the government collected a sum from the muleteers three or four thousand tomans at Qasr and on the road and farmed it out. Undoubtedly the farmer collected as much again as the original 4000 tomans and the officials as much again. Then the other bad characters on the road whom the road guards should repel the road guards having no pay exact fees under the name of safe passage ("salama ru"). There was no strong governor to put a stop to this state of affairs. Therefore now that we have taken possession of this province in order to stop this disorder and make a proper organization firstly we abolish the 4000 tomans, secondly we appoint two hundred and ten sowars under four officers from the frontier to Ain Kush, an those officers under the command of Sardar Muzaffer. Near town to Kangawar thirty men under one officer. For their pay eighteen thousand tomans has been fixed their clothing and fuel is a separate expence, because the guards must be on the road. i have arranged a place just as is done on the Enzeli-Tehran, Tehran-Khorasan, Tehran-Kerman and Shiraz Tehran-Tabriz frontier roads though each road has differences. The arrangement is as follows: each Camel one kran, horse or mule one kran, donkey half kran, to be collected at the Customs House in addition no one has the right to exact from them a single dinar from the frontier to Kangawar, should the guards take anything the government will return it. As this will not cover more than a third of the expence of the guards therefore from every half load that arrives at the Customs House the merchants must pay fifteen shahis as on the Enzeli-Tehran and Tabriz-Tehran is collected from merchandize. In this way we hope that this disorder will be stopped. We have appointed Mr. Thomas Rassam to collect this, to attend daily at Customs and collect it you must give him every assistance that he may carry out his duties.

Translation of telegram from Salar ed Dowleh Sahna.

> Through Thomas Rassam. Customs director.
> You make the collection of the road guard money
> dependant on the permission of the Central
> Administration, do not wait the reply carry out your
> orders.

[Ain Kich about 8 miles west of Kermanshah]

Mr. Rassam sent a telegram to Molitor apprising him of this order by Salar al-Dowleh, which was in contravention of art. 3 of the Customs Regulations. He added that Salar al-Dowleh in person had told him that if he did not carry out these orders he would take steps to force him to do so. The prince sent similar orders to the government of Kermanshah. 26 August 1911.[105]

Meanwhile, the Bakhtiyari government in Tehran was trying to raise a force to oppose the ex-Shah's forces. On 12 August 1911, Ja`far Qoli and Gholam Hoseyn, two Bakhtiyari chiefs telegraphed from Isfahan that they had raised 2,000 *savars*, who would hurry to the defense.[106] Only four days later the same chiefs complained that the *savars* still had not received their rations and fodder (*jireh va `aliq*), to which end 30,000 *tumans* had been promised. They themselves had expended 50,000 *tumans* to buy horses for these *savars*. The cost for rations and fodder from Isfahan to Tehran was 20,000 *tumans*. In Isfahan, the daily expenditure was 1,500 *tumans* for 3,000 *savars*.[107] The lack of funds continued to bedevil the effectiveness of the government forces, which problem was only partly alleviated by a loan from Great Britain and Russia.

Makes a Bid for the Throne Himself

On 3 Ramadan or 28 August 1911, Salar al-Dowleh learnt about the ex-Shah's defeat on 12 August 1909. Mardukh, who brought him this news told the prince: "now the field is yours, if you go forward you will

---

105. FO 248/1031, Enclosure in McDouall to Tehran, no. 82 of 24/08/1911 (English translation plus Persian text)

106. Afshar 1367, p. 2007, doc. 3 (the hijri date 16 Shah`ban = 12 August; the solar date 22 Asad = 19 August).

107. Afshar 1367, pp. 2007-08, doc. 4. The money was still not paid and the permission for a loan for 10,000 *tumans* was not given either. Afshar 1367, p. 2008, doc. 5.

hold the crown and throne." (*digar meydan meydan-e shoma ast*). This news did not discourage him, in fact he also saw this as an opportunity to advance his own claim to the throne. When the ex-Shah was still in Iran, Salar al-Dowleh had called Mohammad Ali shah and himself the latter's *vali-`ahd* or heir-apparent.[108] However, after the ex-Shah's defeat, Salar al-Dowleh made a bid for the throne for himself. He allegedly struck money with the text: *Sekkeh bar zar mizanad salar-e din - yavarash bashad amir al-mo'menin*" On the reverse side stood: al-Soltan Abu'l-Fath Shah Qajar, however, numismatists, so far, have never seen any such coin.[109] He also was seen with a *jiqeh* on his hat and in his proclamations he also styled himself 'Shah' and in his telegrams addressed the cabinet as 'Our Ministers' and the *Majles* as 'Our Majles.' On 19 September 1911, Salar al-Dowleh in telegrams to the *Majles* referred to himself as 'Our Majesty' or as He referred to himself as Salar al-Dowleh *Shahehshah-e koll-e mamalek-e Khuzestan, Lorestan va Iraq-e Ajam*, and announced that he would be in three days in Qom.[110]

On 6 September 1911, Salar al-Dowleh defeated Amir Mofakhkham in Malayer district; many arms fell into his hands, and the town was plundered. He continued to advance towards Tehran unopposed, while Amir Mofakhkham withdrew to Soltanabad, where his cousin Sardar Zafar had 500 Bakhtiyari reinforcements.[111] However, the two Bakhtiyari chiefs did not face the prince again, for on 10 September 1911, Amir Mofakhkham marched via Golpeygan and Khvansar to Bakhtiyari country and Sardar Zafar and Sardar Jang left to Qom. They had 1,500 well-armed men with them and left a bad impression because they left without a fight. As a result, the people of Soltanabad wrote to Salar

---

108. Soltani 1386, p. 183; Mardukh, p. 293.

109. Yaghma'i 1363, p. 140; Bamdad 1347, vol. 1, p. 49; Enayat 1340, p. 315.

110. Enayat 1340, p. 315; Mostowfi 1324, vol. 2, pp. 594, 598; Bamdad 1347, vol. 1, p. 50; Shuster 1968, pp. 134-35; *The New Hazell Annual and Almanack*, vol. 28 (1913), p. 305; IOR/L/PS/20/261/4, 'Persia. No 3 (1912). Further correspondence respecting the affairs of Persia.', Barclay to Grey 19/09/1911, p. 159 (no. 352).

111. IOR/L/PS/20/261/4, 'Persia. No 3 (1912). Further correspondence respecting the affairs of Persia.', Barclay to Grey 11/09/1911, p. 154, (no. 334); IOR/L/PS/20/261/5, 'Persia. No 4 (1912) Further correspondence respecting the affairs of Persia', p. 23-24 (no. 53); Adhari 1378, doc. 40; Dowlatabadi 1362, p. 138; Hamadani 1354, p. 381; Eyn al-Saltaneh 1377, vol. 5, p. 3507 (500 Bakhtiyaris were killed); Kasravi 1350, p. 190. According to Malekzadeh 1328, vol. 6, pp. 292-93, the Bakhtiyaris fought very well when attacked, but Amir Afkham, who was watching from afar, ordered his troops to withdraw as he had already decided to go some place else. However, the result was a defeat and loss of arms, which Malekzadeh ascribes to Amir Afkham's support for the ex-Shah.

al-Dowleh asking for his protection. He replied the same day, writing that if the request had not arrived he would have come with 30,000 men and 22 guns to destroy their town completely. Two days later 400 of his men occupied the town led by the well-known robber Abbas Khan Chenari. During his stay the prince collected 50,000 tumans in taxes. The poor people of the Soltanabad district were first fleeced by the Bakhtiyaris and then by Salar al-Dowleh, who appointed Seyf al-Dowleh, brother to Eyn al-Dowleh, as governor.[112] In Tehran, people, especially outspoken defenders of the Constitution such as Mo`tazed al-Dowleh, were afraid that at any moment Salar al-Dowleh would enter the city, where some 1,000 Democrats and others, who had taken rifles from the arsenal, guarded the gates, where cannons had been placed, day and night.[113]

As a result of the defeat of the Bakhtiyari force many local princes, officials and landowners believed that the central government would be defeated and therefore, to improve their future position or because they felt or were threatened, they joined Salar al-Dowleh's troops with their own men. Of course, after the prince's defeat these landowners were punished by Tehran. One of the landowners whose property was plundered by a force led by the infamous Abbas Khan Chenari, was Nazem al-Olama Malayeri, who was especially targeted, because he was an enemy of Hajji Seyf al-Dowleh, the governor appointed by Salar al-Dowleh.[114]

DEFEATED AT BAGH-E SHAH

Going around Soltanabad, Salar al-Dowleh went to Nobaran with 4,000 men intending to march to Tehran either via Saveh or Zarand. According to one source, whom Eyn al-Saltaneh believed to be lying, the prince had 20,000 men, whose column stretched for 24 km; he had a music band

---

112. IOR/L/PS/20/261/5, 'Persia. No 4 (1912). Further correspondence respecting the affairs of Persia', p. 21 (no. 51); Malekzadeh 1328, vol. 6, pp. 293-95 (in Malayer, he was joined by another 1,000 Kurds and Lors and his total force was estimated to be 30,000 strong); Mostowfi 1324, vol. 2, pp. 594, 598; Eyn al-Saltaneh 1377, vol. 5, p. 3543 (people did not know who were worse, the Lors or the Bakhtiyaris); Bamdad 1347, vol. 1, p. 50; Shuster 1968, pp. 134-35; *The New Hazell Annual and Almanack*, vol. 28 (1913), p. 305. Salar al-Dowleh received men, arms and ammunition from Amir Afshar in Zanjan. Adhari 1327, docs. 37-38.

113. Vaziri 1352, p. 53; Kasravi 1350, p. 191.

114. Hashimi 1389, pp. 605-06 (docs. 1-12).

complete with drums (*balaban*), 16 guns, and the troops were divided into seven sections. These troops launched plunder raids as far as Saveh; many looters returned home after having bagged their spoils, according to Mo`tamadi. When the prince chose the route via Saveh a combined force of 2,000 men consisting of Armenians under Yeprim Khan and Bakhtiyaris, under Sardar Mohtasham and Sardar Bahador, were sent to oppose him. The Bakhtiyaris of Sardar Zafar from Qom also joined them. The battle took place on 27 September at Bagh-e Shah, 13 km from Saveh (144 km from Tehran - between Nobaran and Qom) and Salar al-Dowleh's force of some 4,000 men consisting of Kalhors, Lors and other tribesmen were completely routed, suffering 300 deaths. The tribesmen fled, leaving their cannon, and Salar al-Dowleh, who probably was at Nobaran, fled into the direction of Hamadan. Government forces did not pursue him, although these had suffered few losses, as the Bakhtiyaris were too busy looting. Because the defeated rebel prince had only been pursued as far as Hamadan, it was feared that he might try and raise new troops, because the force that had defeated him was busy plundering, while there was complete disorder of which anyone might have taken advantage. In fact, at Salar al-Dowleh's request, Nazar Ali Khan Amra'i even aided some beleaguered supporters of the prince at Eshtrinan. It was also reported that Salar al-Dowleh had contacted Sowlat al-Dowleh Qashqa'i and Qavam al-Molk asking them to oppose the Bakhtiyaris.[115]

The total rout, first of the ex-Shah's forces, and then followed by that of his brother, meant that the only undefeated royalist force in Iran was that of Shoja` al-Dowleh in Tabriz, who, after these two defeats (Mohammad Ali and Salar al-Dowleh), became discouraged, also due to many desertions from his ranks.[116] The people of Tehran on learning

---

115. Dowlatabadi 1362, pp. 183-87; Vaziri 1352, p. 53; Kasravi 1350, pp. 192-94; Uzhan Bakhtiyari 1344, pp. 238-44 (description of the battle at Saveh and Eshtrinan; claims Salar al-Dowleh had 30,000 men against 2,000 Bakhtiyaris); Mardukh, p. 294; Eyn al-Saltaneh 1377, vol. 5, pp. 3552, 3570-71 (here it is reported that at Saveh the prince had 22,000 men, who were mostly armed with muzzle-loaders (*sar-por*), daggers, swords and cudgels for looting. His mountain guns had been no match for the Schneider guns (3- and 5-shot) that the government forces had); Hashimi 1389, pp. 606 (during their flight Salar al-Dowleh's troops continued plundering the villages they passed trough).

116. IOR/L/PS/20/261/5, 'Persia. No 4 (1912). Further correspondence respecting the affairs of Persia', p. 23-24 (no. 53). IOR/L/PS/20/261/5, 'Persia. No 4 (1912). Further correspondence respecting the affairs of Persia', pp. 23-24 (no. 53); Adhari 1378, doc. 39, 46-47, 50, 52 (plunder); Malekzadeh 1328, vol. 7, pp. 65-67, 117; Dowlatabadi 1362, pp. 141-44, 172-79, 181-82; Hamadani 1354, p. 382; Eyn

Salar al-Dowleh's defeat slaked a sigh of relief, because everybody had been afraid and greatly worried.[117] After Mohammad Ali's forces were defeated and in reaction to the confiscation of the properties of Sho`a` al-Saltaneh and Salar al-Dowleh on 4 October 1911, the Russian Legation intervened to protect its financial interests (Salar was heavily indebted to the Russian Bank) stating he was a Russian subject, thus, preventing the confiscation of Salar al-Dowleh's property.[118]

DESPITE DEFEAT LOCAL SUPPORTERS HOLD THE INITIATIVE

On 8 October 1911, a telegram arrived from Sardar Zafar and Sardar Jang, who were in Hamadan, addressed to olama and merchants of Kermanshah, announcing their impending arrival in Kermanshah and instructing them to arrest Azad al-Soltan until officials arrived to investigate his exactions. The prince learning this fled to the Turkish Consulate. In the evening Hajji Sayyed Habib, Malek al-Tojjar went there with others demanding the return of 1,600 tumans he had paid the prince, who, being helpless paid him. When the text of the telegram became known the population robbed any Kalhor they met in the streets. Sardar Mozaffar Da'ud Khan Kalhor left for Delgosha, the government house at 1.6 km outside the city. The next morning he brought Azad al-Soltan there. Some notables went there and tried to induce him to come to the

---

al-Saltaneh 1377, vol. 5, pp. 3534, 3543, 3560-63 (when in Hamadan the prince threw his two guns into a pond). For a short description of the battle and the carnage of dead and wounded afterwards, see Moore 1914, pp. 60-61; see also Malekzadeh 1328, vol. 7, pp. 53-64 and Saki 1343, p. 349; Soltani 1386, p. 182. Dowlatabadi 1362, p. 181 reports that if the Bakhtiyaris had pursued the prince they would have been able to end the rebellion. People of Saveh and the various neighboring villages that had been plundered complained about the treatment they had received from both government officials and the rebels. Adhari 1378, p. 23 (docs. 43, 47-48). Hamadani 1354, p. 383 (After Salar al-Dowleh's defeat Amir Mofakhkham went on pilgrimage to Kerbela realizing that people knew that he was a partisan of the prince).

117. Dowlatabadi 1362, p. 183. However, shortly thereafter there was a lot of gunfire to be heard in Tehran during the night and people were sure that Salar al-Dowleh had come and they could not sleep all night. The next morning it became clear that a camel driver had fallen into the city's moat and the guards believed that the prince's army had come. The poor camel man was hit by some 2,000 bullets. Eyn al-Saltaneh 1377, vol. 5, p. 3544.

118. Mostowfi 1324, vol. 2, pp. 594, 598; Bamdad 1347, vol. 1, p. 50; Shuster 1968, pp. 134-35; Malekzadeh 1328, vol. 7, pp. 68-69; *The New Hazell Annual and Almanack*, vol. 28 (1913), p. 305; Mo`ayyer al- Mamalek 1361, pp. 102, 108, 111. At that time, it became known that Salar al-Dowleh had put some 300,000 tumans of extorted money in the Bank. Eyn al-Saltaneh 1377, vol. 5, p. 3546.

city and carry on the government swearing to support him. The prince refused saying he would accompany the son of the Vali to join his brother Salar al-Dowleh. Ahmad Mirza from the Kezzel (Khezel) tribe came with 50 *savars* from Salar al-Dowleh and gave the prince a secret message from his brother. McDouall believed that the prince wanted to go to Najaf and appeal to Akhund Khorasani, as he had been forced by his brother to come to Kermanshah; he took more interest in agriculture than politics. Faced with his refusal the notables in consultation with tribal chiefs sent a telegram to the Prime Minister saying that in spite of their telegram the city was left without a governor and in a state of anarchy. Then Salar al-Dowleh arrived with a great force and they had no choice but to submit and support him. Some were forced to accompany him, but fled when he engaged government forces. If there was an impartial governor they will follow him, otherwise they will resist. They signed a telegram, which was sent to others for their signature. Mohtasham al-Dowleh cut out "otherwise will resist" from the text, but he did not sign it. Ehtesham al-Dowleh, the Kerend chief refused to sign as he had been forced to join by Salar al-Dowleh and had documents to prove it. Some merchants were forced to affix their seals. Late in the afternoon the Sardars sent another telegram from Hamadan instructing Mohtasham al-Dowleh to assume the duties of governor and arrest the telegraph superintendent, who had suppressed telegrams but also circulated false ones. There was a crowd in the Telegraph office, which immediately wanted to beat up the superintendent, who was then arrested. McDouall commented that if soon no governor arrived with sufficient force the city would fall back into anarchy.[119]

Although Salar al-Dowleh's whereabouts were unknown, rumors abounded. It was said that he had fled to Tabriz,[120] but it was more likely that he had gone to Kurdistan, from where at the end of October 1911 the prince proclaimed that he had entered Tehran. The same message was also sent to merchants in Tabriz,[121] although it is doubtful that it misled anyone. It would seem that the prince had rallied some support

---

119. FO 248/1031, McDouall to Tehran, 10/10/1911; IOR/L/PS/20/261/5, 'Persia. No 4 (1912). Further correspondence respecting the affairs of Persia', p.139 (no. 53); Eyn al-Saltaneh 1377, vol. 5, p. 3548; Vaziri 1352, pp. 57-59 (for a description of the last days of Azad al-Soltan's administration); Mardukh, pp. 294-97 (for a view of Azad al-Soltan's timid character and the role of the Turkish consul).

120. Jurabchi 1363, p. 78.

121. Ettehadiyeh and Sa'vandiyan 1366, pp. 102-04.

among the Lors, for in October 1911, Salar al-Dowleh was pursued by Sardar Bahador Bakhtiyari, who defeated him near Borujerd killing and wounding 500 of the 2,000 men the prince had with him.[122] This development is somewhat surprising, because on 21 October 1911, Nasir Bakhtiyari, complained to Tehran that the Bakhtiyari force was already two months in Hamadan doing nothing. The only action they had been involved in was the killing and capture of some 100 men of Abbas Khan Chenari, who himself had fled.[123] Moreover, rations were not paid. On 22 October 1911, Ja`far Qoli Bakhtiyari complained that the payment of *jireh* was in arrears. Because the men were men discouraged, he had promised that they would be paid before 27 October. However, when that did not happen he wired Tehran on 25 October 1911 reporting that his *savars* were about to disperse. He complained about the lack of any reply, while the need was great among the *savars*.[124] This was followed by further telegrams from the chiefs demanding action. Wages still had not been not received, to which telegrams no reply was given.[125]

Despite Salar al-Dowleh's defeat on 27 September 1911, Salar Homayun, one of his agents in Kermanshah, demanded Molitor to hand over the Customs revenues to him. Molitor delayed doing so, while asking the government for military assistance, because there were still many supporters of Salar al-Dowleh in the city, whose possible violent reaction he rightly feared. Moreover, the environs of Kermanshah were being plundered by Amanollah Khan, the rebel son of the Vali of Posht-e Kuh, while the Kakawand supporters of Salar al-Dowleh were plundering the Chamchamal district. The situation within the city remained precarious. In October 1911, one of the notables asked Molitor for the money to pay for the organization of a local militia, but he refused, as it would anger Salar al-Dowleh's party in the city. The Russian consul advised Molitor to close the Customs for a few days and remain at home.[126] The prince's supporters were not only active in the Kermanshah area,

---

122. IOR/L/PS/20/261/5, 'Persia. No 4 (1912). Further correspondence respecting the affairs of Persia', Barclay to Grey 25/11/1911, p. 227 (no. 299).

123. Afshar 1367, p. 2008-09, doc. 6.

124. Afshar 1367, p. 2010-13, docs. 8, 10, 12.

125. Afshar 1367, p. 2013-14, docs. 13-15.

126. Soltani, Nahzat, 211; Vaziri 1352, p. 61; Destree 1976, pp. 211-13; Hamadani 1354, pp. 384-5; Adhari 1378, p. 24 (doc. 54). After his brother's defeat `Azad al-Soltan fled to Kerbela. IOR/L/PS/20/223, 'Who's who in Persia. Calcutta: General Staff, India, 1916', p. 55.

but also in Soltanabad. On 11 October 1911, the British vice-consul in Soltanabad reported that the district was unsettled and that Salar al-Dowleh's men were still collecting taxes in some parts, who himself was then on his way with some 5,000 men to Lorestan via Malayer and Nehavand. Hajji Seyf al-Dowleh, brother of Eyn al-Dowleh, his appointed governor sought asylum in British vice-consulate and later left for Tehran.[127]

The ex-Shah's and his brother's partisans were still quite active near Kermanshah in October 1911. Fearing an attack on the city, which was in a state of some disorder, many people, including the governor, Ehtesham al-Dowleh left for Baghdad and Kerbela at the end of October 1911. Salar al-Dowleh, who showed up again in the neighborhood, appointed Farrokh Khan Ilkhani to replace him, but the head of Hajjizadeh clan was unable to maintain order. In November 1911, the situation in Kermanshah became increasingly worse due to killings and the rise in robberies such that McDouall placed British flags on warehouses containing British goods. On 27 November, McDouall wired Tehran that he feared the pillaging of the city.[128] On 21 November 1911, news was received that a force of Bakhtiyaris had defeated Salar al-Dowleh, who had fled with the chief of the Deyrawands to Khorramabad. This news, which may refer to the event that took place in early October (see above), made Amanollah Khan, the rebellious son of the Vali, decide to depart from Delgoshah and leave the Kermanshah area.[129]

Due to the unsettled and insecure situation in the city and province people continued to flee to the holy places in Iraq. The British vice-consul at Kerbela reported on 30 November 1911 that the number of pilgrims was higher than usual due to the influx of refugees from Kermanshah, about 4,000 of them; princes, Khans, merchants, and others. Ehtesham al-Dowleh, the former governor of Kermanshah was one of them. He told the British vice-consul that in a discussion with Salar al-Dowleh the

---

127. IOR/L/PS/20/261/5, 'Persia. No 4 (1912). Further correspondence respecting the affairs of Persia', p. 60 (no. 139).

128. IOR/L/PS/20/261/6, 'Persia. No 5 (1912). Further correspondence respecting the affairs of Persia', p. 35 (no. 89); IOR/L/PS/20/261/4, 'Persia. No 3 (1912). Further correspondence respecting the affairs of Persia.', p. 132 (no. 302); Hamadani 1354, pp. 386-87; Adhari 1378, docs. 53-56 (attack on government buildings such as police and telephone; also road robberies and general insecurity); Vaziri 1352, pp. 61-62.

129. IOR/L/PS/10/212, File 211/1912, 'Turkish Arabia Summaries,' p. 5; Hamadani 1354, pp. 386-87.

latter told him that Mohammad Ali and he had instructions from the Russians prior to their return. They were released on two conditions: (i) if successful in regaining the throne they had to place the civil and military administration under Russian control and all decisions had to be taken with Russia's concurrence; (ii) failing to do so, Russia would do everything to create chaos in Iran to create a situation for justified intervention. Ehtesham al-Dowleh further said that Salar al-Dowleh wanted civil war. Therefore, he and others wanted to apply for Turkish citizenship; others would do so in the Consulates inside Iran. Akhund Khorasani had told Ehtesham al-Dowleh that he regretted the situation, but had not indicated that he would take a position.[130]

TAKES KERMANSHAH, AGAIN

There were continued skirmishes between government forces and rebels in December 1911. Caravans were plundered and trade routes were closed and Abbas Khan, grandson of Sharif al-Molk killed villagers, plundered and burnt 27 villages belonging to Vakil al-Molk; the Customs was closed since the end of November, while the population of entire villages moved to Turkish territory.[131] Therefore, on 1 Dec 1911, Khosrow Bakhtiyari wired from Hamadan that there was a need to pursue Salar al-Dowleh who was gathering men and growing in strength. Also, his *savars* were being discouraged by the long idleness, non-payment and sickness. He again asked for reply to earlier telegrams.[132] However, Tehran had more problems than Salar al-Dowleh and was as yet unable to take forceful action. However, it sent A`zam al-Dowleh as acting-governor of Kermanshah, who arrived there in early December 1911. His arrival led to fights between his and Farrokh Khan's followers, led by the notorious Mohammad Ali Genel. However, on 15 December the city was quiet and the next day Salar al-Dowleh with a small force arrived, who had been invited to come to the city by a group of mainly religious leaders such as Aqa Mahmud, Aqa Mohammad Mehdi, and Aqa Rahim. Initially there was still some fighting between government forces and

---

130. IOR/L/PS/10/212, File 211/1912, 'Turkish Arabia Summaries,' p. 5.

131. Destree 1976, pp. 211-13; Adhari 1378, p. 25 (docs. 55-57, 59, 62). At that time Mojallal al-Saltaneh was trying to raise tribal support for the ex-Shah in Kurdistan. Dowlatabadi 1362, pp. 72-73.

132. Afshar 1367, p. 2014-15, doc. 16.

the rebels. A`zam al-Dowleh, the acting governor, and some of his supporters fled to the British Consulate and took asylum to avoid that the city would be plundered. At that time Salar al-Dowleh took the Customs revenues by force. Molitor had no choice as Salar al-Dowleh threatened him and his staff.[133] The prince appointed Salar Homayun governor of Kermanshah and Farrokh Khan governor of Kangavar who, at the end of December 1911, threatened to sack that town, if it did not surrender to him.[134]

On 18 December 1911, the British and Russian consuls met with Salar al-Dowleh. He told them that he had news that some people at Saqqez had invited the Turks, and they replied that they would report it to their Legations. He then told them that he had given orders to repair the telegraph line and re-establish the postal service. As to A`zam al-Dowleh and others, who were in *bast* in the British Consulate he would pardon them and gave his parole that their property would not be interfered with. However, the presence of A`zam al-Dowleh and four others leaders (his son Fakhim al-Dowleh, Abu'l-Hasan Khan deputy of the *anjoman*, Hajji Rostam Beg, Mahdi Pahlavan Reza and Emad al-Ra`aya) in Kermanshah was not advisable, it would be better if they were absent for two months. If he allowed them to stay, and even if they did nothing, their enemies might cause disorder and accuse them of it. He gave his word that they would be safely conducted to the border, or to a safe place on the road to Tehran, and each consul could send a man or two to observe. McDouall pointed out that in Shiraz Nezam al-Saltaneh had given his word, but that Qavam al-Dowleh still had been attacked and his brother had been killed. Salar al-Dowleh said "I am not Nezam al-Saltaneh,' to which McDouall said, 'yes, but your followers are like the wild Qashqa'is.' McDouall told him he would ask the *bastis* what they wanted. Apart from the five persons that he would pardon the rest might safely return to their homes, but if they again offended and took *bast* they would be tried and if found guilty punished, to the consuls' satisfaction. The

---

133. IOR/L/PS/20/261/6, 'Persia. No 5 (1912). Further correspondence respecting the affairs of Persia,' Barclay to Grey 21/12/1911, p. 29 (no. 87); IOR/L/PS/20/261/6, 'Persia. No 5 (1912); Further correspondence respecting the affairs of Persia', p. 35 (no. 89). IOR/L/PS/20/261/5, 'Persia. No 4 (1912). Further correspondence respecting the affairs of Persia', Barclay to Grey 22/12/1911, p. 136 (no. 318); Malekzadeh 1328, vol. 7, p.159; Adhari 1378, p. 26 (doc. 62); Dowlatabadi 1362, p. 72; Hamadani 1354, pp. 387-90 (Farrokh Khan died on 22 December 1911); Vaziri 1352, pp. 61-63 (with names of those who sought asylum in the British Consulate)..

134. Adhari 1378, doc. 61; Hamadani 1354, pp. 388-89; Vaziri 1352, p. 63.

consuls then said that two of their subjects had their properties seized; Salar al-Dowleh told them to give the details in writing and that he would look into it. He had no news from Mohammad Ali Mirza since two months; he intended to stay for Moharram and spend the winter in Lorestan and Kurdistan. In spring he would collect his forces and march to Tehran. He had not wanted to come to Kermanshah but Farrokh Khan had begged him. He had dispatched governors to Hamadan, Malayer and Koliya`i. On arrival he had only 200 *savars*, which were joined by locals, about 700, but he said that Nazar Ali Khan and his son Sardar Mozaffar would be here in two days with their men.[135] The five *bastis* were ready to leave for Hamadan, provided they would have solid guarantees for their safety. McDouall suggested that guards and a guarantee from Sardar Mozaffar would be sufficient. Salar al-Dowleh said that this would take too long, and that they should leave before Moharram when feelings ran high. Finally, he agreed that two agents from both Consulates and from two leading *mojtaheds* could accompany the safe-conductees. Beyond Kangavar they would be safe. McDouall sent a message to Salar al-Dowleh and added that it was not his function to send *savars*, but if the Russians would so would he.[136]

> From the Salar ud Dowleh
> December 28, 1911
>
> To the British Minister
> Y.E.
> I have no doubt that Y.E. is well informed that when the Azam ud Dowleh arrived here collected the rebels and after ten days of fighting in which many people were killed he took refuge in the British Consulate with his followers. We have arrived here with all the sardars of Luristan and Kermanshah. The country is in perfect order and security. In view of what he has done during the last six years the Azam ud Dowleh cannot remain in this province and therefore we have accepted all his proposals. 1stly (sic) their own security and that of their people in the town. 2ndly

---

135. FO 248/1031, McDouall to Tehran, 19/12/1911; Hamadani 1354, pp. 386-87 (on 21 December Nazar Ali Khan was in Kermanshah), 392 (he and the Vali left the city on 05/02/1912).
136. FO 248/1031, McDouall to Tehran, 21/12/1911; Hamadani 1354, pp. 389-91.

Their security on the way as long as they are within the
boundary of the country in our possession. 3dly three of the
Ulema should accompany them to the border of the country
in our possession. This was also accepted by the Ulema of
Kermanshah who have given a written assurance to that
effect to the Consulate. 4thly, not being satisfied with this,
they proposed and we accepted that four of the chief Ulema
of this country should go to the Consulate and give them
assurances as to their security on the way.
In the meantime Agha Mohamed Mehdi the Mujtahed
interceded on their behalf in the name of the Koran that we
should forgive them and notwithstanding the difficulties
which existed we accepted this and Agha Mahmud the
brother of the Mujtahed above mentioned went to the
Consulate to give them assurance and bring them out but
they did not come. It appears from the above circumstances
that they intend to remain in the Consulate and intrigue for
disorder in the country I request you to send instructions
to the Consul to give assurances to the men in question
and either send them to Tehran or to turn them out of the
Consulate. In doing this not only you have saved the country
of perpetual trouble but you have saved us a lot of trouble for
we shall be grateful to you.
We renew to Y.E. the assurances of our highest respect.
Sd. Salar un Dowleh Kajar
Saheb-Ekhtiar of Khusestan and the Irak-i-Ajem[137]

Meanwhile, Salar al-Dowleh tried to reinforce his position by raising fresh troops of which he allegedly had gathered some 3,000 men to oppose the government. On 2 January 1912, to the great consternation of the city's inhabitants, the prince and his Lors plundered fodder and other provisions from the warehouse of Mirza Ali Khan Qarasuran-bashi. Ten days later it was found that the arsenal had been totally emptied of arms and gunpowder.[138] On 6 January 1912, Salar al-Dowleh demanded payment of 33,800 *tumans* with credit receipts signed by the Imperial Bank of Persia (IBP) manager Hamadan and 42,000 *tumans* from bills on the Ali Akbar Brothers of Borujerd, which he claimed he

---

137. FO 248/1031, letter Salar 28/12/1911 (here also the Persian text).
138. Adhari 1378, p. 26 (doc. 63); Hamadani 1354, pp. 391-92.

had the right to encash. The IBP manager, who had orders not to pay Salar al-Dowleh, had no choice but to pay the prince, who was the only force in town and threatened to take the entire IBP branch treasury if he refused. At that time the IBP had 260,000 *tumans* in cash and notes, of which 120,000 *tumans* had been packed for transport. The rest was in the safe, which was above ground and could easily be demolished and, therefore, fearing greater loss, he paid. Salar al-Dowleh told the British consul that he did not want to fight the Persian government, if they left him alone. If not, he would attack Tehran in the spring. He would be content with an area from Azerbaijan to Khuzestan; he also was willing to pay taxes to Tehran.[139] The *bastis* finally decided that they did not want to leave, despite Salar al-Dowleh's assurance of safe-conduct. Salar al-Dowleh told the Consulate's *monshi* that he could not be responsible for the safty of foreigners if the *bastis* remained in the Consulate, because their presence aroused people's ire. He suggested informing the Russian consul as well.[140] Two weeks later, on the night of 15 January 1912, shots were fired from all sides at the Consulate. McDouall told the Consular guard only to fire if they saw any people in the grounds. The *bastis* and their servants, some 30 people, were all armed and ready to fight, but had orders from A`zam al-Dowleh not to fire unless attacked. In the morning of 16 January, Salar al-Dowleh sent for the British *monshi* and swore he had nothing to do with the shooting incident. He had investigated the matter and was sure that these had been partisans of the *bastis* to inculpate him. He wanted to see McDouall, who let him know that he first needed to punish the culprits, whom he thought were ruffians of Salar Homayun. Nazar Ali Khan sent a message to express his sorrow and informed McDouall that the previous night four of his men had been absent; he had arrested them and if guilty he would punish them.[141]

---

139. FO 248/1053, McDouall to George Barclay, 06/01/1912; Idem, McDouall to Tehran, 06/01/1911; Adhari 1378, p. 26 (docs. 64, 70).

140. FO 248/1053, McDouall to Tehran, 09/01/1912. In mid-February 1912, the government offered the prince a pension of 12,000 *tumans*, if he let to Europe. Dowlatabadi 1362, p. 74.

141. FO 248/1053, McDouall to Tehran, 16/01/1912.

YAR MOHAMMAD KHAN EXPELS SALAR AL DOWLEH

In early January 1912, Farmanfarma was appointed governor of Kermanshah with the task to defeat and oust Salar al-Dowleh. To that end he had two regiments of soldiers, 800 Bakhtiyari *savars* and *mojaheds* at his disposal. However, he had not much faith in the soldiers and therefore, mainly relied on the *mojaheds*. The latter were a force of some 300 men under Yar Mohammad Khan Kermanshahi. Together with a few cannons and maxims this force left Qazvin for Hamadan, where it arrived at the end of January 1912. On 6 February the *mojaheds* took Sahneh, near Kermanshah, and Salar Mokram, who held the place for Salar al-Dowleh fled. Two days later, the *mojaheds*, who constituted the vanguard of a small government force under Yar Mohammad Khan, arrived at Bisetun, from where he wired Yeprim Khan asking for arms and ammunition. Salar al-Dowleh on learning of this threat sent a force against him, but Yar Mohammad, knowing the terrain better than the prince, instead of via the road marched through the hills and entered the city during the night. He only had a few men with him, who took position in a few houses and started firing at daylight. As a result, Salar al-Dowleh, Da'ud Khan Kalhor and the son of Farrokh Khan all fled, apparently believing that their partners had betrayed them. After dark the palace was entered. In the evening all three rebel leaders gathered at Mahidasht and tried to retake the city but were repulsed. During the night a fight took place at the Qarasu bridge, where about 10 *mojaheds* were killed; on both sides some 200 men participated. The rebels then withdrew to Manzileh, east of Kermanshah. A`zam al-Dowleh left the British Consulate where he had taken refuge since 15 December 1911, and took charge of the governorship again. McDouall only allowed A`zam al-Dowleh leave until the government forces had taken the town, as he had promised Salar al-Dowleh. After Salar al-Dowleh's departure from Kermanshah on 8 February, the Constitutional flag was raised. The next morning with a few gunshots the *mojaheds* forced the bazaaris to close the bazaar.[142]

---

142. 'Persia. No 1 (1913). Further correspondence respecting the affairs of Persia', pp. 11-12; Political Diaries vol. 4, p. 518; IOR/L/PS/10/212, File 211/1912 'Turkish Arabia Summaries', p. 6; IOR/L/PS/20/261/6, 'Persia. No 5 (1912). Further correspondence respecting the affairs of Persia', p. 119 (no. 304); Political Diaries vol. 4, p. 518; Malekzadeh 1328, vol. 7, pp. 160-61; Adhari 1378, docs. 71, 73-77; Dowlatabadi 1362, p. 78; Eyn al-Saltaneh 1377, vol. 5, p. 3649; Hamadani 1354, p. 393; Ettehadiyeh and Sa`vandiyan 1366, vol. 1, pp. 136-37; Kasravi 1350, p. 511;

Even though the fighting was over, still some people were killed. For example, Sharaf al-Molk Kurdistani, chief of the Jafs, was not killed during the fighting, because he was at the house of Aqa Mahmud, brother of Aqa Mohammad Mehdi. However, the morning after the fighting (9 February) he was shot with his nephew and two servants by the *mojaheds*. The Kurdistanis in town signed a testimony that it was the *mojaheds* who had killed him and that the townspeople were innocent and sent the document to their tribe to prevent them from killing Kermanshahis. Aqa Mahmud was arrested, also Aqa Rahim, Hajji Aqa Vali, Aqa Sayyed Reza Qomi and the Shaykh al-Eslam of Hersin, all *mojaheds*. Salar al-Dowleh's entire correspondence was found in the palace as was Aqa Mahmud's dispatch case. The extraordinary government commission looked into the case against them. There was no doubt of Aqa Mahmud's guilt; the commission decided he had to pay 4,000 *tumans* and be sent to Tehran with the others. During the night Yar Mohammad Khan, who said he was acting on orders from Tehran, ordered his execution and Aqa Mahmud was hanged at daylight on 12 February. The others were sent to Tehran; Aqa Rahim was also expected to be executed. On 9 February, two officers of the Zanganeh regiment, two executioners, and two others were shot (Salar Rashid Kurdistani, Hajji Rostam Khan, Safar Khan Soltan of the Zanganeh regiment, Shehab Nezam and his brother). The government force consisted of about 200 *mojaheds*, 100 Koliya'i horse and local soldiers and volunteers, perhaps 1,000 in total. They had plenty of ammunition and wired Farmanfarma, who had been recently appointed as governor of Kermanshah, for reinforcements. The city was quiet, but people were in terror.[143] The city was placed under martial law. Sayyed Mohammad Rowzeh-khvan and Na'eb-Sadr took refuge in the British Consulate on 11 February because the *mojaheds* were looking for them. The *mojaheds* accused them of political offenses, but they claimed they could prove their innocence. The former was accused of taken messages from Salar

---

Vaziri 1352, pp. 55-56, 64 (lists names of all the ruffians that fled and of those who were executed), 65-67.

143. FO 248/1053, McDouall to Tehran, 13/02/1912; Malekzadeh 1328, vol. 7, p. 161; Adhari 1378, pp. 26-27 (docs. 73, 75); IOR/L/PS/20/261/6, 'Persia. No 5 (1912). Further correspondence respecting the affairs of Persia', Barclay to Grey 15/03/1912, p. 120 (no. 306); Adhari 1378, p. 27 (docs. 78, 80, 84); Hamadani 1354, pp. 393-94; Mardukh, p. 300; Kasravi 1350, pp. 511-12. According to Dowlatabadi 1362, pp. 79-80 one of the reasons for the arrests and executions was to extort money from the towns people.

al-Dowleh to A`zam al-Dowleh when in bast trying to persuade him to surrender and also of preaching against the Constitution, which latter point McDouall thought he had not. Na'eb-Sadr had always been the go-between for the clergy and the governor and had done the same under Salar al-Dowleh. On 15 February 1912, the local authorities gave written assurances for their safety if they did not leave their homes, out of consideration of the British Consulate that had saved their lives.[144] Although the local population had aided Yar Mohammad Khan in taking the city, the mojaheds behaved as conquerors and rather badly towards their compatriots. This did not make the mojaheds very popular, the more so, while they had only suffered at most 15 men dead and wounded, the towns people had lost more than 500 among the non-combatants.[145]

Salar al-Dowleh went to Mahidasht after he left Kermanshah on 9 February 1912; he sent his wife to Kalhor country and with Sardar Mozaffar and the city Khans he moved to some 16 km from the city camping on crown-lands.[146] His troops plundered all environing villages and he sent messengers all around exhorting people to join his forces. The city was in good order and the defenders were busy fortifying the town. Via the Russian consul a letter arrived from Salar al-Dowleh on 17 February 1912 informing the consuls that he was going to take the town and that consuls and foreign subjects should withdraw to the villages "till he had punished the unruly." He made that point, because some of his followers ascribed their earlier defeat to the presence of Persian officials in the British Consulate, and if they wanted to win they had to destroy it. He said he would allow them to plunder the Consulate and the IBP. Meanwhile, the Kakawands did not let anybody pass into direction of Kangavar. Needless to say that this situation was not good for trade.

---

144. FO 248/1053, McDouall to Tehran, 15/02/1912. The government offered Salar al-Dowleh a pension of 12,000 tumans and restitution of his estates, as he was very poor, on condition that he would keep order in Kermanshah, hand over the city to the governor, and leave Persia. IOR/L/PS/20/261/6, 'Persia. No 5 (1912). Further correspondence respecting the affairs of Persia', Barclay to Grey 12/02/1912, p. 68 (no. 171).

145. Dowlatabadi 1362, p. 79.

146. IOR/L/PS/20/261/6, 'Persia. No 5 (1912). Further correspondence respecting the affairs of Persia', Barclay to Grey 15/03/1912, p. 120 (no. 306); Adhari 1378, p. 27; doc. 81 - at Yar Mohammad Khan's request Yeprim Khan had sent some cannons as the former believed that in that case he could defeat the prince's force, but they had not arrived yet - docs. 83, 85.

SALAR AL-DOWLEH RETAKES KERMANSHAH

At that time, `Ettela' al-Dowleh was president of the court-martial and army commander (ra'is-e qoshun), and president of a special commission. Gates were erected in several places and messengers sent to Farmanfarma, the appointed governor, asking to send reinforcements as soon as possible. Some chiefs, including Sardar Akram, wrote that they submitted to the government. Salar al-Dowleh's supporters were encouraged, because Farmanfarma did not come and did not send arms or troops. The government had only a small force and part of that was willing to desert or help the rebels; the latter formed a large body of troops. On 18 February 1912 skirmishing started. In the night of 21 February there was firing west of Kermanshah where volunteers had made barricades supported by some mojaheds. At sunrise the volunteers joined the rebels, who then occupied Chia Sorkh, a hill suburb of the city. Then they occupied one-third of the bazaar, but were driven back by the mojaheds, who suffered many casualties, but held out at a barricade until the next morning. On 22 February, the rebels (Kurdistanis, Sanjabis, town Khans) entered the city at several points and by 9 p.m. the town was theirs. The government officials and Yar Mohammad Khan fled, the latter without informing his mojaheds, toward Dinavar with much ammunition. On both sides some 40 men killed. On 23 February 1912, Salar al-Dowleh and Sardar Mozaffar went to the palace. When the Kalhors arrived, who had not done much fighting, they started plundering. They did not respect the houses of the Consular staff who flew the Russian or British flag. In the bazaar only the caravanserai of Vakil al-Dowleh, filled with British goods, and the bazzaz-khaneh escaped the looting. During this time also many men, women and children were killed.[147]

The rebels searched everywhere for mojaheds and several were arrested with the help of the towns people who had turned against them because of their oppressive behavior. In total, Salar al-Dowleh hanged 102 Constitutionalists in one day, including `Ettela' al-Dowleh, the

---

147. IOR/L/PS/20/261/6, 'Persia. No 5 (1912). Further correspondence respecting the affairs of Persia', Barclay to Grey 12/03/1912 and 15/03/1912, pp. 117 (no. 297), 121 (no. 307); 'Persia. No 1 (1913). Further correspondence respecting the affairs of Persia', p. 14-15 (no. 22); Dowlatabadi 1362, pp. 80-82 (with a list of plundered warehouses and houses); Adhari 1378, p. 28 (docs. 86, 101-102); Hamadani 1354, pp. 394-95; Kasravi 1350, pp. 512-13; Vaziri 1352, p. 56; Mardukh, p. 301; Malekzadeh 1328, vol. 7, pp. 161-62.

kargozar of Mohammarah. His body was partly burnt and then thrown to the dogs. The others met a similar fate. Due to Yar Mohammad's defeat, Farmanfarma, the new governor, en route to Kermanshah returned to Tehran. Because Hamadan remained in government hands the government in Tehran ordered Farmanfarma to return to Hamadan and face Salar al-Dowleh. He was to leave again with a force of Cossacks. Salar al-Dowleh sent troops to take Kangavar and Sahneh, and intended to march on Hamadan.[148] The prince sent those troops there, because after their expulsion from Kermanshah, Yar Mohammad Khan had fled to Kangavar. Here Sari Aslan, the local governor, supported the government in Tehran. From there, they wired Yeprim Khan asking him for supplies as well as urging him to come in person as soon as possible. They further sent letters urging to send them arms and ammunition, because they had enough men, but not arms, to enable them to destroy the rebel-prince. Salar al-Dowleh sent Sari Aslan a letter reprimanding him for not presenting himself and promising that he would destroy Kangavar. This caused panic among its inhabitants who asked Tehran to send troops to prevent this.[149] Tehran only sent nice replies thanking them for their fervor and to put Sari Aslan's mind at peace he was informed that the ex-Shah had left Iran and now Salar al-Dowleh had to be expelled as well.[150]

Salar al-Dowleh was always looking for ways to get his hands on money and sometimes he did so not by using force, but by false claims with the hint of the use of force. On 14 March 1912, McDouall reported that at the request of the *kargozar* he opened a bag that Salar al-Dowleh had deposited at the IBP, from which the prince claimed 95,000 *tumans* were missing when he returned to Kermanshah. McDouall stated that the claim was false, but Salar al-Dowleh claimed compensation from IBP; he refused to apologize and thus the Bank was in danger.[151] The prince also imposed a forced contribution of the merchants of

---

148. IOR/L/PS/20/261/7, 'Persia. No 1 (1913). Further correspondence respecting the affairs of Persia', pp. 11, 14-15 (no. 22); Political Diaries vol. 4, p. 518; Adhari 1378, p. 28 (docs. 94, 99); Dowlatabadi 1362, pp. 82-83; Eyn al-Saltaneh 1377, vol. 5, p. 3649; Hamadani 1354, pp. 395-97; Kasravi 1350, p. 513.

149. Adhari 1378, pp. 28-29 (docs. 73-74, 81, 83, 87-88, 94-97, 99).

150. Adhari 1378, p. 29 (docs. 77, 98).

151. IOR/L/PS/20/261/6, 'Persia. No 5 (1912). Further correspondence respecting the affairs of Persia.', Barclay to Grey 15/03/1912, p. 121 (no. 307); Malekzadeh 1328, vol. 7, pp. 162-63.

Kermanshah; each had to pay 3,000 to 5,000 *tumans* for his expenses, so that he could dismiss his troops, whom he told to be back by *Nowruz*, because then he would march to Hamadan. Some of his supporters, such as Baqer Khan of the Kakawands, Nazar Ali Khan Amra'i and Hasan Pasha Koliya'i were attacking and plundering villages, notables and anybody on the roads to and from Kermanshah, so that pilgrims remained in Khaneqin afraid to travel to Kermanshah. All these various activities caused economic and human distress and much physical destruction.[152]

RUSSIA AND BRITAIN URGE SALAR AL-DOWLEH TO GIVE UP

On 1 March 1912, Barclay instructed McDouall to suggest, together with his Russian colleague, to Salar al-Dowleh to accept the Persian government's offer "of 6,000 tumans for himself and 6,000 tumans for his family, revocation of the confiscation of his estates, on condition that he keep order at Kermanshah and the places in his occupation, hands them over to a governor appointed by the Persian Government and then leaves Persia with an undertaking not to return to the country without the previous consent of the Persian Government."[153] A few days later, the British and Russian consuls informed Salar al-Dowleh about the offer made by the Iranian government and strongly advised him to accept. However, he refused to do so, but in lieu, on 14 March, he made a counter-proposal in a very long letter, basically demanding the ceding of W. Iran under his rule as a quasi-independent ruler. The two consuls immediately advised him "to make a more reasonable proposal," but he refused, because Tehran would undoubtedly demand changes anyway.[154] During his 'rule' in Kermanshah, Salar al-Dowleh called himself *Farmandari-e koll-e Khuzestan va Lorestan va `Eraq-e `Ajam*.[155]

---

152. Adhari 1378, p. 28 (docs. 89, 90-93, 103). According to Hamadani 1354, pp. 398-99 the prince imposed a contribution from 5 to 50 *tumans* per household. The prince also appointed Ehtesham al-Dowleh as governor of the Thalatheh governorate.

153. 'Persia. No 1 (1913). Further correspondence respecting the affairs of Persia', pp. 9-10 (no. 14); Kasravi 1350, p. 514.

154. IOR/L/PS/20/261/7, 'Persia. No 1 (1913). Further correspondence respecting the affairs of Persia', pp. 15-16 (no. 23) (at that time the prince had only 500 men in the city); Dowlatabadi 1362, p. 84. For the text of this letter, see Appendix III.

155. Mardukh, p. 301.

On 30 March 1912, McDouall was instructed to urge Salar al-Dowleh once again to accept Tehran's terms and hand over the occupied lands to Farmanfarma and to leave Iran. The two Powers fully supported the military action the Persian government was taking, to which end they had made considerable funds available. If he refused, which was contrary to their interests, Russia and Great Britain would not help him get a pension and provide protection in the future. Both consuls met Salar al-Dowleh on 6 April to relate the message, but he refused, saying that, because the Legations were acting a mediators he felt vindicated and declared himself Shah. He had not come to get a pension, but to restore order and religion, to save the country from a corrupt and incompetent government and a child king. He said compare the state of this province with the rest of the country. McDouall said trade in Kermanshah was at a standstill, which the prince denied and said roads were safe. According to McDouall, "He is so filled with his idea of his own greatness that he cannot be convinced to see reality." The next day Salar al-Dowleh left Kermanshah, but not before sending along letter to the two consuls in which he submitted his views and aims (see Appendix III). The prince went to Harunabad, Da'ud Khan Kalhor's headquarters, to speak with local chiefs and arrange their quarrels and collect more men. McDouall did not think the Vali would come. On the same day the two consuls also informed several tribal chiefs and city notables about their message to Salar al-Dowleh. McDouall told the Sanjabi chief the contents of the telegram, who promised to deal with the Kalhors, if Farmanfarma would come immediately with 300 men and guns. Otherwise the tribes would be forced to join Salar al-Dowleh. Farmanfarma who was then at Qazvin, was confident that with his forces he could take care of the problem; also by negotiating with the Sanjabis. Everybody now took the position that the resolution of the Salar al-Dowleh rebellion was in Farmanfarma's hands.[156]

Meanwhile, Salar al-Dowleh had created a commission of justice (*adalat*) consisting of Farid al-Molk, the *kargozar*, Aqa Rahim *mojtahed*, and Malek Mohammad, a bankrupt merchant. On 7 April 1912, Salar al-Dowleh left for Gilan, in Kalhor country, ostensibly to meet with the Vali. He had been in vain trying to have the Vali come to Kermanshah, who finally said that he would meet him in Gilan, provided he would

---

156. IOR/L/PS/20/261/7, 'Persia. No 1 (1913). Further correspondence respecting the affairs of Persia', pp. 18 (encl. 3 in no. 23; no. 24), 53-54 (no.125); Malekzadeh 1328, vol. 7, p. 163; Kasravi 1350, p. 515.

hand over his rebel son Amanollah Khan in chains. Salar al-Dowleh left with 200 men and left the justice commission in charge of Kermanshah with the Ilkhani as executive. There were only 250 levies in the city the rest had gone home. It was said that the Gurans and Kalhors had fought. The Guran-Sanjabi combination was quiet, because they knew that Salar al-Dowleh would not support Da'ud Khan against them and they only joined the prince out of fear of Da'ud Khan in his present position.[157]

McDouall was instructed to make public the communication made to Salar al-Dowleh on behalf of the Legations; the Russian consul had no such instructions, which put the onus on the British. Malekzadeh implied in his comments on these events that the Russians did not want to do anything to hinder Salar al-Dowleh. On 7 April 1912, McDouall first informed Samsam al-Mamalek Sanjabi who told him that his son Ali Akbar had formed a combination against Da'ud Khan Kalhor, but was now quiet as Da'ud Khan was Salar al-Dowleh's most trusted supporter and he was not strong enough to oppose Salar al-Dowleh, if he supported Da'ud Khan. If a man of rank like Farmanfarma arrived with some 500 men and two guns his presence would be sufficient and then they could easily deal with Da'ud Khan. This had to be done quickly, or else the tribes would be obliged to join, or at least send some men to the prince. McDouall also informed Aqa Mohammad Mehdi who at once left for his village and thus there was no ranking *mojtahed* in town, apart from Aqa Rahim. On 3 April 1912, he sent a copy to the Vali and to Qasr-e Shirin to vice-consul Soane for publication and talks with tribal chiefs. McDouall also sent for the Ilkhani, the son of Farrokh Khan, head of the Hajjizadehs in town and *de jure* chief of the Kalhors and told him about the contents of the communication. He said that his position was different as he had properties inside and outside the city, which now were usurped by Da'ud Khan; his first object was to protect the town and he would not yet change his course. On 13 April some 100 of Salar al-Dowleh's adherents met at the house of Aqa Rahim. The principals being the Ilkhani, Salar Mozaffar, and Mashdi Hasan, brother of the late Mo`in al-Ra`aya. Aqa Rahim said the contents of the British message had made him afraid and thought of leaving. The others said there was nothing

---

157. FO 248/1053, Diary no. 3 from March 31 to April 11th 1912. On 7 April 1912, a detachment of 100 Russian troops were sent to Hamadan to avoid that it would fall into the hands of adherents of Salar al-Dowleh. 'Persia. No 1 (1913). Further correspondence respecting the affairs of Persia' Barcley to Grey, 07/04/1912, p. 8 (no. 12); Hamadani 1354, p. 399.

from the Russian consul and the British were the enemy of Salar al-Dowleh. Aqa Rahim suggested writing to Tehran that they were poor inoffensive people and they would submit to anyone who came with force and ask for amnesty. The others refused. They finally wrote a letter to Salar al-Dowleh stating that after he had left the British consul had spread stories that Mohammad Ali had fled and that Salar al-Dowleh must leave and that the government in Tehran was powerful. Therefore, it was imperative that he got the Vali to join and immediately return to Kermanshah with the Vali's forces or they would leave town. If the Vali would not come and he could not do anything they had to see to their own safety. Because the Russian consul said nothing and the Turkish consul was at the prince's service the people thought that only the British were the prince's enemy and when he returned he would make life difficult for British subjects. Salar al-Dowleh had no loyal friends, they only joined him out of fear, some for plunder, others because they had committed too much to him, and some even if they would get government pardon knew that they would be murdered because of their ill-treatment of the people. Only quick action by Tehran could put an end to this, and to prevent that the Vali and the Shaykh of Mohammareh would join Salar al-Dowleh. There was no news from Gilan, only rumors, but it seemed that the Vali would not join Salar al-Dowleh, who "like Sardar Akram is known to be offended at the honour heaped on Daood Khan, a man of no birth."[158]

In April 1912, Salar al-Dowleh again threatened Molitor to pay him the Customs monies; the latter had ordered his colleague Vilain at Qasr-e Shirin to stop all goods destined for Kermanshah. Salar al-Dowleh considered this an act of treason and told him to order Vilain to let the goods depart.[159] By mid-April Salar al-Dowleh had become very unpopular in Kermanshah due to his exactions. He was still in Kalhor country to raise more support.[160] Salar al-Dowleh left Gilan on 28 or 29 April 1912, where he had gone to obtain support of Vali, who only came there after having

---

158. FO 248/1053, McDouall to Tehran, 13/04/1912; IOR/L/PS/20/261/7, 'Persia. No 1 (1913). Further correspondence respecting the affairs of Persia', pp. 9 (no. 14), 52 (no. 125), 54-55 (no. 125); Malekzadeh 1328, vol. 7, p. 164; Kasravi 1350, p. 515.

159. Destree 1976. pp. 247-48.

160. IOR/L/PS/20/261/7, 'Persia. No 1 (1913). Further correspondence respecting the affairs of Persia', p. 38 (no. 84). At the end of March 1912, both the Russian and British consular agent were instructed to jointly inform Mojalal al-Soltan that taking Hamadan in the name of Mohammad Ali, the ex-Shah was contrary to wishes of both Legations. Adhari 1378, doc. 104.

received a safe-conduct from the prince, because Da'ud Khan Kalhor was his enemy. While there, the Vali lived in his own tents and he and his men fed themselves refusing to be the guest of Da'ud Khan Kalhor, "who, he said, was a robber and could only entertain him from his unlawful spoils." The Vali told the prince he could only support the royalist troops under certain conditions: no looting, chiefs should support their men, no molesting of travelers and traders, and no extortion of merchants and others. The prince acceded to these conditions, but the Vali seemed not to have put much faith in this commitment, because he returned home. While in Gilan, Salar al-Dowleh married a daughter of Da'ud Khan, the Vali being present at the wedding. It was said to be the 10th matrimonial alliance of the prince during this campaign. From Gilan he hurried to Kermanshah to face Farmanfarma's advance. The townsmen of Kermanshah were wavering in their support and asked him to declare his intentions and in reply he said he would meet the enemy. He had already summoned Ali Akbar Sanjabi to join him at Gilan, where he did not come due to a feud with Da'ud Khan.[161]

Meanwhile, Salar al-Dowleh did not get his reinforcements, mostly because the various tribes did not trust each other. Samsam al-Mamalek replied to Salar al-Dowleh that given his quarrel with the Kalhors he would not come to Kermanshah as long as they had not left. Moreover, there was trouble on the border caused by the Kalhors and therefore, he could not spare a man. Sardar Mozaffar, the Kalhor chief, in his turn told Salar al-Dowleh that he could not come until the Sanjabi contingent had left Kermanshah and furthermore that he would come when the Vali came. The latter wrote that he would come, but he had an excuse for a delay. This situation was troublesome for Salar al-Dowleh, because he could not do a thing without the Kermanshah tribes. Therefore, he wrote to his supporters that so-and so had already come to encourage them to come as well.[162] On 1 May 1912, Salar al-Dowleh sent a telegram to Townley, the British Minister in Tehran, saying he had been joined by the Vali and that he was returning to Kermanshah and then would march to Hamadan. He had instructed Amir Mofakhkham to march to

---

161. IOR/L/PS/10/212, File 211/1912 'Turkish Arabia Summaries', pp. 7-8. IOR/L/PS/10/212, File 211/1912 'Turkish Arabia Summaries', pp. 7-8; Dowlatabadi 1362, p. 85.
162. Affairs of Persia 1912, p. 74.

Soltanabad and Mojallal al-Saltaneh to Hamadan, where government forces were ready to march to Kermanshah.[163]

DEFEATS GOVERNMENT FORCE DESPITE GROWING QUARRELS AMONG HIS TRIBAL SUPPORTERS

In early January 1912, Abdol-Hoseyn Mirza Farmanfarma had been appointed governor of Kermanshah with the task to suppress Salar al-Dowleh's rebellion. On 6 April 1912, Farmanfarma finally left Tehran for Hamadan with a considerable force. He stopped at Qazvin for a while and on then proceeded to Hamadan, where he arrived four days later. Farmanfarma's troops consisted of levies from his estates in Asadabad, Maragheh and Miyanj, in addition to 400 Bakhtiyari *savars*, 150 Cossacks, amongst whom was Reza Khan Mir Panj Makzimi (the later Reza Shah), who commanded the artillery. There also were levies from the villages of Amir Nezam Qaragozlu and 300 *mojaheds* under Yar Mohammad Khan.[164] A force of 600 Bakhtiyaris under Shehab al-Saltaneh and Ziya al-Soltan followed somewhat later with orders to march to Zanjan and then to wait for further orders. Meanwhile, Amir Nezam, the governor of Hamadan fortified the town. On 3 May 1912, Salar al-Dowleh returned to Kermanshah with 600 men. The Sanjabis and other smaller tribes had not openly broken with Salar al-Dowleh, but had sent no representatives to him in Gilan. The prince told the British consul McDouall that he wanted to fight government troops some 20 kilometers outside Hamadan to avoid casualties among civilians and damage to foreign goods. He asked the consul to convey this to the government in Tehran. The British Minister considered this letter a joke, which had been written before the prince knew that his troops had been defeated at Hamadan. Salar al-Dowleh sent 15,000 men under Da'ud Khan Kalhor, now titled Amir A`zam, to Hamadan to defeat Farmanfarma. The latter took almost one

---

163. IOR/L/PS/20/261/7, 'Persia. No 1 (1913). Further correspondence respecting the affairs of Persia', p. 32 (no. 72).

164. Farmanfarma'iyan 1382, vol. 1, p. 360; Afshar 1367, pp. 2016-17, docs. 18, 20-21 (on 21 November 1911, he complained that promised gunners and soldiers had not come and that Mr. Lecoffre, who was supposed to pay the force's expenditures, had left, the more since all foodstuffs were expensive in Hamadan). On 4 Qus 1329/27 November 1911, he complained that the soldiers had not been paid and were hungry. He asked for wheat and barley to be made available immediately so that they soldiers would not die. Afshar 1367, p. 2018, doc. 22

month to march from Tehran to Hamadan, and on 3 May 1912 he advanced against Mojallal al-Soltan. The two armies met on 5 May; they fired at each other and then fled. "Mujallal winning because he looked round first, and discovered that he and the enemy were playing the same game." Farmanfarma lost three Schneider field guns and some mountain batteries with all their ammunition, and allegedly had only 150 men left. Officially it was said that their breechblocks had been removed before they were abandoned. Farmanfarma withdrew to Hamadan waiting for reinforcements. These were Armenian *fida'is* under Keri Khan, but there was disaffection in their ranks. The Bakhtiyari force at Zanjan was ordered to join Farmanfarma. Meanwhile, Yeprim Khan, with 200 Armenian *fida'is* sent as reinforcement, left Tehran on 7 May and hastened by car to Hamadan to take command of the entire government force. After his arrival on 11 May, Yeprim Khan rallied the government troops, who were reinforced by the Bakhtiyaris.[165]

On hearing about the quarrel between the tribes, Kazem Khan Sanjabi and Salar Arshad Kurdistani, who had been with Mojallal al-Soltan when he defeated Farmanfarma, returned to Kermanshah. Mojallal al-Soltan wrote to Salar al-Dowleh that he should send him reinforcements, instead of leaving some of his force in Kermanshah to deal with the tribal quarrels. Salar al-Dowleh sent some olama to Samsam al-Mamalek, who then visited the prince, who embraced him, called him father and gave him 3,000 *tumans*. Samsam al-Mamalek said the tribes would not accept a government by the Kalhors; if they met there would be a fight; they could not serve in the same army. Salar al-Dowleh promised, 'serve me and you won't have to submit to Sardar Mozaffar.' He asked for 800 men to be sent to Mojallal al-Soltan. Samsam al-Mamalek appeared to have agreed, returned to his village to see his son Ali Akbar, who was the real head of the 'tribal 'combination.' It was expected that if Farmanfarma would defeat Mojallal al-Soltan then they would not join

---

165. IOR/L/PS/20/261/7, 'Persia. No 1 (1913). Further correspondence respecting the affairs of Persia', pp. 37-38 (no. 84); Farmanfarma'iyan 1382, vol. 1, pp. 356-58; Dowlatabadi 1362, p. 84; IOR/L/PS/20/261/7, 'Persia. No 1 (1913). Further correspondence respecting the affairs of Persia', pp. 41 (no. 87), 43 (no. 93), 44 (nos. 96, 98) 53-55 (no. 125), 57 (no. 126), 65-66 (no. 136-37, 140-41), 72; Malekzadeh 1328, vol. 7, pp. 164-65; Kasravi 1350, pp. 516-17; Soltani 1386, pp. 187-89 (Salar al-Dowleh lost 500-600 men, the government 50); Uzhan Bakhtiyari 1344, pp. 244-49. Arshak Gavafian (1858-1916), born in Erzerum, and popularly known as Keri. He was a leader of the Armenian *feda'i*s and a member of the Armenian Revolutionary Federation.

Salar al-Dowleh. Sardar Mozaffar wrote to Ehtesham al-Mamalek of Kerend that he was right to punish the Kalhors. Apparently he was afraid of the strength of the 'combination' and only intended to fight when attacked. He was expected to join at Kangavar for the advance against the governement troops. The Ilkhani was at Sahneh with 300-400 men. Meanwhile, Salar al-Dowleh did not get his reinforcements, mostly because the various tribes did not trust each other.[166]

On 14 May 1912, Salar al-Dowleh met with McDouall to explain, once again, that he was a patriot who only wanted to restore order. He could do it better than the current government and, moreover, he would be more useful to the British than Sardar As`ad, who was beholden to the Russians. Although given their past behavior toward him he had no reason to love the British, but he was convinced only the British government would be able to guarantee Iran's integrity and independence. Therefore, he would do everything to support British interests and had given orders to respect British goods. McDouall asked him about the jihad that Kurdish olama had declared at the instigation of Mojallal al-Soltan, who had told them that the government in Tehran had sold out to Russia and Great Britian and that he had said that foreign goods would be first looted. The prince replied that this was a trick played by his enemies, because Mojallal al-Soltan could not tell such stories without his orders.[167]

SALAR AL-DOWLEH DEFEATED; DEATH OF YEPRIM KHAN

On 19 May 1912, Yeprim Khan, having reconnoitered the enemy's positions, attacked Mojallal al-Soltan. The battle at Surcheh began at 9 a.m. and more or less ended by 4.30 pm, when Yeprim Khan was killed by a sniper. Immediately, panic broke out, because Mojallal al-Soltan's reinforcements arrived at that time, but Keri Khan kept order by ruthless shooting the first men who fled. Then another three hours of fight ensued and Mojallal al-Soltan was defeated; he suffered 300 casualties among which 120 prisoners. Government forces' losses were 30 killed,

---

166. IOR/L/PS/20/261/7, 'Persia. No 1 (1913). Further correspondence respecting the affairs of Persia', p. 74 (encl. 2-4 to no. 166).

167. IOR/L/PS/20/261/7, 'Persia. No 1 (1913). Further correspondence respecting the affairs of Persia', p. 73 (no. 166).

including Yeprim Khan. Salar al-Dowleh's luster waned and he withdrew to Kermanshah with some 80 men.[168] Farmanfarma marched quickly toward Kermanshah to prevent Salar al-Dowleh from reinforcing himself, en route taking Sahneh. On 27 May, the Ilkhani reported that Salar al-Dowleh had defeated the advance guard of government reinforcements. Da'ud Khan Kalhor (Sardar Mozaffar) joined him on the evening of 28 May and camped at Sahneh to make a final stand. In the morning (29 May) government forces attacked with maxims and artillery. Da'ud Khan tried to capture the artillery under Reza Khan, but got his leg shot and withdrew, but died en route. Because Da'ud Khan, his oldest son, as well as many other Kalhor leaders were killed the rest of the tribesmen fled to their own country. The Hajjizadehs of the Ilkhani section fled to the hills. When news arrived of his army's defeat and flight, Kazem Khan Sanjabi was with Salar al-Dowleh and left immediately for his own district. Salar al-Dowleh, Mojallal al-Soltan and his men, with one gun, fled to Lorestan where he took refuge with the Vali. On 30 May 1912, Farmanfarma arrived in Kermanshah without firing a shot; the town remained quiet.[169] To keep it that way, Farmanfarma made it known that he understood that those who had fought with Salar al-Dowleh had done so to protect themselves, or were forced to do so, and he declared a general amnesty provided they did not extend any further support to Salar al-Dowleh.[170]

Since the arrival of Farmanfarma there were no disturbances in the city. However, the situation in the districts remained unsettled, and he took no steps against Salar al-Dowleh's followers, who, in July 1912, still held some villages near Kermanshah. On 7 June 1912, Salar al-Dowleh with 200 men was near Miyandoab, allegedly to force the government

---

168. IOR/L/PS/20/261/7, 'Persia. No 1 (1913). Further correspondence respecting the affairs of Persia', pp. 48 (no. 113), 52 (no. 122), 72-73 (no. 166), 86 (no. 173); Soltani 1386, p. 188 (Salar al-Dowleh lost 500 men, the government 50 men); Eyn al-Saltaneh 1377, vol. 5, pp. 3709-10; Hamadani 1354, p. 401; Adhari 1378, p. 29 (docs. 104, 107-08); Mardukh, p. 303. For a description of the battle and Yeprim Khan's role, see Mo'men 1384, pp. 59-66 and Kasravi 1350, pp. 518-27. Concerning Yeprim Khan's death and funeral, see Eyn al-Saltaneh 1377, vol. 5, pp. 3703-04.

169. Soltani 1386, pp. 188-91; Malekzadeh 1328, vol. 7, pp. 165, 167-75; Hamadani 1354, pp. 402-03; Adhari 1378, p. 29 (docs. 109-111); Eyn al-Saltaneh 1377, vol. 5, pp. 3849-50 (details on this battle by Da'ud Khan); Kasravi 1350, pp. 528-31; IOR/L/PS/20/261/7, 'Persia. No 1 (1913). Further correspondence respecting the affairs of Persia', pp. 65-67 (no. 136-37, 141, 146), 72-75 (no. 166).

170. Soltani 1386, p. 189.

to return his confiscated estates.[171] On 28 June 1912, Salar al-Dowleh wrote that he was in Kurdistan and that tribal chiefs needed to present themselves to him.[172] In July 1912, it was reported that Salar al-Dowleh was at Saqqez and was going to the Tabriz area in a Russian village where Mojallal al-Saltaneh had already arrived. It was also reported that he was collecting additional forces and that Nazar Ali Khan had joined him. As of 2 July Mojallal al-Saltaneh had taken refuge in Ne`matabad, the summer-quarters of the Russian consul, who, in accordance with his Minister's instructions, gave orders to arrest him. He was then taken to Russia, after having signed a document that he would not return to Iran.[173]

FREEDOM FIGHTERS IN GOVERNMENT SERVICE PARTLY DEFECT, PARTLY LEAVE

On 12 July 1912, all Bakhtiyaris and *mojaheds* left for Bisetun and had gone one stage beyond it, because Farmanfarma had no money to pay his troops. He informed Tehran that unless it sent money he was forced to take it from Customs receipts, else the Bakhtiyaris and *mojaheds* would abandon him and depart altogether and Salar al-Dowleh could take over again.[174] The only troops remaining in Kermanshah were the Hamadani *fida'i* regiment and 500 of Farmanfarma's own *savars*, as well as some local troops, and more of the latter were expected. The military leaders were dissatisfied because they had nothing to do and were dispersed over town; also because those who asked for pardon from Farmanfarma were told to come later, implying that he did not trust them, which they

---

171. IOR/L/PS/20/261/4, 'Persia. No 3 (1912). Further correspondence respecting the affairs of Persia', p. 78 (no. 154), 112 (no. 225).

172. Ettehadiyeh and Sa`vandiyan 1366, p. 191.

173. IOR/L/PS/20/261/7, 'Persia. No 1 (1913). Further correspondence respecting the affairs of Persia', pp. 91 (no. 181), 99 (no.191), 111-12 (no. 227). This news contradicted earlier news, according to which Nazar Ali Khan Amra'i and the Vali of Posht-e Kuh, Salar al-Dowleh's principal protectors, had submitted to Tehran, while Salar al-Dowleh was a fugitive en route to Tabriz, fearing that his former allies would arrest him. IOR/L/PS/20/261/7, 'Persia. No 1 (1913). Further correspondence respecting the affairs of Persia', Townley to Grey 24/07/1912, p. 106 (no. 217); Adhari 1378, doc. 112.

174. Political Diaries, vol. 4, p. 586; IOR/L/PS/20/261/7, 'Persia. No 1 (1913). Further correspondence respecting the affairs of Persia', pp. 60 (in April 1912, the government had promised the Armenians new elections, but did not do so), 102 (the Minister of Finance begged for an advance from Russia and Great Britain to pay the troops at Kermanshah, else they would leave), 105, 131.

maintained he could. The British, Ottoman and Russian Consuls met Farmanfarma on 14 July; he told them that the government troops had left without permission and that the presence of 300 *mojaheds* with a maxim and two guns was necessary, because many of the local troops had sided with the rebels in the past and were untrustworthy. Therefore, a loyal group would keep them honest. Salar al-Dowleh was then at Alishtar in Lorestan with Nazar Ali Khan Amra'i, Sardar Akram with about 700 men. Nazar Ali Khan was in regular contact with Farmanfarma and had informed him that Salar al-Dowleh would be willing to submit, if he was offered a governorship. Shortly thereafter he and the Vali made their submission to the government.[175] Salar al-Dowleh also wrote directly to Farmanfarma trying to shame him for what he had done to his family.[176] Farmanfarma again asked the government in Tehran to send him money to pay his troops, else there was the possibility that Salar al-Dowleh would undo all the gains that had been made. At that time he had been able to get the support of 400 Guran *savars*, but they left.[177]

In August 1912, Salar al-Dowleh was plundering parts of Kurdistan. On 15 August there was news that Salar al-Dowleh was 55 km from Kermanshah, and therefore, on 12 August, Farmanfarma left with his army to Senneh to restore order.[178] On 19 August 1912, Yar Mohammad Khan and Mosayeb Qoli Khan arrived at Kermanshah having deserted Farmanfarma one stage from Senneh; they had 300 *mojaheds* with them. They declared for Salar al-Dowleh, who had promised to restore the *Majles*. Yar Mohammad Khan published a notice that his action was not out of enmity to Farmanfarma, but out of desire of the opening of the *Majles* and a change of government. In Kermanshah, they were joined by Salar al-Dowleh's previous supporters.[179] According to Mo'tamadi, the reason for Yar Mohammad Khan's defection was that Farmanfarma, who

---

175. IOR/L/PS/20/261/7, 'Persia. No 1 (1913). Further correspondence respecting the affairs of Persia', pp. 105 (no. 213), 106 (no. 217), 139 (no. 283); Adhari 1378, p. 30 (docs. 110-111).

176. Adhari 1378, p. 30; Farmanfarma'iyan 1341, pp. 500-03.

177. Adhari 1378, p. 30 (doc. 113, 115); IOR/L/PS/20/261/7, 'Persia. No 1 (1913). Further correspondence respecting the affairs of Persia', p. 131 (no. 280).

178. IOR/L/PS/20/261/7, 'Persia. No 1 (1913). Further correspondence respecting the affairs of Persia', pp. 99 (no. 191), 165 (no. 328); Hamadani 1354, p. 407; Mardukh, p. 308 (at that time Salar al-Dowleh was in Buk).

179. IOR/L/PS/20/261/7, 'Persia. No 1 (1913). Further correspondence respecting the affairs of Persia', pp. 129 (no. 279), 165 (no. 328); Hamadani 1354, pp. 407, 409.

did not like the lower class *sardars*, had told Yar Mohammad Khan that he was on his own. It is true that their relationship had been festering from the beginning of 1912. Farmanfarma was very unhappy with Yar Mohammad Khan during the preceding months, even writing that "I will not go with Yar Mohammad Khan to paradise."[180] However, it would seem that the real reason for Yar Mohammad Khan's defection was Tehran politics. The Democrats were hell bent on unseating the current government and were willing to use any means to do so with the objective to have elections for the *Majles*, which had been closed since late 1911. Therefore, the Democrats gave Yar Mohammad Khan, who was one of their supporters, the order to join forces with Salar al-Dowleh. The strange reasoning was that having an alternative government led by Salar al-Dowleh and Yar Mohammad Khan in charge of W. Iran would give the Democrats a strike force to oust the Bakhtiyaris and Naser al-Molk, the Regent, and take control of Tehran and the state. Yar Mohammad Khan knew that the local force that Farmanfarma had left behind did not exceed 500 men, who, moreover, were no threat to his battle-hardened *mojaheds*. He quickly took control of the city, helped by local Democrats, and arrested Seham al-Dowleh, Farmanfarma's deputy-governor and other partisans. That same afternoon, Yar Mohammad Khan published a proclamation in which he called Naser al-Molk a traitor and that he only wanted to re-establish freedom and the Constitution and therefore, would continue to fight until these two objectives had been achieved and the *Majles* reopened. He also sent a telegram to Tehran demanding the dismissal of the Regent, a change of the composition of the Cabinet reflecting that of the *Majles* and the Constitution.[181] Farmanfarma regretted Yar Mohammad Khan's defection after all efforts and expenses made, which, he suggested, would give only new life to Salar al-Dowleh's rebellion.[182] Prior to his defection, Yar Mohammad Khan allegedly in secret had written to Salar al-Dowleh that he was disappointed in doing the government's bidding and that he would support his cause, if he would

---

180. Soltani 1386, p. 192; Farmanfarma'iyan 1382, vol. 1, pp. 358-59; Eyn al-Saltaneh 1377, vol. 5, p. 3654 calls Yar Mohammad Khan 'a bush-cutting gum collector' (*gavan-kan katira begir*). Adhari 1378, pp. 31-32, citing Ali Naqipur, *Yar Mohammad Khan Sardar-e Mashruteh*. Tehran, 1369/1990, pp. 15, 166, 174, ascribes the split to the corrupt traditional elite politicians in charge of the Tehran government as well as to the bad relations between the two men, Yar Mohammad Khan blaming Farmanfarma for the unnecessary deaths of his friends.

181. Malekzadeh 1328, vol. 7, pp. 240-43.

182. Adhari 1378, p. 33 (doc. 116); Kasravi 1350, p. 532.

appoint him commander of his troops, and later as Prime Minister, after he had put him on the throne. In reply Salar al-Dowleh sent 15,000 *tumans* in gold to Yar Mohammad Khan, which he had to collect near Sanandaj. On hearing this Yar Mohammad and 400 *mojaheds* left Kermanshah during the night, and rode to Sanandaj and then personally went around Kurdistan to recruit fighters. He allegedly collected 25,000 men and marched on Kermanshah to seize Farmanfarma and his arms. Farmanfarma knew about his defection and prepared a defense with a force of Sanjabis, some Bakhtiyaris and Armenians.[183]

SALAR AL-DOWLEH RETAKES KERMANSHAH AND LOSES IT AGAIN

On 3 September 1912, Salar al-Dowleh returned to Kermanshah with 500 men and some Kurdish chiefs, among whom Abbas Khan Javanrudi. Yar Mohammad received him warmly; he had 1,000 men, and perhaps more outside the city.[184] After his arrival, Salar al-Dowleh again threatened Molitor and told him that if he did not open the Customs he would retaliate against his staff, who were afraid and demanded that Molitor realize that he put their lives in danger by his refusal to obey Salar al-Dowleh. Molitor was between a rock and a hard place; his anguished staff and merchants urged him to keep the Customs open, which would give Salar al-Dowleh the opportunity to extort money from them. Molitor asked Tehran permission to close the Customs, which did not help much, because the prince took the Customs funds by force. Part of the money seized Salar al-Dowleh paid to Abbas Khan, who promised to dislodge Farmanfarma from Senneh. The tribes took a wait-and-see policy and did not join either side.[185]

At the end of August 1912, Townley reported that the situation in Kermanshah was confused. The government did not know that rebellious *mojaheds* had taken the town; it hoped to recover the town with the help of the Bakhtiyaris levies, 500 of which were with Farmanfarma; 150

---

183. Soltani 1386, pp. 192-93.
184. IOR/L/PS/20/261/7, 'Persia. No 1 (1913). Further correspondence respecting the affairs of Persia', p. 152 (no. 303). According to Hamadani 1354, p. 410, the prince returned on 1 September.
185. Destree 1976, pp. 248-49. While all this was going on the government in Tehran paid 200 *tumans* per month for the upkeep Salar al-Dowleh's wives and children in Tehran. Adhari 1378, doc. 117.

were en route from Soltanabad and 350 were to be sent from Tehran. Farmanfarma stated that all would be well if Tehran would send him 35,000 *tumans*. Yar Mohammad Khan, the rebel leader promised the same result for 40,000 *tumans*, both parties appeared to want to squeeze the government.[186]

The Bakhtiyari tribesmen and the *mojaheds* said they were willing to return if they were paid their arrear pay. There were also complaints that Farmanfarma took the spoils of war to enrich himself and that neither the government nor the troops who took them got any share. ... Before it was clear which side Yar Mohammad Khan and his men was on the central government sent a young Armenian, Mirza Yanz [Yans], former *chef de cabinet* of Yeprim Khan, to resolve the differences between the Moslem *mojaheds* and the Armenians who had remained loyal to Keri Khan. However, he arrived too late and failed in his mission. He not only was unable to convince the Moslem *mojaheds* to return, but he associated himself with the loyal *mojaheds* and the Bakhtiyaris and sent a petition to the government saying that the forces had been fighting for months for the Constitution and the *Majles*, but that the former was ignored and elections for the latter were not even contemplated.

> Copy of a Letter from Persian United Associates
>
> (to the Cabinet. Copy to Sardar Asad, and copy through the Dashnaksutiun to the Diplomatic Boy)
>
> It is of course well known to the Ministry that each member of the army has, from the beginning of the constitutional era, everywhere and at all times supported the independence of the State and protected the constitution. In pursuance of this sacred purpose we have sacrificed ourselves. We have made was and gained great victories, such as the victories of Tehran, Ghilan, Zenjan, Karachedagh, Ardebil, Mazanderan, Astrabad, Salar-ed-Dowleh, Arshad-ed-Dowleh, &c. up to the end. Each individual is still of the same persuasion and will sacrifice himself, and we are convinced that the Cabinet holds the same sacred views as the army.

---

186. IOR/L/PS/20/261/7, 'Persia. No 1 (1913). Further correspondence respecting the affairs of Persia', p. 146 (no. 293).

Seven months ago the Government were forced, on account of external difficulties, to close the Medjliss, and this army corps approved this course and assisted in the execution on account of expediency. The Medjliss was closed; the Cabinet gave explicit promises that the Medjliss would be reopened after the lapse of three months. Seven months have now passed since that promise was made and there is no sign of the reopening of the Medjliss. This has caused us disappointment, and therefore the individual members of the army in general, and the superior and the minor officers in particular, ask the Government to open Parliament, to give exceptionally stringent orders for the holding of elections, and to institute Parliament in a very short time. This will bring about contentment in the country and render the army grateful.

Zia-es-Sultan, Mirza Yanz, Shahab-es-Sultaneh, Kerry, Ghaffar Kazvini, Salar Mansur, Jevad Khan, Gholam Husein Khan Habib, Bahadur-ed-Dowleh (and about 30 more).

After considerable hesitation Farmanfarma's troops were induced to return to retake the city. [187]

On 8 September 1912, Salar al-Dowleh and Yar Mohammad left Kermanshah and with 600 men marched to Kurdistan. They were threatening Senneh, where the governor took refuge in the Turkish consulate, while the inhabitants fled in terror. The government in Tehran did not know where Farmanfarma was, who one week earlier had taken Senneh. Tehran wanted him to leave Senneh and take Kermanshah back from Salar al-Dowleh.[188] When Salar al-Dowleh and Yar Mohammad Khan left the city both forces passed each other without firing a shot; apparently one force took the highway, the other, the rebels, a less frequented mountain road. The other version is that the armies indeed passed in sight of one another without exchanging a blow, because the Bakhtiyaris

---

187. IOR/L/PS/20/261/7, 'Persia. No 1 (1913). Further correspondence respecting the affairs of Persia', Townley to Grey 02/10/1912, pp. 187-89 (no. 370 plus enclosure); Malekzadeh 1328, vol. 7, p. 244. According to Hamadani 1354, p. 410 they left on 10 September; Kasravi 1350, pp. 532-34 (with the Persian text of this letter).

188. IOR/L/PS/20/261/7, 'Persia. No 1 (1913). Further correspondence respecting the affairs of Persia', Townley to Grey19/09/1912, p. 156 (no. 318),174 (no. 338); Malekzadeh 1328, vol. 7, pp. 244-45; Kasravi 1350, p. 534.

and mojaheds refused to fire on Salar al-Dowleh and his men.[189] A third version given is that "the object of each of the Commanders appears to be plunder. The theory current here for some time a tacit understanding between Salar-ed-Dowleh and Firman Firmah is now regarded as probably correct. ... Salar-ed-Dowleh and Firman Firmah may exchange towns."[190] Whatever the truth of the matter, a fact is that the two opponents changed cities without firing a shot

After having returned to Kermanshah on 14 September 1912, there was continued friction between Farmanfarma and the chiefs of the Bakhtiyaris and the mojahed troops. The mojaheds had insulted the Russian flag on the house of a Russian subject and Farmanfarma feared assassination if he did not take action. He informed McDouall that the Bakhtiyaris and mojaheds did not obey him when ordered to pursue Yar Mohammad Khan and they also refused to pursue Salar al-Dowleh. After they had looted some villages he was afraid to do anything. From the Bakhtiyari leaders, Shehab al-Saltaneh and Ziya al-Soltan, McDouall learnt that they were dissatisfied with Farmanfarma, who had taken no steps to punish the rebels and only wrote letters to them rather than using force. He gave appointments to men who were rebels and did not even force them to pay fines to get a government pardon. Also, they did not trust the mojaheds and feared that some might even join Yar Mohammad Khan. An additional problem was that the current mojahed commander did not have the influence that Yeprim Khan had; they were all proud to serve under him, but after his death said why should they serve under an Armenian? They would not fight anymore and had wired Tehran that they were no longer responsible for the security of the province and were leaving. In the afternoon of 19 September 1912, the Bakhtiyaris and mojaheds, some 800 men left the city, returning to Tehran. Farmanfarma immediately asked McDouall to recommend to Tehran that the Bakhtiyaris and mojaheds had to be recalled and money to be given to him to raise a local force. Previously (July 1912) he had said that he needed 300 mojaheds. McDouall felt that a local force could not be trusted as long as Salar al-Dowleh was in Iran. The same held for the tribes, with the possible exception of part of the Sanjabis, because the tribes were only loyal to themselves and not to anybody else, government

---

189. IOR/L/PS/20/261/7, 'Persia. No 1 (1913). Further correspondence respecting the affairs of Persia', Townley to Grey 02/10/1912, pp. 187-88 (no. 370).
190. IOR/L/PS/10/212, File 211/1912 'Turkish Arabia Summaries', p. 5.

or pretender, and were ready to join either side for plunder. A local force in charge of the arsenal would immediately defect to Salar al-Dowleh if he promised it the looting of Hamadan, and probably the nucleus of the defectors would be Hasan, Mo`in al-Ra`aya's brother; in short a situation as bad or worse than tribesmen.[191] When at Kangavar, the chiefs were able to convince the deserting force to stay there until Tehran had sent relief troops. They stated that they had been fighting for the constitution and the *Majles*, and refused to continue fighting when the former was ignored and no hope for the latter to be summoned. However, Tehran was only able to send 150 Bakhtiyaris and no more. Without them the government force in Kermanshah had no fighting value. The British and Russian Ministers told the Bakhtiyari Prime Minister and Minister of War that if they could not raise Bakhtiyari troops and stop them from meddling in politics they would withdraw their support from the Bakhtiyaris. This resulted in part of the Bakhtiyaris at Kangavar returning to Kermanshah, while the rest went to Hamadan to reinforce the garrison there. Salar al-Dowleh was said to have gathered 7,000 men and did not appear to claim the throne any longer but wanted an independent Iran under a constitutional government.[192]

---

191. FO 248/1053, McDouall to Tehran. 19/09/1912; Hamadani 1354, pp. 411-12.

192. IOR/L/PS/20/261/7, 'Persia. No 1 (1913). Further correspondence respecting the affairs of Persia', Townley to Grey19/09/1912, pp, 156 (no. 318),173; Idem, Townley to Grey 02/10/1912, pp. 187-88 (no. 370); Malekzadeh 1328, vol. 7, p. 246; Hamadani 1354, pp. 416-17.

SALAR AL-DOWLEH AND YAR MOHAMMAD KHAN TRY TO RETAKE KERMANSHAH

Although Kermanshah was in government hands again this did not mean that the city was safe and secure. As stated above part of the troops were unwilling to fight given the political situation in the country and had left. Moreover, Salar al-Dowleh threatened the city again, while most of the government troops had gone to Abbasabad. When alerted to the threatening situation its leaders wired the olama that they would be back in Kermanshah by 31 September. Meanwhile, Salar al-Dowleh had wired McDouall that he would leave 27 September for Kermanshah, and on 28 September it was reported that Yar Mohammad Khan was with a force at Kamarian at 55 kilometers from Kermanshah. Farmanfarma repeatedly had asked for funds, as he believed that local levies would fight for him if paid. However, the tribes were not willing to fight for him, even when well paid, unless the Bakhtiyaris force would be there. The 250 Cossacks were not reliable, because it was due to their cowardice or worse that he had lost in May at Hamadan. On 26 September 1912 a large group of people came to the Russian and British Consulates with a petition, an action instigated by Farmanfarma, and the petition only was agreed upon after many meetings and all swearing together. The people really wanted security. Salar al-Dowleh had looted the city in February and the villages were being plundered by both parties. Heavy sums were exacted by Salar al-Dowleh and smaller sums by Farmanfarma. The people would submit to anyone as long as they were left in peace. Farmanfarma had orders to hold the city, but he only had enough men to hold the citadel. The petitioners asked the consuls to protect them, who replied that they only would protect the *bastis*, but not their families and property in the city.[193]

> We the undersigned people of Kermanshah each one representing one community and it is a long time that we are not masters of our lives, property, good name, and honor. Everyone from every side attacks this one handful

---

[193]. IOR/L/PS/20/261/7, 'Persia. No 1 (1913). Further correspondence respecting the affairs of Persia', pp. 175 (no. 434), 202-03 (no. 395); Hamadani 1354, p. 414; Adhari 1378, p. 33 (doc. 120; a day later they sought refuge with the Ottoman consul-general). Eyn al-Saltaneh 1377, vol. 5, p. 3684 refers to the total insecurity in the Hamadan area caused by all sides, whether rebel or government.

of earth. Except killing and plunder it has in the end no other result for the unfortunate people of Kermanshah and especially in these days we see that our honour (irz va namus), lives, and property, are really in danger. Therefore, we are compelled to take refuge in the Consulate. We beg you the representative of a Great Power neighbour to the unfortunates to obtain, in whatever way you know, safety of life, honour, and good name, for we can endure no more and until you give us security of life, property and good name we will not leave the Consulate, and request that the government troops for war and the troops of Salar ed-Dowleh do not enter the town but fight outside.

Seals of *mujtahids* as follows:

> Sultan al-Ulema, Aga Muhammad Mahdi, Aga Shaykh Hadi, Aga Rahim, Imam Juma, Aga Abul Hassan, Aga Shams ed-Din, Haji Aga Wali, Shuja al-Ulema, Zahir al-Ulema, Aga Muhammad Sadiq, Naib Sadr.
> Following princes and Khans. Amin al-Mamalek, Sardar Iljal, Mutazid ed-Dowleh, Zafar Ashraf, Samsam as Sultan, Akram ed-Dowleh, Amir Muqtadir, Mutazid as Sultan, Naser ed-Diwan, Abul Hassan Khan, Mansur ed-Diwan, Shuku` as-Sultan, Haji Hassan Khan Kalantar, Quli Khan, As`ad ed-Dowleh, Muhammad Jawad Mirza, Salar Muhtisham, Sarem as-Sultan, Mirza Ali Khan, Muhammad Taqi Khan, Chiragh Ali Khan, Seyeed i Nizam, Abu Seyeed Khan, Fathullah Khan, Ebrahim Khan, Muawen al-Mulk, Haji Ibrahim.
> Following merchants and traders. Rais et-Tujjar, Haji Seyid Habibullah, Haji Saeyd Baqir, Haji Mulla, Tahir Sarraf, Hussein Hasan, Muhammad Tahir, Muhammad Ali, Malek Muhammad, Haji Ali Akbar, Amanullah Khan. Maled Mohammed, Aga Barar, Sayid Muhammad Ali, Seyid Mohammed, Seyid Mustafa, Shuja el-Nizam.[194]

On 3 October 1912, Salar al-Dowleh and Yar Mohammad Khan with 1,000 men arrived at Miyan Darband at 55 kilometers from Kermanshah.

---

194. FO 248/1053, Petition of *bastis* (for the Persian text, see Appendix IV); IOR/L/PS/20/261/7, 'Persia. No 1 (1913). Further correspondence respecting the affairs of Persia', pp. 203-04 (no. 395).

The two consuls requested that they not fight in the city; they gave Farmanfarma two days to leave the city and face them in the field. Farmanfarma had given his troops orders to leave on 6 October. However, on 5 October 1912 at 2.30 a.m. Yar Mohammad Khan attacked the city. He entered the town through the *darvazeh-ye mahalleh-ye Barzeh Dagh* in the s.e. and the *darvazeh-ye mahalleh-ye Chenani* in the west and took control over a large part of the city. Farmanfarma held the government buildings, the Bakhtiyaris and Sanjabis Chia Sorkh with two guns. At 9 a.m. Yar Mohammad was shot in the head. He had 50 Kalhors with him who fled immediately and came to the British Consulate asking for asylum, which was refused, apart from a few wounded men. The rebels withdrew fighting and there was shooting till afternoon. At that time, some 300 Kurds came to the British Consulate, while under heavy fire seeking asylum. Farmanfarma promised their life if they surrendered. McDouall disarmed them and found that their only arms were some clubs. They were escorted to their own district; the wounded were taken to the Farmanfarma hospital. McDouall estimated that only some 200 persons had died. This number differs significantly from that of Mo`tamadi, according to whom most of Yar Mohammad Khan's force, which was centered in the gardens south-east of the city awaiting news, was shelled by the Bakhtiyaris and Armenians. Even two weeks later they were still burying the about 3,000 dead Kurds. After this defeat the Kalhors tried to join the fight, but they were defeated by the Bakhtiyaris. It was generally believed that Yar Mohammad's death meant the end of Salar al-Dowleh's rebellion. Yar Mohammad's second-in-command, Hoseyn Qoli Khan was able to escape with his men.[195] Thus, finally peace returned to the city after four years of unrest, Molitor, the Belgian Customs officer wrote. Nevertheless, he wanted to leave, because he blamed the Russians for having fomented disorder in Kermanshah as it was one of the main routes through which British goods entered.[196]

---

195. IOR/L/PS/20/261/7, 'Persia. No 1 (1913). Further correspondence respecting the affairs of Persia', pp. 177 (no. 348), 204 (no. 395), 212 (no. 414); Soltani 1386, pp. 192-95; Malekzadeh 1328, vol. 7, pp. 247-48; Hamadani 1354, p. 415; Eyn al-Saltaneh 1377, vol. 5, pp. 3654, 3668; Mardukh, p. 310; Kasravi 1350, p. 535. For details about the battle in Kermanshah and an appreciation of Yar Mohammad Khan, see Soltani 1381, vol. 4, pp. 640-71; see also the contemptuous opinion of Eyn al-Saltaneh 1377, vol. 5, pp. 3665 (Yar Mohammad Khan, the bush cutting gum collector was appointed army commander, governor of Kermanshah and marcher lord (*sarhaddar*) of both Iraqs, while Mojallal al-Soltan became governor of Kurdistan and the prince's deputy). 3760.

196. Destree 1976, pp. 249-50.

SALAR AL-DOWLEH'S KHORASAN AND CASPIAN ADVENTURE (1912-13)

FLEES TO ASTARABAD AND CALLS ON TURKMEN SUPPORT

Salar al-Dowleh, who was in a village outside Kermanshah awaiting news of the outcome of the attack, fled to Sanandaj and was lucky that his escape route had not been cut off. Troops from Hamadan, mostly Armenians under Keri Khan, were about to pursue the prince when news arrived that Mirza Yanz, charged with a mission by Farmanfarma, had been arrested at Qazvin. Suspecting treachery the Armenians refused to march; when Mirza Yanz was released at Tehran's orders it was too late and Salar al-Dowleh was gone. The Bakhtiyaris made an effort to pursue Salar al-Dowleh, but they were unable to catch him. He was said to be in Garrus or even between Hamadan and Qazvin. In mid-October 1912, the Russian Minister believed that Salar al-Dowleh was at 40 km from Tehran, and he believed that the *mojaheds* and Democrats were in league with him. Therefore, he had put the Russian troops at Qazvin on alert.[197] On 16 October 1912, Salar al-Dowleh with a small force was said to be at Hessarak at 50 km from Tehran. For two days it was thought that he might attack Tehran. The government hurriedly gathered troops and gendarmes to put Tehran in state of defense.

---

197. IOR/L/PS/20/261/7, 'Persia. No 1 (1913). Further correspondence respecting the affairs of Persia', pp. 180 (nos. 357, 358), 182 (no. 366), 205 (no. 397); Eyn al-Saltaneh 1377, vol. 5, pp. 3777-78.

However, he proceeded to Sharistanak, north of Tehran in the mountains, where he remained on 22-23 October. According to Eyn al-Saltaneh, not everyone in Tehran was upset by Salar al-Dowleh's approach as many townspeople saw him as the means to be rid of the Bakhtiyari yoke and oppression. In Qom, the olama and sayyeds even took off their turbans during the evening prayer in front of the Fatima shrine praying for the prince's victory. However, the prince disappointed them all, for with some 280 men he continued to Mazandaran. It was only on 27-28 October that the government made a serious effort to pursue him, when 300 Bakhtiyaris, 100 Usanlu *savars*, and 50 Cossacks with two mountain guns were sent against him. Arrived in Nur (Mazandaran) Salar al-Dowleh asked the chiefs of Nur, Kajur and the Khvajehvand to join him. Some chiefs accepted and plundered some Kajur villages.[198] The pursuing force made no serious attempt to capture the prince, who remained in Astarabad district with a small following trying to settle with the central government.[199]

In early November 1912, the British agent at Astarabad reported that Salar al-Dowleh was at Khvajeh Nafas with some 1,000 horsemen and that he had sent men towards Shahrud.[200] Mohammad Reza Khan Afshar, a follower of Salar al-Dowleh, wrote to the Turkmen chiefs inviting them to join the prince, who was at Khvajeh Nafas, awaiting the ex-Shah's arrival.[201] On 4 November 1912, news was received that Salar al-Dowleh, via Nur va Kujur, had arrived at Mahmudabad at the seaside. Earlier, the Minister of Interior had given instructions by telegram to Amir A`zam, the governor of Shahrud concerning Salar al-Dowleh's coming to Mazandaran. On 18 November news was received that Salar al-Dowleh's

---

198. IOR/L/PS/20/261/7, 'Persia. No 1 (1913). Further correspondence respecting the affairs of Persia', p. 205-06 (no. 397); IOR/L/PS/20/261/7, 'Persia. No 1 (1913). Further correspondence respecting the affairs of Persia', p. 211 (no. 414) (A certain Heyder Qoli Khan sought asylum at the Legation; he was believed to be an adherent of Salar al-Dowleh, but he denied it.). According to Adhari 1378, p. 34, the prince traveled to Kamalabad, then to Hesarak, Borghan, Angeh, Shahrestanak to Nur in Mazandaran; see also Adhari 1378, docs. 126-27; Eyn al-Saltaneh 1377, vol. 5, pp. 3780-81, 3785 (also summary of a letter to Amir As`ad).

199. IOR/L/PS/20/261/7, 'Persia. No 1 (1913). Further correspondence respecting the affairs of Persia', p. 239 (no. 475).

200. IOR/L/PS/20/261/7, 'Persia. No 1 (1913). Further correspondence respecting the affairs of Persia', p. 207 (no. 404). Further correspondence respecting the affairs of Persia', p. 207 (no. 404).

201. IOR/L/PS/10/209, File 52/1912 Pt 1 'Persia Diaries', Meshed Consular Diary, no. 48, for th week ending 30th November 1912, p. 1.

savars were at two stages from Damghan. To protect his property Amir A`zam went there on 8 November.²⁰² On 11 November 1912, Salar al-Dowleh, via Do Dangeh and Hazar Jarib, arrived at Nowkandeh, where he had lunch at home of Qahar Khan Salar-e Ashja`. There he wrote 10 letters to various royalist landowners and olama to get their support. His rallying call was that his mission was to save Iran from the domination of the infidel foreigners, but plunder was his real objective. He immediately raised a force of Turkmen that already on 4 November was sighted near Damghan, as noted above. Next, Salar al-Dowleh moved around, from village to the other, and contacted the Russian consul at Astarabad, who rode to see him on 14 November near Hajji YakLag Torkman Ataba'i. Apparently, the Russian consul asked him to go via Qonbad-e Qabus into the direction of Mashhad given that he was responsible for the security of Astarabad town. As Salar al-Dowleh was without real followers he sent a messenger to the Yamut saying that Mohammad Ali Mirza would come to Khvajeh Nafas after one week where they should come to show their loyalty and where wages and provisions would be given. For the moment the Khans did not dare to go to Salar al-Dowleh without the permission of the Russian consul, who on 16 November 1912 rode to Khvajeh Nafas with 30 Cossacks.²⁰³

DEFEATED AT SHAHRUD, SEEKS TURKMEN SUPPORT AND DEAL WITH TEHRAN

Meanwhile, Mosayeb Qoli Khan, one of Salar al-Dowleh's supporters, with some 400 armed men had gone to Shahrud to collect taxes. Amir-e A`zam, the former dismissed governor of Kerman received a letter from Salar al-Dowleh ordering him to receive Mosayeb Qoli Khan. This contact was due to the fact that during his residence in Europe in 1908, Amir A`zam had played a leading role among the reformist Iranian emigres and had been in regular correspondence with Salar al-Dowleh. This exchange of views had led the prince to believe that Amir A`zam

---

202. Vakil al-Dowleh 1362, vol. 1, pp. 329-30. According to Eyn al-Saltaneh 1377, vol. 5, pp. 3791, 3804, Amir A`zam, who had just been dismissed as governor of Kerman, because he had oppressed people and extorted 2-3 *korur tumans*, had fled to Damghan where he joined forces with Salar al-Dowleh and had become his general. A force of 400 Bakhtiyaris, 100 gendarmes and 100 Cossacks sent against him was defeated.

203. Vakil al-Dowleh 1362, vol. 1, pp. 331-33, 340-41, 343.

was one of his true followers. In reaction, Amir A`zam invited Mosayeb Qoli Khan to a lunch and some entertainment. Mosayeb Qoli Khan, whose main camp was at Mojan, 6 *farsakh* from Shahrud, told his men to leave their arms before going into the town. During lunch the governor learnt that fights had broken between his men and those of Mosayeb Qoli Khan and therefore, Amir A`zam ordered them all to be arrested, although some fled. According to Eyn al-Saltaneh, the two leaders got into a dispute and then into a fight, wrestling each other to the ground, in which fight their companions joined. Amir A`zam then rode with his men to Mojan and disarmed Mosayeb Qoli Khan's troops. The booty was said to be 33,000 *tumans*, 500 rifles and 200 horses and mules. Amir A`zam asked Tehran for money to maintain the prisoners, and denied that he had seized any money during their arrest. Because Tehran sent no money, the arrested men were stripped and released thus, reinforcing the robber bands. It is probably this event, viz. that on or before 13 November 1912 it was reported by the Iranian government that Amir A`zam had defeated Salar al-Dowleh between Damghan and Shahrud; the prince was said to have fled to Gumush Tepeh.[204]

On 2 December 1912 it was reported that Salar al-Dowleh met with clan elders of the Ja`fara'i, Ataba'i and Olghi. He told them he had come to fight for Mohammad Ali, not for himself. Until his death he would fight for the improvement of the people of Iran, for which he was ready to fight. He further said: "are you happy that the Russian government sent your daughters to the brothel (*mateshkeh-khaneh*) and makes your sons wear Cossack dress like the Lezgis? In the past they were under Iran's protection now they are under the Russians." They all replied: "we are not at all happy to be Russian subjects. Give us some time to plant barley and wheat then we are at your service."[205] Heydar Qoli Khan Mas`ud al-Soltan was governor of Kord Mahalleh and *kalantar* of the district, but because of extraordinary oppression he dismissed

---

204. Vakil al-Dowleh 1362., vol. 1, pp. 331-32; Eyn al-Saltaneh 1377, vol. 5, pp. 3804, 3866 (another report of the fight between the two men and stated that Mosayeb Qoli Khan had only 40 men with him, which seems more likely), 4061-62; IOR/L/PS/20/261/7, 'Persia. No 1 (1913). Further correspondence respecting the affairs of Persia', p. 209 (no. 410); IOR/L/PS/10/209, File 52/1912 Pt 1 'Persia Diaries', Meshed Consular Diary, no. 47, for the week ending 23rd of November 1912, p. 1; 'Persia. No 1 (1914). Further correspondence respecting the affairs of Persia', Sykes to Townley 22/01/1913, p. 54 (no. 140). For an account giving Amir A`zam's point of view, see Qezelayagh 1349, pp. 358-60 (40,000 *tumans* in cash, carpets, tents, and arms); see also Divsalari 1364.

205. Vakil al-Dowleh 1362., vol. 1, p. 332.

Mohammad Ali Khan Sartip. The latter offered his services to Salar al-Dowleh, who appointed him *kalantar* of the district, fixed the tax rate for rice, which he collected and handed over to the prince. The people of the district also choose for Salar al-Dowleh. At the beginning of December the warriors of the three clans joined Salar al-Dowleh at Khvajeh Nafas, and on 4 December so did the Yamut.[206] After the arrest of Mosayeb Qoli Khan, Salar al-Dowleh and 400 armed men went on a plunder raid and acquired much loot. On 6 December 1912, Amir A`zam received broad support as governor and was appointed governor of Shahrud, Bestam and Damghan; he went to Damghan and raised barricades against Salar al-Dowleh. The prince, who himself had spread the news that the ex-Shah would come, sentenced a man to death who had brought the false news that the ex-shah had arrived and had received a gift for bringing this joyful news (*mozhdeh*).[207]

Sazonov of the Russian Legation tried to resolve the issue by peaceful means and negotiated with the Iranian government to appointed Salar al-Dowleh governor of Gilan rather than using force. Soon after his arrival in the Astarabad area, Salar al-Dowleh put out feelers about the terms offered to him. The prince did not like the ones proposed, which comprised a pension of 12,000 *tumans*, to have all his confiscated undisputed property returned, titles of the disputed ones to be impartially considered, no governorship for the moment, and be allowed to live in Tehran. The Russian consul at Astarabad was instructed to warn him to accept, otherwise pressure would be put on the Turkmen to abandon his cause.[208] Around 25 December 1912, Salar al-Dowleh rejected the terms offered, because he could accept anything from the Bakhtiyaris, who dominated the Cabinet. He said that if Sa`d al-Dowleh would become Prime Minister things would be different, because he would at least offer him an appropriate governorship.[209]

At the end of December 1912 some 700 Turkmen came to Kord Mahalleh. Salar al-Dowleh paid cash wages and announced he would

---

206. Vakil al-Dowleh 1362., vol. 1, pp. 333, 344-45.

207. Vakil al-Dowleh 1362., vol. 1, p. 334. Amir A'zam was also appointed governor of Astarabad. Vakil al-Dowleh 1362, vol. 1, p. 354.

208. IOR/L/PS/20/261/7, 'Persia. No 1 (1913). Further correspondence respecting the affairs of Persia', p. 248 (no. 487); Eyn al-Saltaneh 1377, vol. 5, p. 3861.

209. IOR/L/PS/20/261/7, 'Persia. No 1 (1913). Further correspondence respecting the affairs of Persia', p. 266 (no. 501).

give 5,000 *qrans* as daily pay (*jireh*). This caused concern in Tehran and Ivanov, the Russian consul was ordered to meet with Salar al-Dowleh to settle matters, presumably by having the prince accept the governorship of Gilan. This seems likely in view of subsequent events. On 29 December 1912, Ivanov met with Salar al-Dowleh who agreed that he would dismiss the Turkmen. Ivanov sent 5,000 *tumans* for Salar al-Dowleh's expenses, presumably for his journey to Gilan. On that same day, Salar al-Dowleh mounted the pulpit and told the Turkmen that by telegram he had learnt that Mohammad Ali had arrived at Enzeli, and from there would go to Tehran. Therefore, he would join him by going via Mazandaran. Those Turkmen who would accompany him would get wages. Those that were disappointed left to their camps. On 1 January 1913, when Salar al-Dowleh was at Karkandeh the Russian consul sent the promised 5,000 *tumans*. As agreed the prince paid his men to go to Rasht. Salar al-Dowleh wanted to march via Mazandaran to Tehran. However, at the instigation of the Russian consul the road was blocked by Esma`il Khan Amir Mo'ayyed, and thus, Salar al-Dowleh went to Khvajeh Nafas, where he was joined by others. After three days he went to the Daz tribe. Around 12 January 1913, Salar al-Dowleh returned to Khvajeh Nafas.[210] Around that time, Salar al-Dowleh defeated the government troops of Mazandaran under Amir Saiyid and killed about 20 men. The Russians did not interfere. He withdrew after having gathered sufficient plunder.[211] On 21 January 1913, Townley wired London that Salar al-Dowleh had reached a satisfactory agreement with the Russian Legation and the Persian government, allowing him to live in Tehran, receiving a pension and return of his confiscated properties.[212] As a result, Tehran sent a telegram that Salar al-Dowleh had submitted in January 1913.[213]

However, without waiting for the final arrangments of the agreement, in mid-January 1913, the ever mercurial Salar al-Dowleh left Astarabad. On 26 January 1913, Salar al-Dowleh left Yamut country

---

210. Vakil al-Dowleh 1362, vol. 1, pp. 340-41; IOR/L/PS/20/261/7, 'Persia. No 1 (1913). Further correspondence respecting the affairs of Persia', p. 305 (no. 561) (250 Russian troops + 4 guns stationed in governor of Astarabad's residence).

211. IOR/L/PS/10/209, File 52/1912 Pt 1 'Persia Diaries', Meshed Consular Diary, no. 5, for the week ending 1st of February 1913, p. 1.

212. Political Diaries vol. 4, p. 646; IOR/L/PS/20/261/7, 'Persia. No 1 (1913). Further correspondence respecting the affairs of Persia', p. 296 (no. 541).

213. Political Diaries vol. 5, p. 38; Hamadani 1354, p. 419.

toward Ramiyan and Hajjilar.[214] With a Turkmen force Salar al-Dowleh marched against Nardin (between Shahrud and Bojnord).[215] On 29 January 1913, the governor of Nardin wired that Salar al-Dowleh had arrived at Hoseynabad, 10 km from Nardin with 200 of his own *savars* and some Turkmen. Allegedly, the Goklan spiritual leader Kilich Ishan had promised to join Salar al-Dowleh on condition that he destroy Nardin and its governor, who had killed Mohammad Geldi Khan, the chief of the Goklan two years earlier. Salar al-Dowleh sent letters to the Sardar of Bojnurd and to Durdi Khan, governor of Ament and Incha (on the Atrek) to join him, else it would get worse for them. The Russians were elated by the course of events, and, according to Leleux, the Belgian Customs officer in Mashhad, the entire affair had been orchestrated by the Russian Minister.[216] In early February 1913, Salar al-Dowleh with 300 men took Nardin; the governor had left beforehand. The prince then went towards Sabzavar via Meyamey, on the Tehran-Mashhad road. On 7 February he reached Sabzavar with a small force of some 200 Guklan and Hajjilar and was joined by a bandit, called Jahangir. It was then reported that he intended to march to Mashhad. Meanwhile, the prince was causing some havoc in NW Khorasan. He took many camels and mules from Amir A`zam. The army commander of Mashhad was supposed to march against him but no *savars* came and the guns were rusted. The governors of Sabzavar and Nishapur fled to Mashhad. As a result, the authorities of Mashhad wanted to put the city in state of defense for an expected siege. However, Sykes, the British consul in Mashhad advised them to do nothing without talking to the Russian consul, who had told him that he had instructions not to allow Salar al-Dowleh in places where there were Russian troops. In Tehran, the Russian Minister said that Salar al-Dowleh was at Khvajeh Nafas, which is interesting in light of Leleux's remarks, as the prince clearly was not.[217]

---

214. Fortescue 1920, pp. 30, 33; Kazembeyki 2003, pp.195-96; Vakil al-Dowleh 1362., vol. 1, pp. 329-33, 340-41, 343; 'Persia. No 1 (1914). Further correspondence respecting the affairs of Persia', p. 24 (no. 51).

215. 'Persia. No 1 (1914). Further correspondence respecting the affairs of Persia', p. 24 (no. 51).

216. IOR/L/PS/10/209, File 52/1912 Pt 1 'Persia Diaries', Meshed Consular Diary, no. 5, for the week ending 1st of February 1913, p. 1.

217. IOR/L/PS/10/209, File 52/1912 Pt 1 'Persia Diaries', Meshed Consular Diary, no. 5, for the week ending 1st of February 1913, p. 1; IOR/L/PS/10/209, File 52/1912 Pt 1 'Persia Diaries', Meshed Consular Diary, no. 7. for the week ending 15th February 1913, p. 1; IOR/L/PS/20/261/7, 'Persia. No 1 (1913). Further correspondence respecting the affairs of Persia', p. 299 (no. 551); Idem, 'Persia. No 1 (1914). Further

GOES ON LOOTING SPREE; ENDANGERS DEAL WITH TEHRAN

Salar al-Dowleh spent the week at Sabzavar, collecting money in the usual manner, i.e. by force. He robbed people and seized the government granary at Mazinan. Then the Russian consul told him he had to accept the governorship of Gilan or he would lose Russian protection. Meanwhile, *savars* were collected from everywhere in Khorasan to attack the prince, as he was greatly disliked by the provincial authorities. For example, the manager (*motavalli-bashi*) of the Imam Reza shrine in Mashhad hated Salar al-Dowleh as he knew of several children that had been eaten due to the famine caused by Salar al-Dowleh in W. Iran.[218] Salar al-Dowleh's presence in Khorasan caused much unrest. Mohammad, the notorious Nishapur bandit had joined him and their joint forces burnt three villages near Sabzavar, and they even robbed and disarmed the men of the Kirai regiment in Sabzavar itself.[219] The Russian officer sent to the prince at Sabzavar to see whether his intentions were peaceful returned to Astarabad, because he believed that the prince had some coup in mind.[220] On 10 February 1913, Townley reported that the new Persian cabinet decided that it could not allow such a dangerous person as Salar al-Dowleh to reside in Tehran. After long discussions and after heavy pressure by Russia the governorship of Gilan was again offered to him. Because Salar al-Dowleh was on a plundering expedition having arrived at Sabzevar, Tehran had sent a force against him and considered withdrawing the offer of the Gilan governorship to him.[221] Salar al-Dowleh realizing that Amir A`zam blocked his way into Khorasan and seeing no further advantage in probing any further accepted to submit and become governor of Gilan and returned to Astarabad, to go from there to Rasht.[222]

---

correspondence respecting the affairs of Persia', p. 24 (no. 51); Vakil al-Dowleh 1362., vol. 1, pp. 345.

218. IOR/L/PS/10/209, File 52/1912 Pt 1 'Persia Diaries', Meshed Consular Diary, no. 7. for the week ending 15th February 1913, p. 1.

219. 'Persia. No 1 (1914). Further correspondence respecting the affairs of Persia', p. 80 (no. 202) ("After the raid in the Sabzavar area, Mohammad the bandit returned to Nishapur and Salar al-Dowleh went to Bandar-e Gaz, where he still is. He refuses pension and governorship of Gilan.")

220. IOR/L/PS/18/C144, 'Extracts from Annual Persia Reports, 1906, 1909, 1910, 1911, 1912, 1913 regarding loans, and complete reports for 1908 & 1913', pp. 15.

221. IOR/L/PS/20/261/7, 'Persia. No 1 (1913). Further correspondence respecting the affairs of Persia', p. 307 (no. 564).

222. Vakil al-Dowleh 1362, vol. 1, p. 345.

At that time, the end of February 1913, the British government also believed that this would better, when the Persian government raised no further objection to Salar al-Dowleh's appointment at Rasht and see how things worked out.[223] However, opposition to this position grew. The Regent, who was in London, wired the Persian Cabinet that if Salar al-Dowleh would be appointed governor of Gilan he would not return. The Russians told the Cabinet that they had given their word to Salar al-Dowleh that he would be appointed governor of Gilan, and, therefore, it was difficult to go back on it.[224] However, then Salar al-Dowleh made matters worse for himself, as usual. In exasperation, Townley reported to Grey that "This lunatic prince has now renewed his demand that during his tenure in Gilan" a Cossack guard of 200 men with two officers had to be attached to him. The Iranian government asked Great Britain and Russia to induce the prince to go to Europe as it was unable to agree to such an outrageous demand.[225] London agreed and Grey instructed the British ambassador in Russia to inform his counterpart that Salar al-Dowleh was not fit for such an important appointment.[226] For once the Russian Foreign Minister agreed, and consented that it would be better that the prince went to Europe; he washed his hands off the prince and would instruct his Legation in Tehran accordingly.[227] Not only the Cabinet did not want the prince as governor of Gilan. There was also considerable alarm in Rasht in early March about the appointment of Salar al-Dowleh as governor. The latter seemed to prepare himself for his new function, because on 13 March 1913, he arrived at Astarabad from Sabzavar. After long negotiations Salar al-Dowleh left Sabzavar agreeing to go to Gilan. As reason he gave that the tobacco at Sabzavar was too bad for him to smoke. Leleux paid him 4,000 *tumans* for his travel expenses to Rasht.[228] According to Townley, "At the moment that

---

223. 'Persia. No 1 (1914). Further correspondence respecting the affairs of Persia', Grey to Townley, 25/02/1913, p. 16 (no. 7).

224. 'Persia. No 1 (1914). Further correspondence respecting the affairs of Persia', Townley to Grey, 13/03/1913, p. 36 (no. 73).

225. 'Persia. No 1 (1914). Further correspondence respecting the affairs of Persia', Townley to Grey 18/03/1913, p. 41 (no. 89).

226. 'Persia. No 1 (1914). Further correspondence respecting the affairs of Persia', Grey to Buchanan, 22/03/1913, p. 43 (no. 101).

227. 'Persia. No 1 (1914). Further correspondence respecting the affairs of Persia', Buchanan to Grey 23/03/1913, p. 44 (no. 104).

228. 'Persia. No 1 (1914). Further correspondence respecting the affairs of Persia', p. 59 (no.143).

the Prince had reached this wise decision he was at the head of an infinitesimal force of badly-armed followers and Amir A'zam dominated him with a much superior force of Government troops. Even then Salar did not accept the situation with good grace but returned to Asterabad in a very sullen frame of mind without in any way having made a genuine act of submission to the Government, which he has never ceased to treat with contumely and disrespect."[229]

Tehran had instructed Amir A'zam to welcome Salar al-Dowleh with 500 Damghani *savars* and two cannons, but Salar al-Dowleh ignored him and went to Fenderesk and on 12 March 1913 arrived in the villages there. That same day the Russian consul Ivanov welcomed Salar al-Dowleh on his entry into the city. After lunch Salar al-Dowleh went to Kafshgiri at two *farsakh* from Astarabad. The next day he went to Kord Mahalleh. On 17 March he arrived at Bandar-e Gaz where he received 3,000 *tumans* for his expenses, after which he returned to the village of Gaz. Because of harsh Russian rule most people of Astarabad, the Yamut and the clan chiefs of the Ja'fara'i joined Salar al-Dowleh; esp. the Yamut urged him to take Astarabad; from Goklan until Ja'fara'i country they were ready to pay 5 *tumans* per household cash if he would get rid of the Russians.[230] From his move to Gaz, it seemed that Salar al-Dowleh had accepted Tehran's offer, because Tehran gave instructions to receive the prince with suitable honors. He would be traveling by boat, with only a few servants, from Bandar-e Gaz to Rasht. The governor of Gilan submitted his resignation to the Cabinet in Tehran, writing with some sarcasm that in view of the efforts and troubles H.H. Salar al-Dowleh had given for Iran's independence the authorities had thus rewarded him.[231]

On 12 March 1913, at the request of the Iranian government, Foreign Secretary Grey asked Townley in Tehran to urge the Russian government to agree that Salar al-Dowleh should leave to Rasht. Moreover, the Persian government was ready "to increase his pay, if he resided in Europe." It also feared that riots would break out because of Salar al-Dowleh's appointment.[232] The British consul in Mashhad reported

---

229. 'Persia. No 1 (1914). Further correspondence respecting the affairs of Persia', Townley to Grey, 12/05/1913, pp. 100-01 (no. 235).
230. Vakil al-Dowleh 1362., vol. 1, p. 349.
231. Adhari 1378, p. 35 (docs. 133-34).
232. 'Persia. No 1 (1914). Further correspondence respecting the affairs of Persia', Townley to Grey, Grey to Townley 12/03/1913, p 35.

that in March 1913, a secret agent of Salar al-Dowleh was sent from Krasnovodsk to Rasht to report on the local situation and attitude of population. He then had to go to Bandar-e Gaz to report his findings to Salar al-Dowleh.[233] However, this probably refers to the departure of Mirza Aqa Khan, Salar al-Dowleh's secretary, who arrived in Rasht on 12 March 1913.[234] It might also refer to Qahar Khan, who was said to have gone to Rasht on 20 March to report to the prince about the situation there; others said that he fled out of fear for the Russian consul, while again others said he had gone there to welcome the ex-Shah.[235] This suggests that the prince really had his eyes on Rasht, which he wanted to take by force, as is also indicated by his earlier intended foray into that direction, which was thwarted by Russian intervention.

On 21 March, at the orders of the Russian Legation, Ivanov went to the village of Gaz to make Salar al-Dowleh move. It was agreed that he would disarm his *savars*, who were in Dashti Kolah [?] near Gaz. However, they refused to return their arms. They were urged to do so several times and the third time the chief of the *savars* killed Salar al-Dowleh's servant who had threatened that he would take the arms by force from them and the *savars* departed towards central Iran. Ivanov again insisted that Salar al-Dowleh leave for Rasht. However, the prince wanted remain and said that he would sent a deputy to Rasht to take care of the governorship. After having stayed for two weeks in Gaz, Ivanov with 50 Cossacks and two cannons returned to Astarabad. As a result, Ivanov reported "most unfavourably about him, and the feeling grew on all sides that he would prove an impossible Governor." Meanwhile, Salar al-Dowleh collected taxes in Gaz and environs, where some 50 Astarabadi and Enzeli Qajars were with him, with horse and arms.[236] Around 10 April 1913, Salar al-Dowleh was back at Kord Mahalleh where Ivanov visited him.[237]

---

233. IOR/L/PS/10/209, File 52/1912 Pt 1 'Persia Diaries', Meshed Consular Diary, no. 13, for the week ending 5th of April 1913, p. 1

234. 'Persia. No 1 (1914). Further correspondence respecting the affairs of Persia', p. 80 (no. 202).

235. Vakil al-Dowleh 1362, vol. 1, p. 349.

236. Vakil al-Dowleh 1362, vol. 1, pp. 350-51; 'Persia. No 1 (1914). Further correspondence respecting the affairs of Persia', Townley to Grey, 12/05/1913, p. 101 (no. 235).

237. Vakil al-Dowleh 1362, vol. 1, p. 352. At that time, some former partisans of the prince (brothers of the Ilkhani) returned to Kermanshah where they stayed in the

In the evening of 17 April 1913, Salar al-Dowleh learnt that Amir A`zam had orders from Tehran to take him to Russia. However, he only went to Astarabad to check on Salar al-Dowleh, who was reported to be collecting men to return to Khorasan. The next morning with 50 *savars* and 100 foot under Ashja` al-Molk the prince marched to Karkandeh. The Yamut and other clans were ready to start plundering, and 400 men came to Kord Mahalleh. Meanwhile, Amir A`zam with 50 *savars* arrived at the Russian Consulate on 19 April. Salar al-Dowleh had mobilized a force of foot and horse and wrote to Ivanov, stating that when Amir A`zam left the Consulate he would arrest him immediately. Ivanov said if Salar al-Dowleh would hurt even one Astarabadi he would send his Cossacks to put a rope around his neck to take him to the Consulate. Salar al-Dowleh desisted from taking further action, but now told the Turkmen chiefs that the succession to the throne was not limited to his brother. "I qualify as well and the consul has no right to stop me. In Iran I am my own man and law. I am ready to fight the Russians." He moved his camp to Nowkandeh. Salar al-Dowleh's words had a mobilizing impact on Turkmen and men of various groups joined his cause.[238]

Meanwhile, the Persian government did not want Salar al-Dowleh as governor of Gilan any longer and hoped that Russia would induce him to go to Europe. Tehran took this position, because the rebel prince had not submitted to the central government by accepting its conditions, while the population of Gilan opposed his appointment. Going ahead with his appointment only would create problems, Tehran argued.[239] However, Russia put great pressure on the Persian government to send Salar al-Dowleh immediately to Rasht. The government in Tehran still felt that it could not agree as Salar al-Dowleh had not submitted and therefore, asked the British government for advice.[240] In fact, the position of the Persian government hardened. It had decided to resign rather than agree to Salar al-Dowleh's appointment. The Regent also wired from

---

house of Sayyed Hasan Owjaq, because they were afraid of the population's reaction to their past misdeeds. FO 248/1073, Kermanshah Diary no. 16, ending 17/04/1913.

238. Vakil al-Dowleh 1362, vol. 1, pp. 353-54; IOR/L/PS/10/209, File 52/1912 Pt 1 'Persia Diaries', Meshed Consular Diary, no. 18, for the week ending 3rd of May 1913, p. 1.

239. 'Persia. No 1 (1914). Further correspondence respecting the affairs of Persia', Townley to Grey 13/04/1913, p. 65 (no 156).

240. 'Persia. No 1 (1914). Further correspondence respecting the affairs of Persia', Townley to Grey, 16/04/1913, p. 88 (no. 159).

London that the Cabinet had to resist and not appoint him. Townley advised the Cabinet not to resign, but also pointed out to London that public opinion was against Salar al-Dowleh's appointment.[241] As a result, Grey instructed Buchanan, the British ambassador in St. Petersburg to inform the Russian Foreign Minister that Russia should not insist on Salar al-Dowleh's appointment, but rather that it should insist that Salar al-Dowleh leave to Europe for a while.[242] Although the Persian Cabinet did not resign, it was still against Salar al-Dowleh's appointment as governor of Gilan. The Minister of Foreign Affairs told Townley that the Cabinet did not know what was worse, to appoint Salar al-Dowleh or send an armed expedition against him. If the prince would go to Rasht, the Cabinet feared that he would head a movement of malcontents, who were now in Europe, such as Sepahdar, while also within a short time he would make himself impossible in Rasht, and therefore, it would not be fair to Persia to insist on the appointment of such a man. Also, he had not disarmed his 500 armed Turkmen followers, among whom were many bad characters. Moreover, he had not satisfied any of the government's conditions. Therefore, the Cabinet was leaning toward sending a military force against him.[243] Russia felt that it had a moral obligation to Salar al-Dowleh and therefore, argued that it could not change its position. In good faith, it had passed on the Persian government's promises via its Legation to the prince. If Salar al-Dowleh would not be appointed governor of Gilan serious disorders were likely to arise in the N.E. provinces of Persia on the Russian border, which would force Russia to intervene to protect its interests.[244] The official Russian position was that not Salar al-Dowleh, but the Persian government was to blame for the entire mess. Because the Persian government had disregarded its moral obligation toward the prince, he again had mobilized a Turkmen force and had occupied Sari. The result was that this action had provoked unrest in the Turkmen steppes and in the provinces of Astarabad and Mazandaran. This unrest was a menace to Russian

---

241. 'Persia. No 1 (1914). Further correspondence respecting the affairs of Persia', Townley to Grey 17/04/1913, p. 68 (no. 167).

242. 'Persia. No 1 (1914). Further correspondence respecting the affairs of Persia', Grey to Buchanan, 18/04/1913, p. 69 (no. 170).

243. 'Persia. No 1 (1914). Further correspondence respecting the affairs of Persia', Townley to Grey 25/04/1913, p. 72 (no. 179).

244. 'Persia. No 1 (1914). Further correspondence respecting the affairs of Persia', Buchanan to Grey, 26/04/1913, p.74 (no. 182).

subjects and Russian economic interests in those parts. Therefore, the Persian government was totally responsible by reneging on its promises to Salar al-Dowleh. He had disbanded his followers in March 1913 contrary to what Tehran said and had fulfilled his promises to the Persian government. As a compromise, Russia suggested that Salar al-Dowleh would not take up the governorship of Gilan personally, but would nominate a representative to rule on his behalf. He then could go on leave to Europe. If the Persian government did not agree to this proposal it had to take steps to disband the prince's troops and restore order.[245] As a result, the Persian government invited Salar al-Dowleh to live in Tehran for a while and then receive governorship. It considered appointing Sepahdar when he retuned from Europe. However, if Salar al-Dowleh would come to Tehran, the Persian government would be in state of constant uneasiness, according to the British Minister.[246]

SALAR AL-DOWLEH INVADES AND PLUNDERS MAZANDARAN

On 25 April, Mehdi Shah, a former supporter of the Constitution and brother of Mirza Sa`dollah Khan Ilkhani, with 200 government (*velayati*) *savars*, 400 Yamuts, and with Salar al-Dowleh went to take the government of Mazandaran. Some Mazandarani chiefs fled, but others joined him. Among the latter, E`zam al-Molk and Amir Mokarram, two royalist landowners, were prominent supporters. Governor Amir Akram, was instructed to oppose the prince, but the government had no adequate military force in Mazandaran to oppose Salar al-Dowleh.[247] Although the British reported that Amir-e Akram's force had routed Salar al-Dowleh's Turkmen, between Sari and Ashraf, this was but a minor border skirmish, although the Turkmen lost 8 dead, 12 wounded, including a notorious leader. After this so-called victory, the governor of Mazandaran fled to Astarabad.[248] This light armed opposition was easily overcome

---

245. 'Persia. No 1 (1914). Further correspondence respecting the affairs of Persia', Buchanan to Grey 07/05/1913, p. 86 (no. 209).
246. 'Persia. No 1 (1914). Further correspondence respecting the affairs of Persia', Townley to Grey 01/05/1913, p. 77 (no. 194).
247. Vahidniya, Seyfollah ed. 1362, p. 110.
248. Vakil al-Dowleh 1362, vol. 1, pp. 354-55; Kazembeyki 2003, pp. 195-96; Vahidniya, Seyfollah ed. 1362, p. 110; 'Persia. No 1 (1914). Further correspondence respecting the affairs of Persia', Townley to Grey 01/05/1913, p. 77 (no. 194).

and Mehdi Shah marched ahead. He then plundered some villages belonging to opponents. Salar al-Dowleh paid the family of the killed Turkmen 100 *tumans* and 20 *tumans* to those wounded. On 10 May, after a commitment given by Ivanov, the Turkmen returned. In mid-May 1913, Salar al-Dowleh took Sari, which town felt the strength and greed of his grasping hand. Next, Mehdi Shah with 100 *savars* wanted to seize Barforush to demand 50,000 *tumans*, but the Russian agent did not allow them to enter, as the Russian army was there. In Mazandaran, Salar al-Dowleh demanded 220,000 *tumans* in taxes and after its collection he intended to return to Astarabad.[249] The prince had a large enough force to upset local officials. The governor of Mazandaran had fled to Tehran and the one of Astarabad seemed to have gone over to the rebel, or so it was believed. Salar al-Dowleh sent bombastic telegrams to Tehran announcing that he would come there soon and boasted about what he would do to the Cabinet. He behaved in a high-handed manner, collecting taxes, and firing and appointing governors. Mehdi Shah, at his instruction, wired all Khans in Mazandaran that they had to come and join him with their *savars*. Most out of fear for the Russians did not come, but a few came.[250]

Despite his destructive activities, Russia still argued that Salar al-Dowleh was more sinned against than sinning, because the Persian government had dragged its feet in finishing the negotiations and it should honor the promises made.[251] However, Russia at almost every step of the way had acquiesced in, and even helped Salar al-Dowleh's activities, in Khorasan, Astarabad and Mazandaran. This was not only the view of Leleux, the Belgian Customs administrator in Mashhad, but even of some of the regional Russian press. In June 1913, the newspaper *Ashkabad* published an article from its Barforush correspondent questioning Russia's total absence of taking action against Salar al-Dowleh's actions that negatively impacted Russian trade, apart from the loss of prestige Russia suffered, while, when all these depredations were happening, a whole Russian army detachment was looking on. The Russian

---

249. Vakil al-Dowleh, vol. 1, pp. 353-58, 373 (with the text of a signed document from the Russian consul that Salar al-Dowleh also collected 4,000 *tumans* in taxes in Enzan); 'Persia. No 1 (1914). Further correspondence respecting the affairs of Persia', p. 106 (no. 237).

250. Vakil al-Dowleh, vol. 1, p. 359.

251. IOR/L/PS/18/C144, 'Extracts from Annual Persia Reports, 1906, 1909, 1910, 1911, 1912, 1913 regarding loans, and complete reports for 1908 & 1913', pp. 15.

consul at Astarabad had gone to Bandar-e Gaz with the intention to have Salar al-Dowleh's men disarmed, but shortly thereafter he returned. Instead of disarming the prince's troops, Russian troops withdrew from Barforush, Bandar-e Gaz and Mashhad-e Sar to the dismay of the people there. The departure of 100 Cossacks from Astarabad was also said to be due to Salar al-Dowleh's movements.[252]

On 21 May 1913, Salar al-Dowleh went from Sari to Barforush. Because the Russian garrison had vacated Barforush, the town fell into Salar al-Dowleh's hands without a fight and here also he extorted money from its hapless inhabitants; in total he was said to have collected 330,000 tumans in taxes and fines in Mazandaran. The government official Amir Tupkhaneh Shoja` al-Saltaneh accepted an appointment from Salar al-Dowleh.[253] On 28 May 1913, Salar al-Dowleh left Barforush with a small party and went by ship to Bandar-e Gaz and to Rudsar robbing the Customs houses at Bandar-e Gaz and Mashhad-e Sar, which also had no Russian troops any longer.[254] This plunder operation supplied him with much needed funds. It was only then that finally Russia interfered directly by initiating measures to prevent the future robbing of the Customs receipts. Hearing that Salar al-Dowleh had taken the customs receipts of Gaz and Mashhad-e Sar, the Russian Legation immediately ordered its consul at Astarabad to have its military occupy the Customs offices, as the Customs receipts were security for the Russian loans to Iran, and to see to it that Customs duties were collected on behalf of the Persian government. Also, people who had been paid with these stolen funds had to return the money.[255]

It was then that Salar al-Dowleh, realizing that he could expect no further help from Russia, changed his attitude. He submitted to Tehran and asked leave to settle on one of his estates until the Persian government wanted to ask him to serve. He also asked permission to come to

---

252. IOR/L/PS/10/209, File 52/1912 Pt 1 'Persia Diaries', Diary Military Attache no. 21, for the week ending the 7th Jun 1913, p. 2.

253. Vakil al-Dowleh, vol. 1, p. 358.

254. 'Persia. No 1 (1914). Further correspondence respecting the affairs of Persia', p. 120 (no. 272); Adhari 1378, p. 36 (doc. 137).

255. 'Persia. No 1 (1914). Further correspondence respecting the affairs of Persia', Townley to Grey 28/05/1913. p. 94 (no.228); Idem, Townley to Grey, 08/06/1918, p. 118 (no. 270).

Karaj to talk with the Minister of Interior.[256] However, Townley reacted that this so-called change in attitude was hardly sincere, because he was acting high-handedly in Mazandaran. Nevertheless, the Persian government accepted his peace hand, but also prepared an armed force to attack him.[257] A Bakhtiyari force under Salar Bahador, with two maxims and two Schneider guns, was being prepared to assist the government force that had taken up position at 32 km from Sari. Unfortunately, Salar Bahador declined to lead this force for personal and official reasons, but he assured Townley that his replacement would see to it that there would be no pillaging, an activity the Bakhtiyari tribesmen made a habit of being engaged in.[258]

MARCHES TO RASHT, DEFEATED AT TONKABON, FLEES TO KURDISTAN

On 3 June 1913 the government force entered Sari. On 5 June 1913, news arrived that the force sent by Tehran had arrived at Firuzkuh. With some horsemen, Salar al-Dowleh went from Barforush to Khorramabad (now Shahsavar), the capital of Tuna district, the rest was dismissed. He then went to Amol with 20 men.[259] In Salah al-Din Kalay (between Nur and Now-Shahr) Salar al-Dowleh had hired a boat to take him to Rudsar.[260] From there, he wanted to go by ship to Rasht to claim his governorship by the might of his arms. His small 300-men force, consisting of Quchani Kurds under Rashid al-Soltan, Hojjatollah Khan Kermanshahi, Ilbegi-ye Afshar, and further Turkmen, went over land to Rasht, but had to pass through the Tonakebun district, which was owned by Sepahdar. Salar al-Dowleh did not want to fight his way through and therefore, sent Mozaffar al-Mamalek Nuri Esfandiyari to Khorramabad to ask Amir

---

256. 'Persia. No 1 (1914). Further correspondence respecting the affairs of Persia', Townley to Grey 14/05/1914, p. 91 (no. 220). At that time he also wrote a letter to Farmanfarma full of complaints, accusations, demands, and self justifications. Ettehadiyeh and Sa'dvandiyan 1366, vol. 1, pp. 201, 203, 205.

257. 'Persia. No 1 (1914). Further correspondence respecting the affairs of Persia', 16/05/1913, p. 91 (no. 221).

258. 'Persia. No 1 (1914). Further correspondence respecting the affairs of Persia', Townley to Grey 12/05/1913, p. 100-01 (no. 235).

259. Vakil al-Dowleh, vol. 1, pp. 358-60; Vahidniya, Seyfollah ed. 1362, p. 111; IOR/L/PS/18/C144, 'Extracts from Annual Persia Reports, 1906, 1909, 1910, 1911, 1912, 1913 regarding loans, and complete reports for 1908 & 1913', p. 30.

260. Adhari 1378, p. 37 (docs. 138-39).

As`ad, oldest son of Sepahdar, who had massed his force there, to be allowed to pass without hindrance. Amir As`ad probably had instructions to let Salar al-Dowleh's men pass, because Sepahdar was favorably disposed toward the prince. However, according to Eyn al-Saltaneh, Amir As`ad received Salar al-Dowleh's representative three times telling him that he would not let his force pass, because he had orders from Tehran. At the end of May 1913, due to a misunderstanding, a group of horsemen, among whom Ja`far Qoli Khan, the 14-year old son of Amir As`ad, unexpectedly ran into some of Salar al-Dowleh's men; shots were fired and the son died. Next Salar al-Dowleh's men got into a fight with the vanguard of Sepahdar's men, who were all killed. Then, the rest of the Tonakebuni force attacked and surrounded Salar al-Dowleh's men. After a 3-days battle Salar al-Dowleh's force was practically annihilated. The Tonakebunis took 40 men prisoner and killed 60. Of those taken prisoner, some had surrendered, as they had no place to go, and were allowed to return home, some were arrested and were sent to Tehran, while others fled during the night. Among them was Rashid al-Sultan Quchani, a notable Kurdish chief and Salar al-Dowleh's commander, who was captured later.[261]

Salar al-Dowleh learnt the news of his followers' defeat and flight while waiting at Rudsar (Kalachay). Amir As`ad with a large force approached to arrest Salar al-Dowleh, but fortunately for him suddenly a group of Russian soldiers came and blocked the entry to Rudsar. Benefiting from this Russian protection Salar al-Dowleh escaped by boat, supposedly to Russia. However, he went to Rasht, where he landed on 3 June 1913 at a place a day's march from the town, accompanied by 70 men. It was expected that he would enter the city that same night or the following morning. The Persian government argued, because Rasht was under Russian occupation, that it could not send troops there. Indeed, Salar al-Dowleh intended to enter the town to which end he had wired the commanding officer of the Persian Cossacks in Resht to join

---

261. Adhari 1378, pp. 36-37 (quoting *Vahid* 32 [Tir 1353/1974], p. 4), 38 (docs. 139-41); Eyn al-Saltaneh 1377, vol. 5, pp. 3872-79, 4136-37. According to Khal`atbari, Salar al-Dowleh's force numbered a few thousand, which is hard to believe, given the nature of the terrain of Tonakebun as well as Vakil al-Dowleh's and the British account. Vahidniya 1362, pp. 111-15. For another description of the fight, see Vakil al-Dowleh, vol. 1, pp. 362, 364-65 (fight and arrest of other followers); 'Persia. No 1 (1914). Further correspondence respecting the affairs of Persia', Townley to Grey, 08/06/1918, p. 118 (no. 270); Idem, p. 120 (no. 272). For the report of the interrogation of some of the prisoners, see Adhari 1378, doc. 143.

him. They would have done so, if the head of the telegraph office had not alerted Tehran. The latter then fled to the British vice-Consulate, while spreading the news that the prince had occupied the town. M. Sabline, the Russian Chargé d'Affaires, who always had opposed Salar al-Dowleh's appointment, contacted the commanding officer of the Cossack Brigade to instruct his men in Rasht not to join the prince.[262] Thus, Salar al-Dowleh was not allowed into Rasht due to Sabline's firm position. The prince only remained for a few hours in a garden outside the town, before leaving. Even though Salar al-Dowleh did not enter Rasht his approach alarmed many people. When Vothuq al-Dowleh was approaching Rasht and heard that Salar al-Dowleh was nearby he fled to Enzeli and on 5 June left by boat to Baku.[263]

From Rasht, via Fumen and Masuleh, Salar al-Dowleh went into the Talesh-Dulab direction aiming to reach the Shahseven, it was believed. The prince had only 30 men with him. The Persian government now really wanted to finish with him. Persian Cossacks and Bakhtiyaris were directed to prevent him from coming to either Mazandaran or Kurdistan. In the Talesh, near the village of Derow, he sent some messengers to ask Zargham al-Saltaneh permission to stay in his summer-quarters. At that time, Prime Minister Eyn al-Dowleh telegraphed the chiefs of the Talesh governorate that Salar al-Dowleh had rebelled and was coming their way and that they had to arrest him. Zargham al-Saltaneh sent his brother with some armed men to the prince's camp, but he learnt about the order to arrest him via his messengers and fled. Shortly thereafter a message arrived for Zargham al-Saltaneh from Rashid al-Molk (army commander and governor of Khalkhal), who was then in Tabriz, that Salar al-Dowleh had to be welcomed with all honors, but it was too late. The prince with seven men had ridden into the direction of Zanjan trying to get to

---

262. Vakil al-Dowleh, vol. 1, pp. 377, 393, 399 (there were rumors that the ex-Shah and his two brothers would again invade via Tabriz, Gilan and Gumesh Tepeh); Vahidniya, Seyfollah ed. 1362, pp. 116-17; Kazembeyki 2003, p. 196; Adhari 1378, doc. 138; 'Persia. No 1 (1914). Further correspondence respecting the affairs of Persia', Townley to Grey, 03/06/1913, p. 108 (no. 239); IOR/L/PS/18/C144, 'Extracts from Annual Persia Reports, 1906, 1909, 1910, 1911, 1912, 1913 regarding loans, and complete reports for 1908 & 1913', pp. 15, 30. According to the British, Nekrassov, the Russian Consul-General in Rasht aided and abetted Salar al-Dowleh. IOR/L/PS/20/223, 'Who's who in Persia. Calcutta: General Staff, India, 1916', p. 320. Nevertheless, five of Salar al-Dowleh's men were arrested in Rasht and sent to Tehran. Adhari 1378, doc. 148.

263. 'Persia. No 1 (1914). Further correspondence respecting the affairs of Persia', Townley to Grey, 08/06/1918, pp. 118 (no. 270), 120 (no. 272).

Kermanshah or Kurdistan. According to one report the governor of Zanjan intentionally did nothing to stop the prince, which gave rise to criticism that the Cabinet did not really exerted itself to capture the rebel prince.[264] However, British sources reported that at Zanjan a government force was able to cut him off, but he escaped (with the governor's connivance?) and it was feared that he might make trouble again; the prince's companions were arrested.[265]

Salar al-Dowleh with Lor chiefs

---

264. Adhari 1378, p. 38 (doc. 147).

265. Daftar-Rava'i 1363, pp. 237-38 (for this service Zargham al-Saltaneh was given the title of Sardar Moqtader Taleshi); Eyn al-Saltaneh 1377, vol. 5, pp. 3882, 3884; 'Persia. No 1 (1914). Further correspondence respecting the affairs of Persia', Townley to Grey, 04/06/1913, p.110 (no. 241); Idem, Townley to Grey, 08/06/1913, p. 110 (no.245); Idem, Townley to Grey, 18/06/1913, p. 115 (no. 258); Idem, Townley to Grey, 08/06/1913, p. 118 (no. 270); Idem, p. 120 (no. 272); IOR/L/PS/18/C144, 'Extracts from Annual Persia Reports, 1906, 1909, 1910, 1911, 1912, 1913 regarding loans, and complete reports for 1908 & 1913', pp. 15, 30.

Movements in Kurdistan and Kermanshah and Exile (July-September 1913)

The flight from Rasht via Talesh to Zanjan may have been all along Salar al-Dowleh's plan, or perhaps his plan B, in case his foray into the Caspian provinces would not be successful. Because, in April 1913, there was a rumor in Kurdistan that, from Zanjan, Salar al-Dowleh had written to his supporters in the town and among the tribes. In reaction, fearing raids and plunder, the merchants in Zanjan wrote to their correspondents in Senneh not to send them any goods. The director of Customs at Senneh reported that the prince had written to his supporters there that he had left Mazandaran for Zanjan and was coming to Senneh. "His adherents ardently expect him."[266] Also in April, Hajji Soltan al-Olama, the Imam Jom`eh of Kurdistan and a supporter of Salar al-Dowleh was summoned by Asaf al-Divan, the assistant-governor, who showed him letters that he had written to various chiefs announcing the imminent arrival of the rebel-prince and urging them to join him. Asaf al-Divan had the mullah beaten and then sent him to Kermanshah. He further wrote to Farmanfarma not to allow this man return to Senneh, because this would lead to trouble. Also, news was circulating in the city that the prince would arrive shortly, which the British Consulate in Kermanshah quickly discredited by making it

---

266. FO 248/1073, Kermanshah Diary no. 17, ending 24/04/1913.

known that at that time the prince was in Bandar-e Gaz.[267] Nevertheless, the rumors that the prince had occupied Mazandaran and would come to Kurdistan, which then did not have a governor, caused much anxiety in Kermanshah.[268] It also resulted in activities by Salar al-Dowleh's local supporters.

> I am informed that Mahmed Khan, ex-mujahid, the chief of police [of Kermanshah], one of those who deserted Yar Mohamed when that officer declared for Salar ed Dowleh, and who has caused general satisfaction by his organization of the town police, is very anxious about the future. I understand that he had reported to Farmanfarma that under pretence of gambling there are nightly meetings of adherents of Salar ed Dowleh at the house of Salar Mozaffur, and he fears that they are in consultation with Salar ed Dowleh. This Salar Mozaffur is a man of low character and responsible for many of the executions and plunderings when Salar ed Dowleh was here. He was for some time in "bast" at the Ottoman consulate but has now been pardoned and favoured by Farmanfarma, probably because he can tell where some of the loot left behind, when Salar ed Dowleh left, is concealed. This was the man who negotiated between the town people and Salar ed Dowleh to bring that prince here from Luristan in December 1911. Stories of renewed activity by Salar ed Dowleh are being circulated by his adherents.[269]

In May 1913, Salar al-Dowleh's supporters in Kermanshah continued to spread stories of his victories and his occupation of various towns. They were believed to be in secret contact with him via dervishes or pilgrims. The fact that Farmanfarma had started making new fortifications only reinforced the belief among the population that Salar al-Dowleh would be coming and this increased their anxiety.[270] There was also an increase in the plundering of villages, which was said to be due to the rumors of Salar al-Dowleh's successes and his expected return, and "to

---

267. FO 248/1073, Kermanshah Diary no. 18, ending 01/05/1913.
268. FO 248/1073, Kermanshah Diary no. 21, ending 22/05/1913.
269. FO 248/1073, McDouall to Legation, no. 49, 24/05/1913.
270. FO 248/1073, Kermanshah Diary no. 22, ending 29/05/1913.

the absence of any punishment for such offenses."[271] On 5 June 1913, there was finally an end to the rumors, because on that day Farmanfarma received news from Tehran that Salar al-Dowleh had fled and was instructed to take steps to arrest him, if he came to Kermanshah.[272]

Meanwhile, from Zanjan, Salar al-Dowleh continued to Garrus (Bijar), evading all half-hearted attempts to arrest him en route, and from there to Kurdistan. In Garrus, he took the daughter of Hajj Ali Reza Khan by force as well as 30,000 *tumans* from the government's revenues, and his plundering tribal supporters caused much destruction of life and property.[273] The Russians felt embarrassed by the prince's actions and sent Persian Cossacks under two Russian officers to arrest Salar al-Dowleh who had fled to the Jaf Kurds. Townley commented that "The slickery customer is back to his old haunts." The Bakhtiyaris who had been intended for the expedition to Mazandaran and the Cossacks for Zenjan were ordered to pursue him. In mid-June 1913, Salar al-Dowleh was at Divandarreh, 10 *farsakh* from Senneh, where the Kalbegis had joined him. He wrote to many people and sent messengers to Senneh, saying that he had come to restore order, that these districts were especially his, and he appointed Vakil al-Molk as its governor. Meanwhile, Eyn al-Dowleh, the Prime Minister, telegraphed Asaf al-Divan, the governor of Senneh, that troops were en route, that this time no pardon would be given to the rebels, and that he had to see to it that the prince was unable to raise a force. This news was said to have a positive effect on the people of Senneh, where the prince was said not to be welcome. Salar al-Dowleh also sent a letter to Aqa Habibollah, the agent of the IBP in Senneh, writing him not to flee again, but to trust him and "to greet the traders his dear children from him." Salar al-Dowleh wrote to Soleyman Khan, the son of Da'ud Khan Kalhor, that he had come to revenge his father. He showed the letter to the Kalhor *kadkhodas* who told him not to join the prince again, and therefore, he sent an evasive answer. The heads of the other tribes were also in correspondence with the rebel-prince, but it was believed that they used this as leverage to get Farmanfarma agree to their demands and that it was very unlikely that they would join him. Nevertheless, people in Kermanshah were very worried, because they knew that the prince's supporters were in contact with him. Also, that

---

271. FO 248/1073, Kermanshah Diary no. 23, ending 05/06/1913.
272. FO 248/1073, Kermanshah Diary no. 24, ending 12/06/1913.
273. Adhari 1378, docs. 166-69; Eyn al-Saltaneh 1377, vol. 5, p. 3900.

he would come to take control of the Customs, being in need of money. Farmanfarma intended to send Sayyed Akbar Shah and Ra'is al-Tojjar to advise Salar al-Dowleh to remain where he was, in which case he would intercede for him with the government. However, when pointed out that the two emissaries were not to be trusted he abandoned this plan. Officials at Miyan-Band intercepted a bundle of letters from Salar al-Dowleh to Salar Mozaffar, Hasan Mo`aven al-Ra`aya, the Kalhor chiefs, and others, as well as their replies to him, which they handed over to Farmanfarma.[274]

Farmanfarma made preparations to oppose him, to which end he had recently received reinforcements. Nevertheless, the notables of Kermanshah criticized him for not being firm with Salar al-Dowleh and his followers. Farmanfarma had allowed former supporters of the prince to return to Kermanshah, including Salar Mozaffar, the prince's main supporter and responsible for most of the exactions and executions during his stay in the city. In May 1913, Farmanfarma even invited him to an official military review at the *Meydan*. "This caused much cursing by the native spectators and soldiers, including the Cossacks, who were cursing the Farmanfarma and the government for allowing it."[275] The governor told the British consul that he knew what people said and although Salar al-Dowleh as "his brother-in-law and cousin is dear to him," he would act against him if he rebelled. Townley, the British Minister in Tehran also had doubts about Farmanfarma, because "his loyalty is somewhat doubtful, and he is as arrant a coward as Salar." It was known that Salar Mozaffar had sent a messenger to Salar al-Dowleh, who was reported to have arrived in Qaratowreh district, 14 *farsakh* from

---

274. FO 248/1073, Kermanshah Diary no. 26, ending 26/06/1913; Shahedi 1381, pp. 654-55. 'Persia. No 1 (1914). Further correspondence respecting the affairs of Persia', p.149 (no.307); Idem, Townley to Grey, 18/07/1913, p. 125 (no.282); IOR/L/PS/18/C144, 'Extracts from Annual Persia Reports, 1906, 1909, 1910, 1911, 1912, 1913 regarding loans, and complete reports for 1908 & 1913', pp. 15; IOR/L/PS/10/212, File 211/1912, 'Turkish Arabia Summaries,' p. 12; 'Persia. No 1 (1914). Further correspondence respecting the affairs of Persia', Townley to Grey, 07/07/1913, p. 124 (no. 277); Adhari 1378, doc. 1; Hamadani 1354, p. 426.

275. FO 248/1073, Kermanshah Diary no. 21, ending 22/05/1913. Farmanfarma had invited all unsavory bad characters, who fled after Salar al-Dowleh's defeat, back into town with the argument that it was safer as he could keep an eye on them. Therefore, people suspected that the governor himself was a supporter of the rebel-prince. FO 248/1073, McDouall to Legation, 24/05/1913. Even in November 1913, McDouall reported "the policy of Farmanfarma appears to be to support adherents of that prince [Salar al-Dowleh] against his opponents as he supports the Kalkhani against the Sinjabis." FO 248/1073, Kermanshah Diary no. 46, ending 13/11/1913.

Senneh, where there was no one to oppose him.²⁷⁶ It may well be that Salar Mozaffar carried a proposal from the governor, because Prime Minister Eyn al-Dowleh replied to Farmanfarma's offer to negotiate with Salar al-Dowleh "that the prince had caused so much loss to life and property that negotiations would be impossible and measures were being taken to capture him." Farmanfarma sent official copies of the telegrams from the Telegraph Office to the tribal chiefs concerning the troops en route and measures taken against Salar al-Dowleh. The Sanjabi and Kalhor chiefs forwarded the letters sent by the prince to Farmanfarma. When letters from Salar al-Dowleh arrived for two Qalkhani chiefs, on duty with 200 men in Kermanshah, they fled. On 22 June, in Senneh, notables, olama and tradesmen held a meeting to decide whether or not to receive Salar al-Dowleh. It was unanimously decided to refuse him entry and the notables were asked to mobilize men to take care of the town's defense. They wrote the prince that supplies were short and they feared the anger of the government, therefore, he was not welcome and if he would come they would oppose him. On 29 June the notables with some 1,000 men left to oppose Salar al-Dowleh, who only had some 100 Kalbegi and 50 Turkish Jafs with him at Kuleh, at some 8 *farsakh* from Senneh. Unable and unwilling to meet with this force, Salar al-Dowleh fled from that location.²⁷⁷ However, he remained at about 10 *farsakh* from Senneh, but moved each day to a different village. He still had a small force of Kalbegis and Jafs with him, and tried to extort 5,000 *tumans* from a village headman by torture. On 4 July 1913, a force led by Russian officers with four guns and 50 loads of ammunition arrived and camped outside Kermanshah.²⁷⁸

At that time, the prince requested the Russian consul to have the Russian officers recalled, who led to the Cossack force sent after him. The prince clearly believed that he would have been able to have the Cossacks defect to his side, as had happened in Astarabad. "Salar humorously observed that if the officers remained with the force he would be compelled to flee to Luristan, but if the officers were recalled

---

276. 'Persia. No 1 (1914). Further correspondence respecting the affairs of Persia', Townley to Grey, 23/07/1913, p.126 (no. 285); see also pp. 126-27 no. 287, p.149 (no.307); IOR/L/PS/18/C144, 'Extracts from Annual Persia Reports, 1906, 1909, 1910, 1911, 1912, 1913 regarding loans, and complete reports for 1908 & 1913', pp. 15; FO 248/1073, Kermanshah Diary no. 25, ending 19/06/1913.
277. FO 248/1073, Kermanshah Diary no. 27, ending 03/07/1913.
278. FO 248/1073, Kermanshah Diary no. 28, ending 10/07/1913.

he could make his own terms with the [Persian] Cossacks."²⁷⁹ This was a real possibility, as we have seen in the case of Rasht and Astarabad (see above). Also, McDouall reported, "It is a well-known fact that the Persian Cossacks are sympathizers of the prince as proved by their flight at Surjeh last year. They probably would have retreated in May 1912 when Farmanfarma engaged the rebels, if Da'ud Khan had not been killed, because their Iranian commander told McDouall if the battle had lasted another half hour they would have been defeated.²⁸⁰

On 6 July 1913, the Russian-officered force from Tehran left with two guides to Senneh, where it arrived on 9 July; also from other directions troops were hemming the prince in. The Cossack force's task was twofold: i. to arrest Salar al-Dowleh; and ii. "to issue a notice to the evildoers of Kurdistan that the Persian government ordered disarmament and collection of revenue and justice, if they did not obey and there was fighting no intercession would be accepted." One Mir Mehdi Khan called Sardar Jang by Salar al-Dowleh and known as Mir Mehdi Shah Astarabadi had been charged by the rebel-prince to raise a force of Kalbegis and take control over Garrus. When the prince fled, Mir Mehdi was captured by a son of Aqa Habibollah and handed over to the governor of Senneh who asked Tehran for instructions. It was said that Salar al-Dowleh was among the Turkish Jafs, who every year came to graze their herds in Iran. They were five *farsakh* from Divandarreh where the government troops were. The Kalbegis had left their district and were at some distance from these troops.²⁸¹

What happened then is somewhat unclear. According to printed British reports, after having stayed four days in the Cossack camp Salar al-Dowleh by misleading the Russian officer in charge of the Persian Cossacks was freed on parole. He said that he wanted to visit a sick friend and after having given his word of honor that he would return that same evening he was allowed to leave. Instead of returning he sent a note

---

279. 'Persia. No 1 (1914). Further correspondence respecting the affairs of Persia', p.149 (no. 307); Idem, Townley to Grey, 18/07/1913, p. 125 (no. 282); IOR/L/PS/18/C144, 'Extracts from Annual Persia Reports, 1906, 1909, 1910, 1911, 1912, 1913 regarding loans, and complete reports for 1908 & 1913', pp. 15; IOR/L/PS/10/212, File 211/1912, 'Turkish Arabia Summaries,' p. 12; 'Persia. No 1 (1914). Further correspondence respecting the affairs of Persia', Townley to Grey, 07/07/1913, p. 124 (no. 277).
280. FO 248/1073, McDouall to Townley, 28/08/1913.
281. FO 248/1073, Kermanshah Diary no. 29, ending 17/07/1913.

saying that he wanted to try his luck again. Salar al-Dowleh was said to have gathered tribal forces and intended to attack Kermanshah.[282] In his immediate reporting, McDouall wrote that the Russian captain informed the governor of Divandarreh that he had an interview with Salar al-Dowleh and would see him again. He would arrange matters and further that the Kalbegis had submitted. On 15 July 1913, Salar al-Dowleh came to the Cossack camp and surrendered. The captain wrote to the governor of Divandarreh to send Mir Mehdi, who was imprisoned in Senneh, and another message to the director of Customs of Senneh to arrange the Kalbegi taxes. The governor complied and the kadkhodas of Divandarreh wrote that Salar al-Dowleh had left the camp to say farewell to the Jaf chiefs and then would return. However, he did not return and the next morning sent a message that he was ill. The Russian officers were much disturbed about this breach of faith. On 20 July 1913, Captain Zabulinsky telegraphed Farmanfarma that Salar al-Dowleh intended to go to Kermanshah and that he was in pursuit. Farmanfarma then sent copies to all chiefs and local governors ordering them to be ready to oppose the prince. Salar al-Dowleh's supporters in the city made it known that the Russians had allowed him to escape on purpose. According to McDouall, it was not expected that any tribe would support the prince, except perhaps for some Gurans. On 22 July a telegram reported that the prince had left to Marivan and Avroman and would try to reach Kermanshah.[283]

However, when the prince had been brought to Kermanshah McDouall reported that then the Russian officers stated that Salar al-Dowleh had not surrendered in Kurdistan, but had come in under a safe conduct and left. A letter from them was intercepted in which they wrote to the prince that, "as arranged, they were returning to Kermanshah. Here they say they hoped to arrange a meeting and settle the matter." Salar al-Dowleh also had asked the Russian consul to come and see him, who had refused as it might be misunderstood.[284] This course of events suggests that the Russians had been trying salvage the value of their asset by arranging a governorship for Salar al-Dowleh and

---

282. 'Persia. No 1 (1914). Further correspondence respecting the affairs of Persia', Townley to Grey, 23/07/1913, p.126 (no. 285); see also pp. 126-27 no. 287, p.149 (no.307); IOR/L/PS/18/C144, 'Extracts from Annual Persia Reports, 1906, 1909, 1910, 1911, 1912, 1913 regarding loans, and complete reports for 1908 & 1913', pp. 15.

283. FO 248/1073, Kermanshah Diary no. 30, ending 24/07/1913. Later the name of Capt. Zabulinsky is given as Zabulowsky.

284. FO 248/1073, McDouall to Townley, 28/08/1913.

a pardon and financial incentives for his supporters. His departure from the Cossack camp, as suggested by his supporters, was part of the plan as was his slow advance towards Kermanshah, while creating confusion about his intentions through his urging of tribal chiefs to join him. However, once near Kermanshah, he immediately contacted the Russian consul and agreed to come in willingly, not as a prisoner, but as a man willing to negotiate. However, this plan failed to achieve its objective, because the British refused to play along and insisted on the ouster of the prince, to which Russia reluctantly agreed.

Whatever the truth of matter, towards the end of July 1913, Farmanfarma received a letter from Ja`far Soltan of the Avroman informing him that Salar al-Dowleh was with him and going to Javanrud. In fact, Farmanfarma told McDouall that the prince was at Paveh at Javanrud, three stages from Kermanshah.[285] Salar al-Dowleh seemed to have had no followers at all at this stage; he had visited most chiefs in disguise, but only received evasive replies. Only Bahram Soltan (Qalkhani Guran) and Fatah Beg (Walad Begi Jaf) promised support, but, as they were too weak, only on condition that other forces joined him as well. Meanwhile, Salar al-Dowleh's wife, daughter of the Vali of Posht-e Kuh, arrived from Tehran with her son, en route to Posht-e Kuh.[286] Salar Mozaffar openly received from and sent messages to Salar al-Dowleh. There was no news whether the prince had gathered a force.[287] On 19 July the Cossack force arrived from Kurdistan. Salar al-Dowleh had written to the tribal chiefs to join him, who forwarded his letters to Farmanfarma. "He sent in to the Russian doctor for medicine a week ago [mid-August] and said he was tired of life and worn out with travels." Mid-August 1913, he was with Mahmed Beg Sharafbeyni, not far from the oil-wells at Chia Sorkh. He was said to have gone to Kalhor country to the house of Abdollah Khan Farrash-bashi hoping to see Soleyman Khan and induce him to join his cause. His supporters were Fatah Beg, Walad Begi Jaf, Mahmed Beg of a section of the Sharafbeyni and two

---

285. FO 248/1073, Kermanshah Diary no. 31, ending 31/07/1913.

286. FO 248/1073, Kermanshah Diary no. 32, ending 07/08/1913. Hasan Pasha Khan, former chief of the Koliya'is and adherent of Salar al-Dowleh, saw the arrival of the rebel-prince as an opportunity and together with some other Khans attacked the current chief, his nephew Hoseyn Qoli Khan. Initially, the fight was inconclusive and still ongoing, but finally the nephew lost. FO 248/1073, Kermanshah Diary no. 29, ending 17/07/1913.

287. FO 248/1073, Kermanshah Diary no. 33, ending 14/08/1913.

border Shaykhs. It was assumed that he might be able to raise only 100 men, according to Farmanfarma even 400, although the prince in his letters claimed 6,000 men; the 100 figure probably was nearest to the truth.[288] After Salar al-Dowleh found that he was unable to raise troops he surrendered to the Cossack force sent after him, whether this was by design or by force of circumstances. It happened as follows. From Nilavar, a Sanjabi village, Salar al-Dowleh corresponded with Farmanfarma. The prince sent Sadeq al-Mamalek, one of his staff, to Farmanfarma, who sent Salar Mozaffar to Salar al-Dowleh. On 20 August, the Russian officers and consul had a long discussion with Farmanfarma. Salar Mozaffar also was involved, and one Russian officer told McDouall that the Turkish consul had sent Salar Mozaffar to the prince to warn him that they intended to capture and expel him. Salar Mozaffar sent a messenger to Farmanfarma, who arrived in the morning of 25 August and the governor went to the Russian Consulate. It appears that when Salar Mozaffar reached the prince he was on his way to Lorestan, but stopped. The other Russian captain told McDouall that his colleague would bring the prince back, dead or alive. In the evening, a Russian officer and others left and met up with Salar Mozaffar and together went to the prince's camp. The representative of the Russian Consulate bore the Russian flag and Salar al-Dowleh dismounted and kissed the flag. In the morning of 28 August, Salar al-Dowleh arrived in Kermanshah, accompanied by Capt. Zabulowsky, the *monshi* of the Russian Consulate, Mohammad Baqer Mirza, chef de cabinet on behalf of Farmanfarma, 6 Russian and 50 Persian Cossacks. He was taken to the Russian Consulate, but it was unclear whether he was a prisoner or a refugee temporarily under Russian protection. McDouall who spoke with the prince wrote that he seemed to be "unstrung in his nerves." Salar Mozaffar told his friends that the prince was willing to surrender if offered 50,000 *tumans* in cash and the governorship of Kermanshah and Kurdistan, with an adequate salary.[289] Salar al-Dowleh was kept at

---

288. FO 248/1073, Kermanshah Diary no. 34, ending 21/08/1913.

289. FO 248/1073, Kermanshah Diary no. 35, ending 28/08/1913; Adhari 1378, pp. 39-40. According to IOR/L/PS/10/212, File 211/1912, 'Turkish Arabia Summaries,' p. 10; 'Persia. No 1 (1914). Further correspondence respecting the affairs of Persia', p. 160 (no. 324), p.151 (no.311), Salar al-Dowleh was taken to Kermanshah of 25 August and on 27 August to the Russian Consulate, which dates are at odds with the Kermanshah Diary no. 35. The Cossack escort may have been sent, because Qasem Khan Sanjabi wrote to Farmanfarma that Salar al-Dowleh had asked him for an escort of 50 men to take him to Kermanshah. FO 248/1073, McDouall to Towley, 28/08/1913.

Delgosha, where the Russian consul lived during the summer. Here he was kept under strict supervision, although treated "as a honoured prisoner, whose personal safety is guaranteed," while a Russian officer was always with him. Only a few locals were allowed to see him. Mahmud Khan Hajjizadeh wrote him a letter, sent through his wife, promising the support of 100 men and that the Kakawands were also ready to do so. The Russian consul made sure that nobody who wanted to kill the prince could get access to him. Farmanfarma suggested that Salar al-Dowleh be offered the governorship of Zanjan, but Tehran replied that the matter was none of his business and that he should stay out of it. It would be resolved by the Russian Legation and the Ministry of Foreign Affairs.[290] Via Farmanfarma, Salar al-Dowleh tried to get British support for an appointment as governor of Zanjan, but Townley replied that since earlier he had refused British good offices, he had now to take what was offered to him. Sabline, the Russian Chargé d'Affaires, wanted him sent to Europe with a pension.[291]

The Russians first intended to allow him to stay in Tehran under surveillance. Buchanan, the British ambassador in St. Petersburg told the Russian government that London would not agree and insisted on a payment of a pension to the prince, who had to be exiled and sent abroad, forfeiting the pension if he returned. The Russian Minister of Foreign Affairs agreed and instructed the Legation in Tehran accordingly.[292] With the good offices of the Russians Salar al-Dowleh negotiated the payment of a pension of 10,000 *tumans* or £1,800 per year and an outfit allowance of £600 from the Persian government on condition that he went to Switzerland. If he would return to Persia he would lose his pension and Russian goodwill. Despite being a serial plunderer and extortionist, Salar al-Dowleh was very impoverished. He had only one large property remaining that was mortgaged to the Russian Bank for a debt of £50,000. It was also secured on a guarantee of Arbab Jamshid, a bankrupt Zoroastrian banker whose affairs had been taken over by the

---

290. FO 248/1073, Kermanshah Diary no. 36, ending 04/09/1913. It was said that the prince demanded the governorship of Kermanshah and Kurdistan, which, in McDouall's view, was contrary to British interests, given the prince's anti-British sentiments.

291. 'Persia. No 1 (1914). Further correspondence respecting the affairs of Persia', Townley to Grey, 02/09/1913, p. 160 (no. 325).

292. 'Persia. No 1 (1914). Further correspondence respecting the affairs of Persia', Buchanan/St. Petersburg to Grey/London, 23/07/1913, p. 126 (no. 286).

Iranian government. Given this situation he had no choice but to accept, the more so, if he would not accept, Russia would deport him.[293]

On the night of 6 September broadsheets (shabnamehs) were thrown into the houses of Arfa` al-Mamalek, the monshi of the Russian consulate, and of Mohammad Baqer Mirza, who were with the party that brought in Salar al-Dowleh. The writers of the broadsheets stated that they formed a secret society and they warned foreigners and Iranians who had brought Salar al-Dowleh on the promise of safety and to settle his affairs that it was now clear that the prince was kept prisoner and if he was not released they would kill those responsible. Farmanfarma had the matter looked into, and on 10 September arrested Mirza Hasan Mo`aven al-Ra`aya and Salar Mozaffar and put them in chains. In the city it was said that the Russians wanted the prince to have a governorship, while the British objected to this. According to McDouall, the Russian consul had not heard from his Legation concerning the prince for 15 days, indicating that ongoing discussions between the British and Russian governments were difficult.[294] Regarding the broadsheets and the subsequent arrests it appears that Salar al-Dowleh's supporters had wanted to rescue him.

> At a meeting, said to have been held in the house Seyid Sherif Khan Cabuli, it was arranged that they should be in a garden under the terrace of the house now occupied by the Russian consul with a ladder and horses and Salar ed Dowleh should break through a thin wall of a latrine overlooking this garden and descend by a ladder. One of those present, Mirza Habibulleh Khan a friend of [the] late Yar Mohammed fearing for his safety revealed the plot and two men, as reported, were arrested. The actual writer of the shabnameh was one Mirza Gul Mohammed in employ of Meshdi Hassan who is himself illiterate. On 13th Salar

---

293. 'Persia. No 1 (1914). Further correspondence respecting the affairs of Persia', Townley to Grey, 17/09/1913, p. 152 (no. 319); Idem, Townley to Grey, 07/10/1913, p. 164 (no.339); Fortescue, Military Report, pp. 30, 33; Eyn al-Saltaneh 1377, vol. 5, p. 3947 (he left Tehran in a car); Kazembeyki 2003, pp.195-96; Colby and Churchill 1914, p. 534; Sharif Kashani 1362, vol. 3, p. 789; Political Diaries vol. 5, pp. 200-01; Ettehadiyeh and Sa`vandiyan 1366, vol. 1, pp. 211-14; IOR/L/PS/18/C144, 'Extracts from Annual Persia Reports, 1906, 1909, 1910, 1911, 1912, 1913 regarding loans, and complete reports for 1908 & 1913', p. 15; Adhari 1378, p. 39 (docs. 156-57).

294. FO 248/1073, Kermanshah Diary no. 37, ending 11/09/1913.

Mozaffar was sent by Farmanfarma for Salar ed Dowleh and has not been seen since.[295]

On 14 September 1913, Capt. Zabulowsky and a party of Cossacks left Kermanshah, on the 15th another party and on the 16th Reza Khan (the later Reza Shah), who commanded the Cossacks in Kermanshah for some years, left with his men. It was believed that Salar al-Dowleh left with the first party.[296] Although the arrest of the prince was an action sanctioned by the British and Russian Legations, McDouall was not always immediately informed, because it was only after the departure of the Cossacks that he learnt that Salar al-Dowleh, contrary to what he believed, was still in the Russian Consulate as was Salar Mozaffar, who was not allowed to leave. Mashdi Hasan had been released.[297] It is of further interest to note that information about the negotiations about the prince's future was hardly available in Kermanshah, because a few days prior to Salar al-Dowleh's departure Salar Mozaffar sent a message to the Kalhor chiefs not to pay any money to Farmanfarma, because Salar al-Dowleh would be shortly appointed governor of Kermanshah at Russia's request.[298] Salar al-Dowleh with a few servants, including Salar Mozaffar, left on 5 October for Rasht and Europe. He was accompanied by Captain Zakharchinkov, the Russian physician and Persian Cossacks. Farmanfarma sent a farewell party of *savars* that went as far as the Bid-e Sorkh pass. Before Salar al-Dowleh left, he told his local wife, a princess, that he had arranged with the IBP in Kermanshah to pay her expenses in his absence. However, when she asked the IBP she found that no funds had been provided.[299] Salar al-Dowleh arrived in Baku on 23 October 1913. A Russian officer escorted him all the way to the Swiss border, where his pension was monthly paid by the Russian Legation.[300]

---

295. FO 248/1073, Kermanshah Diary no. 38, ending 18/09/1913.
296. FO 248/1073, Kermanshah Diary no. 38, ending 18/09/1913.
297. FO 248/1073, Kermanshah Diary no. 39, ending 25/09/1913.
298. FO 248/1073, Kermanshah Diary no. 40, ending 02/10/1913.
299. FO 248/1073, Kermanshah Diary no. 41, ending 09/10/1913; Hamadani 1354, p. 430 (the prince arrived on 10 October in Hamadan and left on 12 October).
300. 'Persia. No 1 (1914). Further correspondence respecting the affairs of Persia', Townley to Grey, 17/09/1913, p. 152 (no. 319); Idem, Townley to Grey, 07/10/1913, p. 164 (no.339); Fortescue, Military Report, pp. 30, 33; Eyn al-Saltaneh 1377, vol. 5, p. 3947 (he left Tehran in a car); Kazembeyki 2003, pp.195-96; Colby and Churchill 1914, p. 534; Sharif Kashani 1362, vol. 3, p. 789; Political Diaries vol. 5, pp. 200-01; Ettehadiyeh and Sa'vandiyan 1366, vol. 1, pp. 211-14; IOR/L/PS/18/C144, 'Extracts

However, the prince was undaunted and had not learnt anything from past experience. He told his Russian secretary he was going there for a rest, but would be back in Persia next spring, probably via the south. He indeed tried, unsuccessfully, to open negotiations with the Bakhtiyaris the following year.[301] In Europe, Salar al-Dowleh after a short stay in Switzerland first went to Paris. From there he went to Brussels and onwards to London with a letter of recommendation from the Grand Master to the 'Mason brethren' to give financial support their fellow-member Salar al-Dowleh as he was short of money.[302]

---

from Annual Persia Reports, 1906, 1909, 1910, 1911, 1912, 1913 regarding loans, and complete reports for 1908 & 1913', pp. 15; Adhari 1378, p. 39 (docs. 156-57).

301. Shahedi 1381, pp. 654-55.

302. Ehtesham al-Saltenah 1366, pp. 701-03. He tried to use his contacts with the Freemasons to try to get his properties back and even to be allowed to return to Iran, but none would go out of their way to help him. Adhari 1378, p. 43.

Salar al-Dowleh's Alleged Activities During WW I

GERMANY ACCEPTS THE HELP HE OFFERED

Even before WW I started on 28 July 1914, so did the rumors about Salar al-Dowleh's pro-Axis activities. In early July 1914, the British Resident in Bushehr received the following news from Bahrain. "This week a Dervish with servant arrived here by sailing vessel from Dilwar a Tangistan port. They left by steamer 'Barala' for Bunder Abbas. Persian merchant of Bahrain says that Dervish talks like royal Prince and Kurdistan coolies who met him recognized him as Salar-ad-Dowleh immediately. Dervish caught one of the Kurds by the ear and asked him why he salaamed to him as he was Dervish and not the Salar."[303] This clearly was a case of mistaken identity, because Salar al-Dowleh was in Switzerland. Although it would have been possible to travel from there to Iran in two months, it seems unlikely, also because travel had become more difficult due to the events that led to the outbreak of the war. Moreover, in April 1914 Salar al-Dowleh was in Switzerland, where he lived in Zürich under the name of Mahmoud Persan. Also, his pension was paid by the Russian Legation, on condition that he lived in Switzerland. He bitterly complained that his pension was insufficient, as he had about 10 Persian attendants with him. If he would request the

---

303. IOR/L/PS/11/81, file P 3059/1914. Tel. no. 775, Resident Persian Gulf to Secretary Government of India, 10/07/1914.

Russian Minister to be allowed to travel to Italy or France, the latter had instruction to inform him "that he could not be permitted to leave the country without the special sanction of the Persian Government." Because the Russian government feared that Salar al-Dowleh either wanted to secretly leave Switzerland or establish relations with people in Iran, who opposed the government, the Russian Minister had to have the prince watched. However, Mr. de Bacheracht told his British colleague in Bern that local conditions made that nearly impossible. On 9 June 1914, the Russian government instructed Mr. de Bacheracht to warn the prince: "1. to abstain from all attempts against the existing Government in Persia; 2. That in the present state of public opinion in that country such attempts would be completely abortive." 3. The Russian government did its best to restore order in Iran and Ahmad Shah on reaching majority in July would try to improve the situation of his Qajar relatives; therefore, the prince had to wait, else the Russian government would lose interest in his fate. 4. The Russian government also would consider some grievances that the prince had brought to its notice. Although the prince was not under Russian surveillance he was nevertheless monitored by them. On 28 March 1914, Mr. de Bacheracht had written Salar al-Dowleh that the Russian government had information that certain Russian subjects had undertaken to manage his property in Iran and to raise agitation in his favor. If this was true the Russian government informed the prince that in future it would decline to help him. In reply, Salar al-Dowleh came in person to Bern showing Mr. de Bacheracht two contracts with a Russian subject named Moshtari, dated Berlin 26 January 1914, in which he gave Moshtari full power to manage his properties and to exploit certain mining concessions. There was no mention of political matters in the contract.[304]

It thus would appear that he still was in Switzerland, because it is there where his name once again appeared in the official correspondence. On 18 September, Grant Duff (Bern) informed London that the Persian Minister in London had wired Tehran that Salar al-Dowleh wanted to leave Zürich for Berlin, but the German consul had refused to give his Russian passport a visa. Salar al-Dowleh informed Mr. de Bacheracht "that unless he receives answers to certain letters sent to

---

304. IOR/L/PS/11/76, P 1464/1914, Grant-Duff, Bern to FO, 05/04/1914. The prince lived at the 'Hofburg,' Hofstrasse 116, Zurich VII, the same address where Einstein lived from 10/08/1912 until 19/03/1914.

Monsieur Sazonof he will leave Switzerland." The Russian Minister although instructed to stop Salar al-Dowleh from leaving, believed that he would do so anyway.[305] Being unable to go to Berlin, the prince opted for a location that was closer. On 30 September 1914, in Bern, Salar al-Dowleh proposed to the German ambassador to lead a German-supported liberation movement in Iran against the Russians and British. In reply, Berlin contacted its ambassador in Istanbul for advice. The German ambassador replied in the affirmative, adding that the prince was "mad" and that he was nothing but a useful tool, because somebody else would have to be in charge of the operation. He stipulated that the prince's collaboration and his departure to Istanbul had to be kept a secret and that he had to travel under a fictitious name.[306]

The Iranian government must have learnt about Salar al-Dowleh's activities, because it was worried that the prince would initiate activities at the border or inside Iran. This is suggested by the fact that in September 1914, the Minister of the Interior wired the governor of Khorasan to learn whether there were rumors about activities by Salar al-Dowleh, because the Persian authorities believed that with German money he and the ex-Shah might make trouble in the Astarabad or Ardabil area.[307] In October 1914 there were reports that Salar al-Dowleh had returned to Kurdistan and was collecting troops, but the Russian Legation in Tehran did not know whether he had left Switzerland. In reply to a request for information, London informed its Minister in Tehran that the Russian ambassador in Bern had informed his British colleague that around mid-September 1914, Salar al-Dowleh had left for Milan.[308] Both British and Russian Ministers in Tehran were sufficiently disturbed by the possibility of another rebellion by Salar al-Dowleh that they discussed the possibility of using the Cossack Brigade to undertake

---

305. IOR/L/PS/11/82, P 3699/1914, Tel. no. 92, Grant Duff, Bern to FO, 18/09/1914.
306. Gehrke 1377, vol. 1, pp. 87-89; Bast 1377, p. 36; Idem 1997, p. 14; Adhari 1378, p. 40-41.
307. IOR/L/PS/10/210, File 52/1912, Pt 2,"Persia Diaries," Meshed Diary no. 37, for the week ending September 12, 1914, p. 1; Eyn al-Saltaneh 1377, vol. 5, p. 4026 (who suggests that it may have been a fake Salar, who wrote a letter to Amir As'ad demanding blood-money (*diyeh*) for his dead men and plunder; Amir As'ad gathered troops). It was only in 1917 that Mohammad Ali Mirza left Odessa fearing to be captured by the Bolsheviks and came with his family to Istanbul. Ehtesham al-Saltaneh 1366, p. 723.
308. IOR/L/PS/11/84, P 4167/1914, Tel. 310, Townley, Tehran to Grey, London, 23/10/1914.

an expedition against the prince in Kurdistan. However, the Russian Minister believed that the Brigade was not the right tool, because many of its Russian officers had been recalled and the area of operation concerned a part of the country where hostilities between Russian and Turkish troops might take place. Therefore, it would be better to use the Gendarmerie for that purpose, according to Townley; he did not think that the prince had a large following, and therefore, preferred to position all reliable troops on the road between Hamadan and Tehran to be able to control any possible popular movement.[309]

Salar al-Dowleh arrived in Istanbul probably in mid-October 1914, where, according to the Iranian embassy, the Germans paid him 500 liras per month. The German ambassador, von Wangenheim, introduced Salar al-Dowleh to Enver Pasha and other Turkish leaders, who were not very enthusiastic about the possible role that the prince might play.[310] Ehtesham al-Saltaneh, the Iranian ambassador in Istanbul reported that he had Salar al-Dowleh watched. The prince was accompanied by his uncle, Rokn al-Saltaneh, a son of Naser al-Din Shah, who was the one-eyed man accompanying Salar al-Dowleh.[311] On 18 November 1914, Ehtesham al-Saltaneh met with the German ambassador, von Wangenheim, intimating his own and the Iranian cabinet's pro-German sentiments, in this way hoping that Salar al-Dowleh would not be sent to the border. Later, he also offered his services as go-between with the Iranian Prime Minister to allegedly arrange joining the Axis and asked that Salar al-Dowleh not be sent to the border. However, by that time it was too late. Earlier, the German ambassador in Istanbul had already urged the Turks to send the prince as soon as possible to the Iraq-Iranian border to take advantage of the unsettled political situation inside Iran and the determination of the prince to take action. The Turks who at first had been unwilling to support this action changed their mind after Iran

---

309. IOR/L/PS/11/84, file P 4382/1914, Tel. no. 320, Townley, Tehran to Grey, London. 03/11/1914.

310. Bast 1377, pp. 36, 40. The payment was conditional on the Iranian government joining the Axis, if not the prince would be sent to Germany. Adhari 1378, p. 41 (docs. 169-70).

311. IOR/L/PS/11/85, P 4570/1914, Tel. 352, Townley, Tehran to FO, 21/11/1914; Litten 1925, pp. 230-31 (Mohammad Reza Mirza Rokn al-Saltaneh returned to Switzerland after his nephew's internment). According to IOR/L/MIL/17/15/11/3, 'Who's Who in Persia (Volume II)', p. 324, "he is now living in Switzerland where he alternatively offers his services to us and to the Germans , but he is unable to do anything for either."

had declared its neutrality on 29 October 1914. At that time, the German Chargé d'Affaires in Tehran, Rudolf von Kardorff was trying to induce the Iranian authorities to join the Axis countries. Therefore, he asked Berlin not to send Salar al-Dowleh to the border. His request was strongly supported by Prince Reuss, the Minister in Tehran (then in Germany) and Max von Oppenheim, the well-known German Middle-East expert and traveler. However, due to the slowness of communication, Salar al-Dowleh's departure could not be stopped and, about mid-February 1915, he was in Baghdad.[312]

RECALLED FROM KHANEQIN (FEBRUARY 1915); RUMORS ABOUT HIS RETURN

In December 1914 the government in Tehran sent a wire to its ambassador in Turkey asking him to report whether Salar al-Dowleh was still in Istanbul, which showed the Cabinet's great interest in his whereabouts.[313] In February 1915, Samsam al-Mamalek, the governor of Qasr-e Shirin and chief of the Sanjabi tribe as well as the director of Customs at Qasr-e Shirin both reported that Salar al-Dowleh and Amir Heshmat with 1,000 Turkish soldiers had come to Chia Sorkh, where the Bajlan, Fatah Beg Jaf and some Jaf tribesmen had joined them. He also was said to have contacted his father-in-law, the Vali of Posht-e Kuh.[314] Samsam al-Mamalek informed the governor of Kermanshah that one of his men, who knew Salar al-Dowleh, had gone there and returned and had seen no sign of him.[315] Meanwhile, Prime Minister Mostowfi al-Mamalek lodged a protest with the German Chargé d'Affaires and the Turkish ambassador. However, the Turks denied that Salar al-Dowleh was with them. Nevertheless, Ehtesham al-Saltaneh formally asked Istanbul to

---

312. Bast 1377, pp. 39-44; Gehrke 1377, vol. 1, pp. 88-89. Ehtesham al-Saltaneh does not mention any of these events in his Memoirs. Perhaps he intended to deal with them in his planned *Khaterat-e Sefarat -e Eslambul*. Ehtesham al-Saltaneh 1366, p. 723.
313. IOR/L/PS/10/478, File 3516/1914 Pt 1, German War: Persian attitude towards Turkey,' Townley to Grey, 04/12/1914. There was also a report that in December 1914 he was raising troops in Lorestan, but that the Vali did not help him. Adhari 1378, doc. 162.
314. FO 248/1112, Kermanshah Diary 25/02/15; FO 248/1112, McDouall to Legation, 23/02/1915; Bast 1377, p. 44; Adhari 1378, p. 43 (docs. 169-70).
315. FO 248/1112, Kermanshah diary 04/03/1915.

recall the prince.[316] Salar al-Dowleh indeed had been in Khaneqin and had contacted several people, among whom the Vali of Posht-e Kuh. Therefore, in early February 1915, the government of Iran, which had lodged a protest, informed the governor of Kermanshah that the Turkish government had communicated that Salar al-Dowleh had been moved to Anatolia.[317] Wilhelm Litten, who was involved with German activities in Iran and the Kermanshah area in particular during WW I, wrote: "With great unease people discussed that one of the great warring powers would be willing to help [Salar al-Dowleh] to return to Iran. When this news became really true and one of the warring great powers believed that in doing so it would make itself popular with the Iranian population, by having sent this prince to Persia, then this great power must have lost its mind." However, after having been to Khaneqin, Salar al-Dowleh was arrested by the Turks and interned and Litten never mentioned the prince ever having played a role in German-Turkish operations in the border area.[318] Nevertheless, despite his removal, some blamed Salar al-Dowleh for the invasion by Hoseyn Ra'uf Bey and the fierce battle at Kerend between his and Iranian forces in June 1915, due to the prince's alleged collaboration with Turkish forces.[319] In July 1915, McDouall reported that the Turks were still at Sar-e Pol and said that Salar al-Dowleh was with them. They were intriguing with the tribes hoping to create confusion to be able to come back.[320] However, that seems unlikely, because Schönemann, the German consul in Kermanshah, did not want Salar al-Dowleh to be involved with his anti-Allied activities in W. Iran at all, "because he was generally hated."[321]

---

316. Bast 1377, pp. 44-45; FO 248/1112, McDoual to Legation, 27/02/1915. The news about Amir Heshmat was correct as he was really there and later was allowed to travel to Tehran.

317. FO 248/1112, Kermanshah Diary, 12/02/1915; Adhari 1378, pp. 41-42 (citing the newspaper *Ershad* of 26 Asad 1294), 43; Gehrke 1377, vol. 1, p. 138, vol. 2, p. 586, note 327; Adhari 1378, doc. 171. Despite this, in early April 1915, there was yet another rumor that Salar was said to have returned to Khaneqin. FO 248/1112, Kermanshah Diary, 08/04/15; see also Bast 1377, p. 46.

318. Litten 1925, p. 230.

319. Bast 2002, p. 37.

320. FO 248/1112, McDouall/Hamadan to Legation, 21/07/1915.

321. Bast 1377, pp. 46-47.

In 1916, Salar al-Dowleh reportedly was a prisoner in Bursa.[322] In 1917 the rumors about Salar al-Dowleh were rife and confusing. Salar al-Dowleh was reported to be in Soleymaniyeh with Turkish forces in Kurdistan and that he also was intriguing with the Russians.[323] On 18 April 1917, McDouall reported that Salar Mozaffar, a servant of Salar al-Dowleh, offered his master's services if Great Britain would protect him when he came to Persia. He further said that prior to the British advance into Mesopotamia, the Turks had put him at Deir with the intention to have him replace Nezam al-Saltaneh, the leader of the provisional government in Kermanshah. The British Minister in Tehran was not interested at all in the proposal and wrote: "Salar can go to perdition; his servant ought to have been shot."[324] On 14 May 1917, McDouall reported that it was said that Salar al-Dowleh wanted to escape from the Turkish troops with whom he was at the Kurdistan border. The Minister did not believe this news, because one day earlier, according to a Persian source in Tehran, there was news that the Turks allegedly intended to attack Kermanshah via Kurdistan and had Salar al-Dowleh with them.[325] However, such an attack was quite unlikely, as the British had taken Baghdad on 11 March 1917 and the Turkish army was in retreat.[326]

The news about Salar al-Dowleh took a different turn after the defeat of the Turks in W. Iran and in Iraq, for on 21 May 1917, McDouall reported that Salar al-Dowleh's agent expected to be sent to Kurdistan by the Russians to offer him the governorship of the West (Malayer, Tuyserkan, Nehavand, Hamadan, and part of Kurdistan and Lorestan) if he raised Kurdish tribes to help them. McDouall was instructed to check this news with the Russians.[327] Although on 25 May McDouall signaled that he had no news about Salar al-Dowleh, the Minister noted that McDouall had

---

322. IOR/L/MIL/17/15/11/3, Who's who in Persia? p. 350. Another source reports that he "had joined Nizam us Sultanah and the Germans." AIR 20/511, case no. 1945.

323. Moberly 1987, p. 243; IOR/L/MIL/17/15/11/3, Who's who in Persia? p. 350.

324. FO 248/1181, tel. McDouall/Hamadan to Tehran18/04/17. Deir probably is Deir al-Zur in Syria.

325. FO 248/1181, Tel. McDouall/Hamadan to Tehran14/04/1917.

326. FO 248/1181, tel McDouall, Hamadan to Tehran, 14/05/1917.

327. FO 248/1181, Tel. McDouall/Hamadan to Tehran,21/05/1917. According to IOR/L/MIL/17/15/11/3 , Who's who in Persia? p. 350, in 1914 [sic] Salar al-Dowleh "returned to the border area and was said to be in treaty with the Russians for the appointment of W. Persia. These negotiations were denied by the Russians." The year 1914 must be due to an erroneous reading of the original correspondence.

informed him that Salar al-Dowleh wanted to return to Iran.[328] That same day McDouall reported that the General Officer Commanding (G.O.C.) was negotiating with Salar al-Dowleh, but that nothing had been settled. Churchill, the British Legation's Oriental secretary, wrote in a note that he supposed "that G.O.C. has been informed of Salar ed-Dowleh's previous record and that H.I.H. is mentally unbalanced."[329] In mid-June 1917, Marling reported to London that Salar al-Dowleh had been for some time with Turkish troops in Kurdistan and that "Russian Military Authorities appear to be in treaty with Salar ed Dowleh to give him Governorship of Western (Persia) on condition that he raises tribes for them. General Office Commanding after admitting negotiations now denies them."[330] Meanwhile, in early June 1917, the so-called Salar al-Dowleh agent and possible contact of the Russians, Moqtader al-Dowleh, was arrested in Senneh and imprisoned by the Russians in Hamadan and shown to be an impostor.[331] From Hamadan, McDouall confirmed this arrest and reported that the real Salar al-Dowleh agent was in Hamadan, who was still awaiting instructions from the Russians, who denied that there ever had been negotiations.[332] In August 1917, there was a report that Salar al-Dowleh in disguise accompanied by two men had come to the Sanjabis.[333] Later it was reported that the prince had died, but Cox from Baghdad reported that there was no confirmation of Salar al-Dowleh's alleged death.[334] Two weeks later it was reported by a number of people that Salar al-Dowleh disguised as a dervish had come to Tuyserkan en route to Lorestan. Vladimir Minorsky of the Russian Legation in Tehran did not believe it; he thought that Salar al-Dowleh was in Kirkuk or Mosul.[335] In mid-September 1917, there was information that the prince had met the Koliya'i and Lorestan chiefs dressed as a Jaf dervish. Later, in the habit of a mullah, the informant in person had taken Salar al-Dowleh to Qom, who said he was going to Astara.

---

328. FO 248/1181, Tel. McDoual/Hamadan to Tehran 25/05/1917.
329. FO 248/1181, Tel. McDouall/Hamadan to Tehran 25/05/1917.
330. IOR/L/PS/11/127, P 4038/1917, Tel. no. 211, Marling to FO, 15/06/1917.
331. FO 248/1181, Tel. Kennion/Kermansha to Tehran 09/06/1917.
332. FO 248/1181, Tel. McDouall/Hamadan to Tehran12/06/1917.
333. FO 248/1181, Tel. Kennion/Kermanshah to Tehran, 08/08/1917.
334. FO 248/1181, Tel. 3313, Cox, Baghdad, 20/08/1917.
335. FO 248/1181, Tel. McDouall/Hamadan to Tehran 03/09/1917. Idem. tel. Kennion to Tehran 01/0901926, who reported that Salar in disguise or an imposter had passed to Tehran.

However, at that time, the Iranian government believed that he was still in Konya.[336] On 20 September 1917, an imposter acting as if he was Salar al-Dowleh was arrested.[337]

Because of the confusing news about the sightings and activities of Salar al-Dowleh, consul McDouall took some time to bring light where darkness reigned. He reported as follows: In April 1917, a man called Sayyed Mohammad, a brother of the chief of the Fendereski Turkmen, claimed to be a servant of Salar al-Dowleh. He contacted Sayyed Musa, the manager of Salar al-Dowleh's estates and his fierce supporter. Sayyed Musa intended to have the man identified by some Russian Turkmen, and if he was who he claimed to be "he would give him anything he required." Sayyed Mohammad then disappeared and was said to be the same man whom the Russians arrested in Kurdistan, calling himself Salar Moqtader and an agent of Salar al-Dowleh. The Russians had let him go after some time. Then there was a report that Salar al-Dowleh was in Tuyserkan with Khosrow Khan. The authorities tried to arrest him, but he escaped. However, they detained his companion Sayyed Ja`far Kermanshahi for some days. Sayyed Ja`far then came to Hamadan and in vain tried to get funds from Salar al-Dowleh's chief eunuch (*aghabashi*), who returned to Tehran. The man arrested in Soltanabad called himself Sayyed Mohammad Fendereski and thus, was the same imposter and there was no one else.[338] At any rate, in 1917, the British government did not attach great credibility to these reports, as none had been substantiated. Also, both the Iranian and Russian governments believed that the prince was in Turkey.[339]

---

336. FO 248/1181, Tel. McDouall/Hamadan to Tehran 14/09/1917.

337. FO 248/1181, Tel. McDouall to Tehran 28/09/1917.

338. FO 248/1181, McDouall/Hamadan to Tehran 20/09/1917. According to the *kargozar* of Kermanshah the whole affair was a case of personification. The Salar al-Dowleh person was somebody called Mohammad Khan, Salar Moqtader of Fendaresk. FO 248/1181, Kennion, Kermanshah to Legation, 1 October 1917.

339. IOR/L/PS/11/127, P 4038/1917, Tel. no. 336, Marling to FO, 10/10/1917 and handwritten note dated 18/10/1917.

A Failed Second Caspian Adventure (end 1918) and Exile

Whether Salar al-Dowleh was in any way involved in activities on the Western front, i.e. at the Kermanshah front, still remains unclear, but based on the information presented here this seems highly unlikely.[340] Research in Ottoman sources may bring clarity to this issue. During the summer of 1918 it was reported that Salar al-Dowleh had appeared in Iranian Kurdistan, but the British believed that it concerned an impostor.[341] However, his absence from war operations was not due to his lack of interest to take advantage of unsettled times and situations in Iran. Because towards the end of WW I, Salar al-Dowleh tried to enter Iran via the Transcaspian region and raise a rebellion in Astarabad. As stated above, in 1917 he was reported to be in Soleymaniyeh, while in July 1918 he still was said to be in Kurdistan. However, later that year he was again back in Switzerland by arrangement with the Swiss authorities and with an allowance from the government of Iran. By the end of November or early December 1918 he left Switzerland and went to Istanbul. In December 1918 he was reported to have passed through Tiflis on his way to Baku and Enzeli. Therefore, the Iranian government asked the British, who by that time controlled

---

340. Stephanie Cronin, *The Army and the Creation of the Pahlavi State in Iran 1910-1926*. London: Tauris, 1997, p. 65 disagrees, because she writes: "the now pro-Ottoman Salar al-Dawlah, operating in Western Iran," without providing any source for this statement. Khan Malek Sasani, *Yadbudha-ye Sefarat-e Estanbul*, Tehran: Ferdowsi, 1345/1966 never even mentions Salar al-Dowleh's presence in Istanbul.

341. AIR 20/511, case no. 1945.

the border area with Russia, to arrest him when their troops came across him. On 22 December 1918 news was received that Salar al-Dowleh had secretly landed at Krasnovodsk and intended to go to Yamut country in Astarabad province to raise the tribes. A British detachment was immediately sent to arrest him, but he had already left. The Persian government gave orders to the Persian Cossacks in Mashhad to go and arrest him. On 28 December 1918 he was captured by a British detachment based in Krasnovodsk before crossing into Iran, or, according to Sir Percy Cox, near Gumush Tepeh. The prince was accompanied by cousin prince Hoseyn Homayun and some Turkish or Bolshevik agents. The British believed that his planned landing was part of a Turkish plot to raise the Turkmen.[342]

He was immediately sent to Baku from where, via the GOC of the British force there, he sent a telegram to Cox asking "to be allowed to return to Persia under protection of the Legation and without further restoration of his properties and appointment to a Governorship. Failing that he wanted to be sent to England." Ahmad Shah wanted him to be taken to Qazvin or Tehran, and failing that to Great Britain. The Prime Minister of Iran agreed with Cox that this was out of the question as he would become a source of trouble and intrigue. Cox himself suggested Istanbul or Poona, if the Viceroy of India agreed. However, Istanbul was to near to Iran and Poona was considered unsuitable. Finally, Tehran suggested Great Britain or Tehran, provided assurances were given that he would not escape as he had from Switzerland. In that case the government of Iran would pay the prince 1,000 *tumans*/month, as it had done in the case of his stay in Switzerland, while it also would make a one-time grant of £1,000 for his travel expenses for him and his family, whom he had left behind in Istanbul. Once the political situation in Iran had settled the prince might be allowed to return, Cox suggested. London contacted the government of Iran as well as the commanding officer of the Mesopotamia Expeditionary Force about Salar al-Dowleh's fate. London felt that his presence should be kept innocuous until the political situation in Iran had settled. Therefore, it wanted to send the prince and

---

342. AIR 20/511, case no. 1945 (the first document, a handwritten note dated 04/03/1919, states that "He is mad and his name no longer carries much weight in Persia"); Cox/Tehran to Delhi, no. 94, 08/03/1919; Memo no. I (a) 2852, 23/07/1919; IOR/L/MIL/17/15/11/3, Who's who in Persia? pp. 350-51; Fortescue, Military Report, p. 60; Moberley 1987, p. 468; IOR/L/PS/10/211, File 52/1912 Pt 3 'Persia Diaries', Intelligence Summary for the week ending 28th December 1918, number 50, p. 1.

his family to Baghdad to reside there, the more so, since Tehran had agreed to pay him an allowance of 1,000 tumans/month. The British autorities in Baghdad agreed to have him come, but preferred to have him proceed onwards to Egypt or elsewhere, because "Baghdad is really too near Persia to be a suitable residence for him. He has spent most of the last four years with the Turks and will always be a centre of intrigue." At that time London did not yet have a firm idea what further to do with the prince.[343]

On 13 May 1919, the prince, accompanied by his secretary prince Hoseyn Homayun, his servant Esma`il Osmanov and cook Abbas Ali, left Baku and via Enzeli and Qazvin under military escort traveled to Baghdad, where he arrived at the end of that month.[344] Given the prince's proclivity for escaping, his popularity in Kurdistan, and the proximity to Iran, which might lead to unwanted intrigue, it was impossible to find suitable lodgings for Salar al-Dowleh in Baghdad. Therefore, the British authorities in Baghdad proposed to house him comfortably in the POW camp in Hinaidi, an arrangement that had to be temporary and Baghdad wanted to know when the prince would be sent to Switzerland or Great Britain? As he would reside in a POW camp, neither he nor anyone else accompanying would be allowed to leave the camp and would be subject to the same regulations as the other prisoners. If the prince wanted to employ a servant outside the camp to buy provisions then that servant was allowed to bring those to the camp's entrance, but he was not allowed to enter the camp or have any communication with the prince or his companions. On 2 June 1919, Salar al-Dowleh arrived in the camp, where he was housed in a tent on the banks of the Tigris with all luxuries, complete with an electric fan. Cox had made special point of that, writing that the prince would not appreciate the heat and "it is not desirable that should he return here full of resentment against us." Therefore, at the end of July 1919, the British authorities also decided to henceforth allow

---

343. AIR 20/511, case no. 1945 (Troopers, London to General, Baghdad, secret, 01/03/1919; Extract telegram no. 32, Cox/Tehran to FO and Baghdad, 16/01/1919; SoS India to Viceroy 02/03/1919; Tel. no. 2796, Political Baghdad to SoS India, 08/03/1919; Cox/Tehran to Delhi, no. 94, 08/03/1919; General Baghdad to Troopers, London, no. I (a) 2404, 29/03/1919; Troopers, London to General, Baghdad, no. 76852 (MIR), 07/04/1919; Adhari 1378, doc. 181 (dated 9 March 1919) mentions that Salar al-Dowleh was in Baku.

344. AIR 20/511, case no. 1945 (Onetis, Baku to General, Baghdad, secret, no. 1.1140, 12/05/1919; NorPerForce to GHQ, no. 1, 1291, 23/05/1919 (under escort of 1 officer, 3 n.c.o.'s, and 12 other ranks 1/4 Hants by lorry convoy).

him to have periodical riding exercises. This was done twice a week accompanied by one n.c.o. and two men as an escort. According to Eyn al-Saltaneh, the expense of the prince's detention amounted to 3,000 liras/month, which the British charged to his properties in Iran.[345]

Having asked his wife to join him in Baghdad, he, on 31 May 1919, asked the British authorities to find out whether she had already left Istanbul. By the end of June 1919 his wife let him know that she was unable to join him, because she could not stand the journey to Baghdad, which news greatly perturbed him. Salar al-Dowleh then asked the British authorities to be allowed to go to Najaf, where he was willing to swear an oath that without their permission he would never return to Iran. After Najaf he wanted to go to Europe or Istanbul, or failing that to Aleppo, because he found the climate in Baghdad insupportable. In a telegram of 29 June 1919, the British authorities in Baghdad, who wanted to be rid of him, asked London whether they might let him leave for Aleppo after he had taken the oath. On 9 July Baghdad asked London whether it could decide on the options given in its 29 June telegram, because an indefinite nature of prince's residence in the POW camp was not desirable. On 6 August London informed Baghdad that on 31 July it had instructed the High Commissioner in Cairo to make arrangements for Salar al-Dowleh's residence in Aleppo, if he did not see any objection to this. However, Cairo considered it undesirable that the prince would reside in Aleppo and thus it was back to square one for the authorites in Baghdad.[346]

On 30 July 1919, the prince's servant Esma`il Osmanov, a Montenegran, requested to be allowed to leave to Saloniki or Baku, because he had a blind and penniless mother in Istanbul. However, the British authorities in Tehran, Baghdad and London did not want Salar al-Dowleh to have any communication with the outside world, and his servant's departure would provide such an opportunity and therefore,

---

345. AIR 20/511, case no. 1945 (Tel, Civ. Comm. to GHQ no. 5182, 27/05/1919; GHQ to Civil Commissioner, Memo I (a) 2662, 28/05/1919; Political Baghdad to SoS India, no. 6051, 29/05/1919; Cox to Political Baghdad, no. 234, 25/06/1919; Memo no. I (a) 2819, 12/07/1919; Memo no. A 1789/455, 29/07/1919; Eyn al-Saltaneh 1378, vol. 7, p. 5599.

346. AIR 20/511, case no. 1945 (Tel. Perscoms to GHQ, X 56, 31/05/1919; Political Baghdad to SoS India, no. 7237, 28/06/1919; Political Baghdad to SoS India, no. 7677, 09/07/1919; SoS India to Political Baghdad, 06/08/1919; Political Baghdad to SoS India, no. 9085, 09/08/1919.

on 17 August 1919, his departure was considered inadvisable.[347] However, on 19 August 1919, the same British authorities gave Abbas Ali, the cook, permission to accompany the prince's son to Tehran. Likewise, on 30 August 1919, prince Hoseyn Homayun was given permission to return to Iran.[348] Clearly the trend was to end the internship of the prince's companions and therefore, it was no suprise that on 1 September 1919, London informed Baghdad that Salar al-Dowleh was allowed to go to Istanbul where he was allowed to stay no longer than one month, after which he had to go either to France or Switzerland. He also should take the oath at Najaf, as he had promised to do at the end of June. On Tuesday, 2 September, Salar al-Dowleh was informed of this decision as well as that on Thursday a car would take him to Najaf to take the oath. He would be accompanied by Navvab Mohammad Hoseyn Khan, while the Dept. Civil Commissioner asked him whether he wanted to take his son with him. On 15 September 1919 the prince departed for Istanbul.[349]

---

347. AIR 20/511, case no. 1945 (Memo PR 346, 04/09/1919; Memo no, I (a) 2924, 15/08/1919; Memo A-1789/788, 17/08/1919.

348. AIR 20/511, case no. 1945 (Tel. A5652, 18/08/1919 plus separate pencil note; Memo 26547, 30/08/1919;

349. AIR 20/511, case no. 1945 (Tel. SoS India to Political Baghdad, 01/09/1919; A.T. Wilson to Salar al-Dowleh, no. 26808, 02/09/1919.

Salar al-Dowleh and Khuzestan (1924)

The next time we hear about Salar al-Dowleh was in 1924. In the intervening years he had been living in Switzerland. According to Litten, Salar al-Dowleh was still obsessed with becoming Shah and wanted to return to Iran, "a news that was met with dismay by the people of these parts, because they still remembered with great anxiety the murderous plundering that had taken place in the various parts of Iran due to his presence."[350] A compelling opportunity as far as he was concerned was the imminent demise of Qajar rule in Iran. In a surprising development he was invited by the government of Iran to return to his motherland. In probably the late spring of 1924, Reza Khan told his Cabinet with much glee that he had just learned that things were going very badly for Salar al-Dowleh in Europe. He had sent him money by telegram inviting him to return to Tehran, where he would be given a comfortable life and be astonished at the revolutionary changes that had taken place.[351] This formal invitation was confirmed by Salar al-Dowleh himself in a conversation that he had on 10 December 1932 with Mr. Binah, the administrative officer in Haifa, whose office kept an eye on him (see below). He told Mr. Binah that "in 1924 Reza Khan had invited him by wire to enter Persia through Russia, but instead he went via Baghdad to apply to the British to release him from his parole not to enter Persia without their consent. He then returned to Europe as he could not get a satisfactory guarantee for his personal safety from Reza Khan."[352]

---

350. Litten 1925, p. 230.
351. Eyn al-Saltaneh 1379, vol. 9, p. 4800.
352. CO 732/60/11, secret, District Commissioner. My conversation of 10/12/32 with Prince Salar Ed-Dowleh Qadjar.

Perhaps the prince saw it as a last chance to get his properties back, because he indeed went to Baghdad, from where he asked the Persian government for permission to enter the country. To that end, in September 1924, he sent his son Mohammad Reza to the government in Tehran with a request to have the price on his head removed that the *Majles* had placed on his head in 1911, and which, apparently had not been revoked, so that he might return to Iran. According to Salar al-Dowleh's grandson, his father Mohammad Reza was received by Reza Khan, then Prime Minister, who for old times' sake (in 1906, Reza Khan had been in charge of the guard detail guarding Salar al-Dowleh in Eshratabad) went to the *Majles* to have this request agreed to. However, the request was denied and Reza Khan apologetically shrugged his shoulders to Mohammad Reza, who was in the visitor's loge, implying, 'Sorry, I did my best.' Mohammad Reza then was told that he was a guest of the State, meaning that he was under house arrest. He remained in that situation until his mother's brother-in-law asked Reza Shah to allow him to leave and stay with his mother, which request was granted.[353]

It is unlikely that the prince needed British permission to enter Iraq or Iran, as he stated, no such impediment is mentioned in the remaining British official correspondence. Moreover, when the High Commissioner became aware of his presence he did not expel the prince as an undesired, illegal alien and parole breaker, but he ignored him. In late October 1924, Salar al-Dowleh told the Iranian Consul-General in Baghdad that he had stayed with an old friend, Mohammad Hoseyn Khan Navvab, who worked in the office of the British High Commissioner. However, on his return to Baghdad at the end of October 1924, the Navvab did not react to a note the prince wrote asking to see him. This suggests that High Commissioner had just learnt about the prince's visit and forbade his staff to see him, as is clear from the Iranian Consul-General's report.[354]

While waiting for a decision from Tehran whether he was allowed to return, the Shaykh Khaz'al crisis broke out, for whom he had a letter

---

353. Oral communication by Davood Ghajar-Mozaffari (04 August 2017). That his son's visit indeed took place is borne out by Adhari 1378, p. 44 (doc. 185). It is perhaps to this event that the following report refers to. "Salar al-Dowleh had asked permission to return to Iran, but after a heated discussion in the Majles this was refused, because of his reactionary tendencies." AIR 23/391, Extract Intel. Summary no. 15 ending 16 May 1925.

354. Adhari 1378, doc. 185.

from the ex-Shah.[355] Salar al-Dowleh went immediately via Basra to Mohammerah allegedly to stir the already muddy waters, according to Iranian sources. It was even reported that he came by a British man-of-war to Mohammerah. In 1926, the Persian government still maintained that Salar al-Dowleh had taken advantage of the unrest in Khuzestan to make problems.[356] Although the British consul Colonel Peel in Mohammarah indeed mentions that Salar al-Dowleh visited that town and told him to leave, he does not mention any political activity by him. This would also have been difficult as he arrived on 3 October and already left on 11 October for Iraq.[357] Allegedly an agreement had been made between Salar al-Dowleh, the Vali of Posht-e Kuh and Shaykh Khaz`al of Mohammerah to jointly march to Tehran.[358] However, that seems unlikely, because right at that time the Shaykh was engaged in a very serious discussion with the British and the Iranian authorities to find a solution for the conflict with Tehran.[359]

---

355. Adhari 1378, p. 44, doc. 182.

356. Basri 1335, p. 61 (Reza Shah, in these Memoirs, quotes the *Times of Mesopotamia* no. 235 of 6 Nashrin 1924, that the Shah's uncle had come to Ahvaz to discuss the ex-Shah's return). *Shafaq-e Sorkh* editorial 16 August 1926; Adhari 1378, docs. 183-84; Bamdad 1347, vol. 1, p. 50; Eyn al-Saltaneh 1377, vol. 5, p. 3694; FO 248/1382, MFA to Legation, 30/11/1926.

357. Administration Report 1924, p. 46; Political Diaries, vol. 7 (1922-1927), p. 247.

358. According to his grandson, such an agreement had been concluded between Salar al-Dowleh, the Vali and Sheik Khaz`al. Oral communication by Davood Ghajar-Mozaffari (04 August 2017). However, I have not been able to find any evidence, or even a whiff, of such an agreement.

359. IOR/L/PS/18/C221, 'British Relations with Khazal, Shaykh of Mohammerah,' p. 15, paras 41-42.

INCURSION FROM IRAQ (MID-1925)

INTRIGUE IN DAMASCUS AND FINANCIAL PROBLEMS

In Baghdad, on 26 October 1924, Salar al-Dowleh met with the Iranian Consul-General whom he told that the British would settle his problems with the government of Iran, as usual twisting the communication that he had received, as we will see below. He added that the purpose of his trip to Mohammareh had been to make the Iranian government understand that he had the power and force to claim him rights and that the Kurds and Lors on hearing that he had returned immediately would come to kiss his hands and feet; he only had to come to the border and they, with their thousands, would put an end to these barefeet Iranian soldiers and Cossacks. However, in a discussion with Mohammad Hoseyn Khan Navvab, the latter made it clear that his claim on British assistance was unfounded, because only the British Legation in Tehran could handle this matter. Salar al-Dowleh replied that the British consul in Ahvaz had told him that he could not stay there, but that if he had any requests he should address those to the British embassy in Baghdad. The prince was clearly at his wits end, referring to his properties in Iran that had been confiscated, so that he had not even a house to stay in Tehran. His monthly pension of 1,000 *tumans* had been reduced to 500 *tumans* and had not been paid for the last nine months. He was 370,000 francs in debt in Europe and had to take care of his wives and children. Earlier he had sent his oldest son to Tehran to pave the way for his return, but had heard nothing further from him. The Navvab told him that all what he had said was known and detailed in his file and implied that he could not do anything for him. Salar al-Dowleh then told him that he intended to depart for Switzerland.[360] The following day, Salar al-Dowleh, under the alias of Mohammad Reza Khan, went to Beirut and from there traveled to Switzerland.[361]

However, in December 1924 he came to Damascus, probably driven by his financial difficulties. On 5 January 1925, he visited the British consul Walter Smart, who, before his posting in Syria, had served many years in Iran and was fluent in Persian. The prince was deep in debt and wanted to make his case that the British government should support him. He explained that "after my countrymen had invited me to liberate them, I responded as duty bound and went to Ahvaz." Just like in 1910, he had wanted Great Britain to remain neutral, but it did not and "considered it expedient that I should leave Arabistan for Tehran or Iraq, while the British Legation in Tehran should discuss with London how to make final arrangements for the tranquility of me and my family." He further expounded how in January 1919 the British Army "without reason arrested me," and that Eshratabad, Mardabad and all his properties were confiscated on some pretext and thus, he had lost everything. Such is fate, he said, but he had to live. Tehran had fixed his pension at 800 tumans/month. From 1923 to August 1924, three months of his pension remained unpaid, which were only paid in September 1924. However, of the year 1924-25, only 3 months had been paid so far, i.e. the payments of May-December 1924 were still missing. Moreover, from 1921, the Iranian government had reduced his monthly pension by 300 tumans, so he and family had to exist on 500 tumans and this payment was only obtained after pressure from the British Legation. When the British consul Peel told Salar al-Dowleh in October 1924 to leave Ahvaz he claimed that he did so only on condition that Great Britain would arrange some general settlement of his affairs. The prince maintained if the consul at Ahvaz had not agreed that the British government would offer him a general arrangement he could have raised all of SW Persia and establish an independent government of Khuzestan. In this manner,

---

360. Adhari 1378, p. 44 (doc. 185) In Idem, doc. 186 the prince told an official of the Iranian embassy in Beirut that he only had gone to Mohammerah to advise Shaykh Khaz`al to obey the government and that he did not want that a war would break out. For his estates in, e.g., Lorestan, see Adhari 1378, docs. 187-88.

361. Adhari 1378, p. 44 (doc. 186).

British interference had deprived him of taking justice in his own hands for him and his family. He did not want to deal with the Tehran government, but expected Great Britain to take care of him and his large family. He had told the consul at Ahvaz that he needed at least 100 tumans/day for his family with 10 children, four grandchildren and four servants. His debt in Switzerland amounted to 95,720 francs and he was desperate for money. Therefore, he asked Smart whether the British government might not give him an advance on the promised final arrangement, so that he might continue to live in the hotel in Damascus until he made more permanent arrangements.[362]

Consul Smart was very much upset with the prince's visit, the more so, because he intended to place his family in a house in Damascus and go himself to Switzerland. "The restless and irresponsible disposition of this Prince is well-known to you," he wrote to London. But more in particular, the prince's continued presence in Damascus, Smart feared, might lead to intrigue against the Iranian government. Therefore, he didn't like the idea of him being there and he feared his frequent visits, because, if he "were to arrange another of his fantastic rebellions," these visits, in retrospect, would be seen as British support for his cause. Therefore, Smart hoped that London might find the means to induce Salar al-Dowleh to move away from Damascus and as far away from Iran as possible.[363]

The Foreign Office had not much consolation to offer Smart. It informed him that Salar al-Dowleh had distorted what he was told in Ahvaz by Consul Peel, viz. that "his case would be submitted to HMG and Peel was warned not to specify any definite form of assistance nor to hold out any hope of financial support from HMG." Nevertheless, London took some action to help out Salar al-Dowleh, who had complained to the British ambassador in Berne about the irregular payment of his pension. In December 1924, the prince's letter to the ambassador was copied to Sir Percy Lorraine, the British Minister in Tehran, who unofficially asked the Iranian government about the prince's arrears. The Iranian Mininister of Finance, Zoka al-Molk, stated that these payments were complete and only the current quarter's pension was

---

362. FO 684/2/25/29, Translation letter Salar al-Dowleh to Mr. Smart, Consul, Damascus, 06/01/1925 (also encloses the Persian text of the prince's letter); FO 684/2/25/29, Smart to FO, 07/01/1925. For the details of the debt, see Appendix V.
363. FO 684/2/25/29, Smart to FO, 07/01/1925

outstanding, of course based on the lower amount of the pension.[364] On 23 January 1925, Smart sent a letter to Salar al-Dowleh with that information and with the message that this was all the British government could do for him. On 8 February 1925, Salar al-Dowleh replied to Smart in which he contested what the Iranian Minister of Finance had said, alluding to unreliable Persians, and repeated what was owed to him. As if he had not read Smart's letter, he concluded his letter with the phrase that he still waited for Britain's reply as to his finances. Smart forwarded this letter to the Foreign Office on 10 February 1925. He added that in his view £1,200/year (i.e. 6,000 tumans) for the Shah's uncle, even if he had not such a big family, was hardly adequate. Moreover, the prince was running into debt in Damascus as well. He apparently received credit from the Shaykh of Mohammareh as well as locally. Therefore, Smart expected Salar al-Dowleh to rebel again and he suspected that he was intriguing to overthrow Sardar Sepah. He noted that Damascus was ideally situated, because from there via the desert it was very easy to go to Iran as was clear from visits from other Iranians to the city without the knowledge of Tehran. Every malcontent from Iran passing through the desert was certain to meet Salar al-Dowleh. "The East remains incurably romantic, and this Prince's memory is still associated with pillaging on a grand scale, Karguzars hanging over town-Gates, lesser fry over caldrons of boiling pitch, and other picturesque incidents of his medieval progresses through distracted provinces of Persia." Because Smart considered Salar al-Dowleh just to be the man to embark on another such foolhardy enterprise persuaded by reckless malcontents, he suggested that it might be more cost effective if Tehran gave him a better pension on condition that he retire to Europe and not interfere with his homeland.[365]

Smart was so worried about another of Salar al-Dowleh's 'adventures' or shulooks as he called them, that he wrote to his former collegue Havard in Tehran asking him whether he could something about the prince's payment arrears, so that he would keep quiet for some time. "As you know, he is quite mad," and it would be cheaper for Tehran to give him a decent pension than the cost of another of his rebellions. If the Minister, Percy Lorraine agreed perhaps he could mention the matter

---

364. FO 684/2/25/29, draft Tel. FO to Smart, 21/01/1925.
365. FO 684/2/25/29, Smart to FO, 10/02/1925.

to Reza Khan. Smart added that after all at Vothuq al-Dowleh's bidding "we pushed him out of Persia in 1919, and in 1924 by moral pressure. So we did the Persian Government a good turn and Salar a bad turn."[366] Lorraine, referring to Smart's letter, wrote that Great Britain could only unofficially raise the matter, and when he did Zoka al-Molk repeated once again that all payments to the prince had been made.[367] Lorraine also spoke to Reza Khan about the matter, who said that Salar al-Dowleh was lucky that the government had not totally cut him off as a partisan of Shaykh Khaz`al. When Lorraine told him that Salar al-Dowleh was in Damascus and on intimate terms with French authorities he did not make much of it. Reza Khan did not see what advantage it would give Salar al-Dowleh, but asked whether Smart could give more particulars.[368]

Smart reacted that Lorraine was mistaken, because Salar al-Dowleh was not intimate with the French authorities at all; the French Delegate only returned his call after 25 days and the French Advisor of Police did not at all. In fact, the French Delegate had received the prince without effusion and did not even offer him a cigarette. Contrariwise, there was much contact between the prince and French Freemasons as he was one himself. One of the Syrian Masons was even foolish enough to guarantee the prince's purchase on credit of furniture. According to Smart, Salar al-Dowleh only wanted to financially benefit from the Masons. From his side, Salar al-Dowleh did his best to cultivate the French, because he wanted them to take an interest in him, and perhaps give him financial aid, with the promise when he would be Shah to be complaisant towards French policy. Meanwhile, he had taken an expensive house in Damascus and furnished it in "the deplorable and expensive manner affected by the Persian grandees with European experience." He also had a large domestic staff and bought a car. Although it was possibly bought on credit, Smart did not understand how the prince could afford to live in this style with his small and irregularly paid pension. He refused to help the prince get a loan from local bankers. Once again Smart emphasized

---

366. FO 684/2/25/29, Smart to Havard, 17/02/1925.
367. FO 684/2/25/29, Loraine to Chamberlain, 05/02/1925.
368. FO 684/2/25/29, Loraine to Smart, 26/02/1925. One month later, Lorraine checked again with the Iranian Minister of Finance, who said that Salar al-Dowleh's pension had been paid up to end 1924; he added that given Iran's financial situation it was impossible that his pension would be increased. FO 684/2/25/29, Loraine to Smart, 01/04/1925.

that Salar al-Dowleh's big danger was his relationship with discontented compatriots. As an example, he reported that the prince recently had a secret meeting with `Ujaimi Pasha Sa`dun, the ex-chief of the Muntafiq tribe, who had come from Turkish exile recently to Damascus. Salar al-Dowleh urged him to stir up his tribes with those on the other side of the border and free Khuzestan from its oppressor, i.e. Reza Khan. `Ujaimi Pasha laughed. Why should he, because Salar al-Dowleh's pension was not paid, start hostilities against Iran? In fact, when he had to flee from the Ottomans he had been hospitably received in Iran and he felt grateful for that. He later said that Salar "must be mad to make such a proposal to him."[369]

SALAR AL-DOWLEH GOES TO KURDISTAN (APRIL 1925)

During the Kurdish revolt of Shaykh Said in February 1925 Salar al-Dowleh had talked of joining him. Smart believed that given his partiality to the Kurds it was not unlikely that he would join up with Shaykh Mahmud (see below). He also was desperate, because of his financial problems and was much upset by the arrest of the Shaykh of Mohammerah and accused the British of faithlessness to their friends. At the end of April 1925, Smart felt vindicated about his suspicion concerning the prince, when he learnt that Salar al-Dowleh had made inquiries about a car taking him across the desert to Iraq. He left town on 28 April with a certain Zakariyah, a former Turkish *qaimaqam* (district governor), who had acted as his interpreter with `Ujaimi Pasha on 11 April 1925. His entourage said the prince had gone to Beirut, but Smart had some doubt about this. He alerted Baghdad about his suspicion, expressing the hope that the authorities would be able to stop the prince.[370] Smart also checked with the French authorities in Damascus, who told him that the prince had indeed gone to Beirut and from there would go to Egypt. Smart still had his doubts and asked Satow, his British colleague in Beirut to check.[371] Satow replied that Salar al-Dowleh had indeed been in Beirut, but on or about 1 May he had returned to

---

369. FO 684/2/25/29, Lorraine to Smart, 01/04/1925.
370. FO 684/2/25/29, Smart to Lorraine, 29/04/1925 [cc FO, Beirut, Baghdad]
371. FO 684/2/25/29, Smart to Satow/Beirut, 08/05/1925.

Damascus.[372] Although this was untrue, because the prince was in Iran by that time, it was later that Smart learnt how Salar al-Dowleh had deceived the French authorities, whom he first had thought to have facilitated the prince's entry into Iran. He found out that the prince had left Damascus with some companions in two cars ostensibly on a pleasure trip to Ezra at two hours drive south from Damascus. From there he sent back his own car with some of his companions to drive to Beirut and the police seeing a well-known car with royal arms passing, registered it as such in their records. After a few days the car returned to Damascus thus completing the deception. Meanwhile, from Ezra, Salar al-Dowleh crossed the desert.[373]

Using his Kurdish contacts, the prince wanted to get involved with rebellious tribes and use their activities for his own vague ends. Although the border was porous nevertheless Salar al-Dowleh passage was immediately spotted by the British authorities in Iraq. On 28 April 1925 it was learnt that Salar al-Dowleh had passed through al-Kadhimeyn going to the Iranian border, too late for the Criminal Investigation Department (CID) to catch him. On that same day, the Administrator in Kifri asked his colleague in Soleymaniyeh to intercept a high ranking Persian, who had crossed the Shirwan river from the Khaneqin side and stayed the night near Bawanur, "today somewhere near Diziaish and tomorrow intends to cross Esharizur to Avroman." A handwritten notation by an unidentified British official suggested that it might be Salar al-Dowleh. The prince had said that he intended to see Shaykh Mahmud to persuade him to let him have 2,000 men to attack Kermanshah. He believed that his force would grow to 20,000 men and said that he was in contact with Iranian officers who promised to help him.[374] Although the prince's identity was confirmed the British military only received orders to monitor his movements and report to Headquarters.[375] On 10 May 1925, Salar al-Dowleh accompanied by Hajji Ebrahim Beg, Karim Beg, Mohammad Bey, Amin Beg s/o Sewaid Beg, Jaf Begzadeh, a Turkish Yuzbashi, a Turkish officer, another military officer, and three servants arrived at Shaykh Meydan in Warwama Nahiyeh of Halabja Qaza. On 11 May they left and crossed the Sharazor and arrived at Biara on 12 May,

---

372. FO 684/2/25/29, Beirut to Smart, 11/05/1925.
373. FO 684/2/25/29, Smart to Lorraine, 04/06/1925.
374. AIR 23/391, Tel. Admintor Kifri to Admintor Sulaimani, 07/05/1925.
375. AIR 23/391, secret, Aviation to Special Sul, 12/05/1925.

where they stayed with Shaykh Ala al-Din. On 14 May the prince was said to have arrived in Tawilah, where he stayed with Shaykh Ali of that village. A government agent, who was in the house with the prince in Shaykh Meydan, reported that a merchant in Baghdad would sent him some rifles that he had bought from the French in Syria. The Turkish officers had plenty of money and French maps of Azerbayjan. They also had many French books with them. Their objective was to the raise the rebellious Kurdish tribes in Azerbaijan. The prince was in contact with notables in Tehran and with the chiefs of Javanrud. The Special Services Officer (SPS) in Soleymaniyeh commented that if the prince would succeed in raising the Iraqi tribes this would have a deplorable effect on the possible cooperation between Iran and Britain to capture Shaykh Mahmud. If Britain were to allow him to raise the tribes of Avroman and elsewhere ["at the moment we cannot stop him] Iran would not like this and their positive attitude would change. The SPS also reported that Esma`il Aqa Simko intended to raise the tribes in Azerbaijan in rebellion to the Iranian government. According to the SPS this was because the Iranian government wanted to tax and completely disarm them.[376]

On 15 May 1925, Salar al-Dowleh crossed into Avroman country and was with Mahmud Khan Dizli.[377] The British sent an airplane that dropped messages that he had to leave and report to Soleymaniyeh, if not, he was considered to be an enemy. He ignored the message and a few days later entered Iran.[378] On 21 May 1925, Salar al-Dowleh was reported to be with Mohammad Rashid Beg of Waisseh in Avroman country. Shaykh Mahmud reportedly sent Majid Effendi to talk to him.[379] On 23 May the prince was with Mahmud Khan Marivan. The Administrative Inspector of Soleymaniyeh asked whether he should ask Shaykh Mahmud to arrest and bring him to him, to which he received an affirmative reply.[380] On that same day the High Commissioner asked the High Command to have the garrison commander at Halabja monitor

---

376. AIR 23/391, secret. Memo Spec. Serv. Officer Sulaimani, undated (14/05/1925); AIR 23/391, secret, Special Sul to Aviation/Baghdad, 15/05/1925. High Command wanted to identfy the Jewish Baghdad merchant and intercept the arms transport. AIR 23/391, secret, Aviation to Special Sul, 20/05/1925.

377. AIR 23/391, secret, Special, Sul to Aviation, 18/05/1925.

378. Aide-Memoir, FO 371/11401, f. 152-555

379. AIR 23/391, secret, Special Sul to Aviation, 21/05/1925.

380. AIR 23/391, Admin. Inspec. Sulaimani to High Commissioner, 23/05/1923; Idem, High Commissioner to Admin. Inspec. Sulaimani, 24/05/1925.

Salar al-Dowleh's movements and to do everything to get hold of him or his followers or secure their expulsion from Iraq.[381] On 25 May the CO in Halabja was ordered to arrest and expel the prince or any of his followers found in Iraq. "No special expedition was required" and if arrested Salar al-Dowleh should be treated "as an officer prisoner."[382] To allay Iranian suspicions concerning the British position vis a vis Salar al-Dowleh the British asked Tehran to send an Iranian official to visit the border area. Unfortunately, Iran had as yet not recognized the Baghdad regime, in which case it would have had a military attaché at Baghdad, who could have made the visit. King Feysal had written a letter earlier that year to Reza Shah, who had not replied, which made matters more difficult.[383] On 25 May 1925, the Inspector of Halabja received a letter from Salar al-Dowleh addressed to the High Commissioner asking to forward it speedily, if possible by airplane. The prince was then with Shaykh Mohdosman at Durud, which he thought might be in Iranian territory.[384]

Salar al-Dowleh clearly expected that the tribal chiefs in Kurdistan would be willing to support his rebellion, because the commanding military officers in the provinces, including Kurdistan, were "totally corrupt and amassing fortunes." This would give him the opportunity to once again offer his services to 'save the country' under his leadership.[385] As a result, "Sardar Rashid, a notorious chieftain from the Ravansar region, who had already rebelled half a dozen times in the past and been pardoned, again raised the banner of rebellion, in connivance with Salar-ed-Dovleh, many local tribes joining in the revolt for the sake of plunder. This revolt very soon extended towards the north."[386] Salar al-Dowleh had also talked with Shaykh Hosam al-Din, Ja`far Soltan the chief of the Avroman, Mahmud Khan Marivan and the Zaru Khans. Therefore, several Kurdish tribes joined the rebellion drawn by the prospect of plunder.

---

381. AIR 23/391, secret, High Commissioner to Headquarters/Baghdad, 23/05/1925.

382. AIR 23/391, secret, Aviation to OC Troops Halabjeh, 25/05/1925.

383. Aide-Memoir, FO 371/11401, f. 152-555

384. AIR 23/391, Cavto, Halabja to Aviation, 30/05/1925.

385. Aide-Memoir, FO 371/11401, f. 196-203.

386. Arfa 1964, p. 203.

TRIES TO FOMENT UPRISING IN KHUZESTAN AND FAILS TO REACH KERMANSHAH

While the prince was making contacts in Kurdistan, Mohammad Zakariya al-Idrisi, one of his agents, went to Basra on 17 July 1925. On 19 July he went to Mohammerah and on 22 July returned to Baghdad. The next day he told a government agent that he had met with several tribal chiefs in Mohammerah, who were opposed to the Iranian government. "They promised support to Salar-al-Dawlah should it be possible." From this visit and the contact with Simko it is clear that Salar al-Dowleh tried to stir up a rebellion throughout the provinces in Western Iran. In Baghdad, Mohammad Zakariya was waiting for somebody and on the latter's arrival he would inform the prince. It was said that this person was Gen. Kersallidze, an ex-Russian officer, a Bolshevik and Georgian Christian, who recently was in Paris and who would try to enter Iraq.[387] The two ex-Turkish gendarmerie officers accompanying Salar al-Dowleh, undoubtedly unhappy with their low pensions on which they lived in Damascus, had been induced to accompany him because he told them he was a prince and had been recalled by his government. He offered them positions as officers of his staff or as managers of his estates. However, when they arrived in Kurdistan they found out that he was a rebel with a lukewarm following. They were detained for a while, but finally were allowed to leave to Baghdad. They reported that the prince told them that he expected reinforcements and supplies of arms, ammunition and airplanes, and the Kurds thought that the British supported him.[388] Another of Salar al-Dowleh's agents was a certain Mohammad Amin Effendi Eitonni, a Syrian and pensioned lieutenant of the Turkish army, who had accompanied the prince. When he was detained around 12 August 1925, he had Salar al-Dowleh's and Mohammad Zakariya's baggage with him, who had gone to the Kalhor tribe. They had not given a fixed date for their return, but had told him to wait for them at Khaneqin in the house of Mullah Mostafa. The police there had ordered him to go to Baghdad; on examination he had no papers of interest on him.[389]

---

387. AIR 23/391, secret, CID, Baghdad to Advisor Min. of Interior, 28/07/1925.
388. AIR 23/391, Dept. Insp. Gen. Police to Advisor Min. of Interior, 13/08/1925; FO 684/2/25/29, Smart to Lorraine, 04/06/1925.
389. AIR 23/391, secret, CID to Advisor Min. of Interior, 13/08/1925.

In late July 1925, the British received information from Halabja that Ja`far Soltan had promised to help Salar al-Dowleh to take Kermanshah. The British High Commissioner sent a letter to Ja`far Soltan, who, although an Iranian subject, owned villages in Iraq, warning him against such action. Ja`far Soltan then told the prince that unless he showed credentials from the Iraqi or British governments that they supported him, he would withdraw his support. As he could not, Ja`far Soltan wrote to the High Commissioner that he would withdraw his support from Salar al-Dowleh, whose plans had become hopeless by that time. The prince then went to the north of Avroman to try and win over Mahmud Khan Dizli, but here also he initially met with no success, although he remained with him in the border area.[390] In the summer of 1925, the Iraqi government had tried to subdue Shaykh Mahmud, who crossed the border into Iran (Avroman country). He returned in August with Iranian tribesmen and was joined by his ally Mahmud Khan Dizli and also by Salar al-Dowleh.[391] On 1 Moharram or 22 July 1925, a very optimistic Salar al-Dowleh asked the Political Officer, it is not stated where, two cables to be sent to his agent Mohammad Zakariya in Baghdad. One stated: "Proceeding Kermanshah. All tribes Kermanshah Luristan accompanied. Send two drivers. Your presence required. Do not delay."[392] The rebels occupied Saqqez, Baneh and Sardasht and surrounded Senneh. However, Iranian reinforcements were able to expel the rebels who fled to Iraq. Because the road from Hamadan to Senneh via Qorveh was suitable for trucks the Naderi Guards infantry regiment reached Senneh in 48 hours and were shortly thereafter followed by cavalry and a mountain gun section. As a result, the Kurdish forces withdrew and ceded the occupied towns of Saqqez, Baneh and Sar Dasht to the government troops. Sardar Rashid and Salar al-Dowleh fled to Iraq, but Ja`far Soltan, the Avromi chief of Nowsud was left alone as he had remained neutral during the rebellion.[393]

---

390. On 16 May and 10 July, 1925 "I strongly dissuaded Salar to interfere with Persia and also dissuading Jafar Soltan and other chiefs (27/07/1925) from joining him. PG took no action or thanked us." High Commissioner Baghdad to Minister/Tehran, 11/09/1926. AIR 23/391, Translation confi. memo no, 184 of 11/06/1925 by the Mutasarrif Diyala liwa to the Ministry of the Interior, with attachment copy of letter no. 627 of 10/06/1925 from the Qaimaqam of Khaneqin.

391. FO 371/11491, Nicholson/Tehran to Chamberlain. para. B and C. 13/07/1926.

392. AIR 23/391, no date (fol. 40). This was send to his agent Mohammad Zakariya, Imperial Hotel, Baghdad.

393. Arfa 1964, p. 203.

Salar al-Dowleh finding himself in difficulties sent a piteous appeal to the government in Tehran and asked the Iranian commander opposing him for an armistice, which Soltan Kirish Khan refused. The prince was said to have received an unfavorable reply from Tehran and left for Iraq. In Kermanshah it was said that the Russian consul there sent money to the prince, and that on one occasion his messenger was stopped by Iranian troops, who took the money.[394] There also was an offer from a letter from a certain Sardar Muzaffar Int[?] offering to take Salar al-Dowleh to the Prime Minister in Tehran to "make every possible arrangements to correct the matter and secure His Excellency's [i.e. the prince's] life. [...] for he will be saved from troubles and will live happily in the capital of his dominions under the shade of the Sardar [-e Sepah; i.e. Reza Khan]. He must believe that the Sardar has forgiven him."[395] It is unknown whether this letter ever reached the prince, who the author is and what his motives were, but needless to say that this offer, if real, had no follow-up.

FLEES, IS CAPTURED AND EXILED TO SYRIA

After the failure of his incursion, Salar al-Dowleh left the Nowsud area in disguise and went to the Kalhors, with whose chief he had a family relationship (see Appendix I).[396] In a letter to his wife Helen dated 3 September 1925 he put a good face on his desperate situation, saying that "Now it is better because all Kalhur are with me. [...] Everywhere there is effervescence against the General of Persia [i.e. Reza Khan]. I receive letters that they are ready to assist me. Naturally I encourage (it, him?) You will hear shortly that I will conquer all Kurdistan, Karmanshah."[397] However, shortly thereafter he fled via Halabja to Khaneqin,[398] while en route he got into a skirmish with the Iraqi police.[399]

---

394. AIR 23/391, Extract Kermanshah Report no. 7 to 29th August 1925.

395. AIR 23/391, translation of a [partly torn] letter, no. 1276, 22 Amerdar 1304, Ministry of Interior, Government of Kurdistan.

396. Aide-Memoir, FO 371/11401, f. 152-53; Adhari 1378, p. 44.

397. For the text of the letter, see Appendix VI.

398. FO 248/1382, Secr. High Commissioner Iraq to advisor Min Interior, 03/09/1926.

399. See Appendix VI.

In his flight he was helped by Shaykh Mahmud of Soleymaniyeh, a well-known troublemaker.[400]

On 5 September 1925, after a gun fight, the police at Mandalai arrested five of Salar al-Dowleh's men, but the prince himself escaped.[401] However, shortly thereafter, Salar al-Dowleh was arrested at Mandali where he entered Iraqi soil; here his saddle bag was searched (for its contents see Appendix VIII). After consultation with the Iranian government, he was released when he promised that he "would never do it again if allowed to stay in Syria."[402] One Mostafa Chelebi of Khaneqin (the contact person between the prince and his family) who arrived in Baghdad on 25 October 1925 told a British agent that Salar al-Dowleh had left for Syria en route to Italy, about 25 days ago. He had obtained a visa from the Italian consul and traveled via Aleppo.[403]

Smart opposed the recommendation from the High Commissioner in Baghdad that Salar al-Dowleh should be exiled to Syria. He reiterated that in the past he had warned several times that Damascus was the ideal location to reach Iran unobserved, and if only his warnings had been heeded the recent incursion could have been prevented. Smart once again pointed out that if the prince would reside in Damascus, "it must be obvious to all students of his fantastic career that one day, sooner or later, he will start off again on another romantic freebooting expedition." He added that the French would not be able to stop him, however vigilant they would be. According to Smart, there were only two solutions to this problem. One, Iran would be so fortunate to get hold of him and put an end to his activities. The other, was to send him to Europe and pay him an adequate and regular pension, which he would forfeit if he left. Smart expressed the hope that perhaps Reza Khan might be persuaded to accept this. If however, Salar al-Dowleh had to be returned to the French Mandate, Smart suggested Beirut rather than Damascus as his place of residence. There it was easier to control his movements and

---

400. FO 371/11491, Nicholson/Tehran to Chamberlain. para. B and C. 13/07/1926.
401. AIR 23/391, secret, CID to Advistor Min. of Interior, 07/09/1925.
402. FO 248/1382, Shams al-Saltaneh to Minister, Legation 01/02/1926. Ja`far Soltan said that he regretted his participation in the rebellion. Adhari 1378, p. 44 (docs. 190-92).
403. AIR 23/391, secret, CID to Advisor Min. of Interior, 31/10/1925.

the relaxing climate might work as a sedative for his highly-strung nerves. Damascus would be a bad place for him, because his creditors were waiting, unless he had collected some spoils during his last foray.[404] The Foreign Office prefered Smart's option to send Salar to Europe via Basra, if the Iranian government would agree to the terms of an adequate and regular pension.[405] Unfortunately, the Iranian government disagreed and thus, the prince remained living in Damascus. As a consequence, the unfortunate Smart was not rid of Salar al-Dowleh's unwanted attentions. In early November 1925, the prince sent Col. Mohammad Zakariya al-Idrisi, who was with him on his last trip to Kurdistan, who said that the prince was ill and therefore, he sent him with the following message: "if we had any plans in view of the recent dynastic change in Persia, he was at our disposal." Smartly curtly replied that he did not wish to have any relations with the prince after his last adventure and Persian affairs were no concern of his. However, he feared that Salar al-Dowleh would not be deterred by his curtness and undoubtedly would continue to bother him given his financial difficulties. Therefore, Smart reiterated and not without a certain measure of self-interest (or self-protection?) that "In the interest of the Iraqi and Iranian government I recommend he be moved from Damascus."[406]

Salar al-Dowleh's 1925 incursion into Kurdistan had a rather brazen follow-up in 1926, probably due to his financial problems, when on 1 February 1926, Shams al-Saltaneh, one of Salar al-Dowleh's wives, who lived in Tehran (see Appendix I), informed the High Commissioner in Baghdad that when the prince was arrested her husband had 7,000 Rs and £130, or a total value of £800, in his saddle bags and that he wanted these returned to him.[407] On 16 February 1926, Baghdad informed the Legation in Tehran that the saddle bag had been opened by Salar al-Dowleh's servant, who did not mention any money and that he had no further

---

404. FO 684/2/25/29, Smart to FO, 16/08/1925.
405. FO 684/2/25/29, Tel. HC Baghad to London, 28/08/1925.
406. FO 684/2/25/29, Smart to FO, 06/11/1925. In October 1925, the *Majles* had voted to depose and exile Ahmad Shah, and install Reza Khan as the next Shah of Iran.
407. FO 248/1382, Shams al-Saltaneh to Minister, Legation 01/02/1926 (original in Persian).

information about the matter.⁴⁰⁸ Lorraine replied to Salar al-Dowleh's wife in that vein, adding, that neither cash was found nor was this mentioned at that time.⁴⁰⁹

---

408. FO 248/1382, High Commissioner Baghdad, to Percy Lorraine, Tehran 12/09/1926 (quoting letter of 12 September 1925 by the acting *qaemaqami* of Mandali.) For a list of the contents of the saddle bag, see Appendix VIII.

409. FO 248/1382, Percy Lorraine to Shams al-Saltaneh, Tehran 08/03/1926. In 1956, Salar al-Dowleh told Hasan Enayat that when he was arrested in 1926, he had a suitcase filled with jewels and precious items that were confiscated. He had tried every avenue to get these returned to him, to no avail. Enayat 1340, p. 317. However, he did not raise that issue in 1926 and thus, this must be another Salari invention.

LAST INCURSION FROM IRAQ (MID-1926)

PREPARATION AND GOES UNDETECTED TO KURDISTAN (JUNE 1926)

After his 1925 adventure in Kurdistan, Salar al-Dowleh did not return to Europe as Bamdad has it, but returned to Damascus, as detailed above. However, possibly due to his financial troubles, Smart's plea that he be moved to Beirut was heard (whether by the prince or by somebody else), because in early 1926 Salar al-Dowleh was said to be living there. Smart was spot on that the failure to move the prince to Europe would only lead to new trouble, for he certainly planned a new incursion into Iran, as is clear from the contacts he made with Arab military officers in Syria (see Appendix IX). In 1926, due to new rebellions in Kurdistan and Azerbaijan, Salar al-Dowleh once again like a Jack-in-the-Box reappeared on the scene.

When he took up residence again in Syria at the end of 1925, the French authorities informed the British Consul-General in Beirut that they had warned Salar al-Dowleh to abstain from political activities and orders were given to watch him discretely.[410] However, this surveillance was rather incidental, if not sloppy or even non-existent. In fact, it was the British High Commissioner in Baghdad who in July 1926 received information that Salar al-Dowleh intended to leave Beirut for Iran in disguise. He asked the British Consul-General in Beirut to watch him

---

410. FO 248/1382, Beirut to Baghdad, 28/07/1926.

and suggested to the British Legation in Tehran that perhaps the Iranian government might ask the Syrian government to prevent his departure.[411] On 10 July 1926, the British Consul-General in Beirut asked the French to prevent Salar al-Dowleh from leaving Syria. He also tried to find out what Salar al-Dowleh was doing and reported: "At that time he was in Damascus returning a few days ago. He seems to be short of funds and is looking for financing from wealthy people whom he frequents, the purpose of his journey." Even as late as 27 July 1926, there was no report that Salar al-Dowleh had left Syria and thus, implicitly was still under surveillance.[412]

The French authorities were embarrassed by their assurances on 10 July and again on 27 July 1926 that Salar al-Dowleh had not left Syria, when by that time he had already left and reached the Iranian border, and they felt let down by their Public Security office.[413] In fact, it was the British Consul-General who reminded the French that Salar al-Dowleh had left Caiffa (probably Haifa) as he had told them before. Salar al-Dowleh had left Lebanon via the desert without a passport. The British Consul-General asked the French: "Is this correct and what about the surveillance?"[414] The French authorities informed him that indeed Salar al-Dowleh had left Lebanon at the end of June 1926. To save face, they added that they would give orders to find and watch him, they added optimistically.[415] Later the French High Commissioner told the British Consul-General that Salar al-Dowleh had departed in disguise as a shepherd via Nisibin (Nusaybin) with a flock of sheep. If he would return to Syria he would not be allowed to stay there, but would be asked to go to a country faraway from Iran.[416]

In early July 1926, Abdol-Ghani al-Mandalawi, a well-known Kurdish nationalist, received a letter from Ja`far Soltan with a letter for Salar al-Dowleh asking him to come to Avroman, which letter the CDC failed

---

411. FO 248/1382, High Commissioner Baghdad to CG Beyrout, 10/07/1926; Idem, tel. High Commisioner/Baghdad to Tehran 11/07/1926, in which the rumor of Salar al-Dowleh's intended disguised departure was reported and the question was raised whether the French would be able to stop him. AIR 23/391, Tel. HC Baghdad to Minister/Tehran, 10/07/1926.

412. FO 248/1382, Beirut to Baghdad, 28/07/1926.

413. FO 248/1382, CG Beirut to High Commissioner/Baghdad, 10/08/1926.

414. FO 248/1382, CG Beirut to French High Commissioner, 18/8/1926.

415. FO 248/1382, French High Commissioner to Cons. Gen/Beirut, 27/08/1926.

416. FO 248/1382, Con. Gen/Beirut to High Commissioner/Baghdad, 23/09/1926.

to intercept.⁴¹⁷ A friend of Abdol-Ghani al-Mandalawi was asked to report on his activities in particular in relation to Soviet contacts and recent violent intrigue and propaganda. He talked with him and learnt that he did not know the prince personally, but had received a letter from Ja`far Soltan via Shaykh Ala al-Din. Ja`far Soltan informed the prince that conditions in Avroman were favorable for another attempt and he asked him to make haste. On 29 July al-Mandalawi received a letter from Mullah Shaykh Hasan, son of Mullah Shaykh Qader from Halabja that the "Kurdish *hizb*" were ready for action. On 29 July 1926 al-Mandalawi sent letters (*manshurs*) to, among others, Farid al-Saltaneh, the Persian consul in Mosul and his colleague in Najaf as well as to other people. Farid was reported to be very pro-Russian and had a Russian wife. According to the CDC, all that indicated that Kurdish nationalists would shortly make another attempt to rebel in either Iraqi or Iranian Kurdistan or both, but likely only in Iran.⁴¹⁸

MARCHES ON SENNEH AND IS DEFEATED

En route to Avroman country, Salar al-Dowleh was escorted by two of Karim Beg Jaf's men from Kolar to Shemiran, who left him there after stealing two of his horses and some of his goods. It was reported that Ja`far Soltan was said willing to help him.⁴¹⁹ At the end of July 1926, Salar al-Dowleh visited Sayed Khalil Aqa of the Kakai, who gave him two guides to Qaria Chirmagh village. Its chief (*mokhtar*), Ahmad Qader accompanied him to Karim Beg's house at Keller. After talking to him there, the prince went to Qader Mahmud in Jular village, who accompanied him to Ja`far Soltan in Avroman.⁴²⁰

On 31 July 1926, Salar al-Dowleh from Khaneqin, passing through Khurmal in disguise, reached Avroman country, opposite Halabja, to join Shaykh Mahmud who, at that time, had been rebellious for many

---

417. AIR 23/391, secret, CDC to Advisor Min. of Interior, 14/07/1926 (the HC informed Tehran).
418. AIR 23/391, secret, CDC to Advisor Min. of Interior, 05/08/1926. The intelligence agents failed to find any Soviet connection. The report only mentions old news, viz. that the Russian consul in Qazvin had sent an agent to Senneh in March 1923.
419. FO 248/1382, Cowan, Admin Insp. Soleymanieh to High Comm., 09/08/1926.
420. AIR 23/391, Extract from Confi Report of Kirkuk Liwa for August 1926.

years, "and totally out of control." Shaykh Mahmud Dezli had diverted the waters of the important Dilani canal for several summers, while the Avroman also attacked Iraqi officials and troops on the Iraqi side. Reza Neyrizhi and Jahangir Qalkhani were rebellious and Iranian tribesmen tried to escape to Iraqi territory, when pressed by Iranian forces.[421] On 30 July Salar al-Dowleh arrived at Shaykh Meydan with four *savars* of Karim Fattah Beg Jaf; he was disguised as a dervish and then arrived at Tawilah, where Qader Beg provided him with a new escort and he continued to Nowsud, where he arrived on 4 August. His intentions were unknown. He had a rough passage, because each escort robbed him of something, including his horse on two occasions indicating that they did not support his cause wholeheartedly. At Nowsud he visited Shaykh Mahmud at Walajir. He also was said to have had contacts with Simko and Said Taher.[422] Salar al-Dowleh remained at Nowsud at least until 6 August and wrote to the chiefs of Avroman, Marivan, Javanrud and Senneh to raise their forces and attack Senneh. This was ironically 6 days after the British Consul-General in Beirut wrote on 28 July 1926 that, according to the French authorities, Salar al-Dowleh was under surveillance in Beirut![423] On 12 August, consul Cowan wired from Kermanshah that it was confirmed that Salar al-Dowleh was in Avroman and was marching to Senneh with Jafar Soltan's tribesmen.[424] In early August 1926, Salar al-Dowleh wrote a letter to H. Dobbs, the High Commissioner in Baghdad.[425]

> Avroman Frontiers
> Dated the 3rd August 1926
> To:
> H.E. the High Commissioner
> for `Iraq, Baghdad

---

421. FO 248/1382, Tel. High Commissioner Baghdad to Tehran, 09/08/1926; IOR/R/15/1/382, 'File 23/15, 19 I (D 89) Mesopotamia - General', Dobbs/Baghdad to Clive/London 16/12/1926; AIR 23/391, Special Sul to Aviation, 02/08/1926.

422. AIR 23/391, Extract from Report no. ending 5/8/26 Sulaimani.

423. FO 248/1382, Tel. High Commissioner/Baghdad to Tehran, 09/08/1926. The dates of the prince's arrival at Nowsud vary between 2 and 4 August 1926. AIR 23/391, Special Sul to Aviation, undated [f. 66].

424. FO 248/1302, Tel. no. 38, Cowan/Kermanshah to Legation, 12/08/1926.

425. FO 248/1382, Salar al-Dowleh to High Commissioner/Baghdad, 03/08/1926.

After the fall of the great Kadjar dynasty my compatriots who well recognize the rights and pro-Shahinshah from Azerbaijan, the great Ulama of Tabriz, the tribes of Shasawan, the people of Astarabad and the noble tribes of the Turkoman Kadjar have called me to return to Persia. I was about to make movement to Azerbaijan when letters from Luristan, Kermanshah and Kurdistan tribal chiefs were received, and in view of the confidence, familiarity and kindness that I had from the Kurds whom I consider my children I decided to enter my dear country from this side. But owing to the close neighbourhood of the two countries i.e. `Iraq and Persia I deemed it necessary that I should bring to Your Excellency's notice these facts in brief.

I hope that the British Government who on account of the friendship that was existing since two hundred years with the Kadjar family will, on this occasion that I have (by the help of God) decided to recover my rights, respect the rights that were transferred from the Government and the nation of Persia, and maintain lawful and friendly attitude concerning the internal affairs of Persia and be aloof in favour of the national independence the rights of which may also be respected.

As regards my personal question I think I need not reiterate as it is impossible to change my experience and principle that I have had since 30 years past. My personal conviction is that friendship with the British Government is as indispensable as life to the Persian Government. Therefore the British Government can at any time reckon me as one of its sincere friends and I hope that after success, Inshallah, friendship and alliance of the two Governments will also be of my person duty.

Sd/- Salar-ud-Dawlah Kadjar

The High Commissioner did not reply, "because despatch of any reply however unfavourable would have been taken by tribesmen as proof of complicity in Salar al-Dowleh's projects."[426] Unfortunately for the British, this was a belief they could not do much about, the more so since Salar al-Dowleh himself created the impression of British

---

426. FO 248/1382, Tel. High Commissioner Baghdad to Tehran, 26/08/1926.

involvement in a very strong and convincing manner, which also partly explains the support that he received. To prop up his own importance and create an impression that he had something more to offer than just his royal personage, Salar al-Dowleh bruited about that before coming to Kurdistan, he had been in Beirut, where he had told his plans to the Italian consul, who gave him £800 and had promised to write to other Italian consuls to assist him. The High Commissioner added, "Needless to say we don't believe anything he says."[427] But to give even more substance to the contribution that he might make to his Kurdish allies, Salar al-Dowleh had intimated that Great Britain would supply airplanes for his revolution. In fact, the prince had approached several technicians and Arab officers in Syria. One of them, then living in Cairo, even contacted him during the rebellion and asked the High Commissioner in Baghdad that his letter of 20 October 1926 to be forwarded to Salar al-Dowleh.[428] It was also reported that Salar al-Dowleh told everybody that he was supported by Great Britain and was promised funds and arms when successful in taking Kermanshah etc. The chief of police of Erbil reported that Salar al-Dowleh had told Shaykh Mahmud that the government of Great Britain had given him 7 million Rs.[429]

Cowan, the British consul in Kermanshah, informed the British Legation in Tehran on 12 August 1926 that Salar al-Dowleh with Ja`far Soltan was marching on Senneh.[430] This information was forwarded to the government of Iran (Ansari) on that same date by Chargé d'Affaires Nicholson.[431] Reliable reports received on 11 August in Soleymaniyeh also mentioned that Salar al-Dowleh with frontier tribes was marching on Senneh.[432] On 20 August 1926, the British consul in Kermanshah, Cowan reported that it was doubtful that Salar al-Dowleh was with the force that threatened Senneh and Baneh. He further reported that Sardasht was still under siege.[433] One week later Cowan reported that

---

427. FO 248/1382, High Commissioner Baghdad to Nicholson, Tehran, 12/10/1926; AIR 23/391, secret, CDC to Advisor Min. of Interior, 09/10/1926.

428. FO 248/1382, Baghdad to Cairo, 30/10/1926. For the text of this letter, see Appendix IX.

429. FO 248/1283, Police Abstract of Intelligence no. 49, 04/12/1926.

430. FO 248/1382, Tel. Cowan/Kermanshah to Tehran, 12/08/1926.

431. FO 248/1382, 12/08/26 High Commissioner Baghdad to M/Tehran. also the draft Persian version.

432. AIR 23/391, secret, CDC to Advisor Min. of Interior, 15/08/1926.

433. FO 248/1382, Cowan/Kermanshah to Tehran, 20/08/1926.

Kurdish rebels were at Shanin, 50 kilometers NE from Kermanshah and another force at 25 kilometers West from Senneh. Government troops, whose morale was bad, were defeated by these rebels.[434] At the same time the Pishdar Kurds attacked Iranian forces at Sardasht, forced them to withdraw and threatened Sowj Bulagh.[435] The Iranian general staff was afraid that "the ignorant Kurds" would believe that Salar al-Dowleh had outside help, because alone, he was discredited and of no importance. Also, how else could he have crossed Iraq going to Iran, unless with the connivance of Iraqi officials? This line of thinking worried the Chief of Staff, because it might lead to a general Kurdish uprising. In fact, the Iranian Chief of Staff also did not believe that Salar al-Dowleh had been able to slip into Iran via Iraq without the British knowing it. Col. Fraser, the British military attaché in Tehran, told him that Ja`far Soltan believed that the Iranian government had its hands full in Azerbaijan and Khorasan and therefore, he had not much to fear.[436]

In early September 1926, the Special Services Officer of Soleymanieyh received a letter from Ja`far Soltan, who reported that he had looted about 20 villages in the Senneh district and had taken some 10,000 sheep and 1,000 cattle belonging to Mo`tamed and Vakil al-Molk, notables of Senneh. The Avromans took 10 prisoners, 2 automatic rifles and 7 horses. Their losses were unknown. Salar al-Dowleh's advisers told him that logistically his large force could not remain in the field for long and could not take Senneh or Kermanshah, but he insisted. He actually sat 14 days outside Senneh hoping that the Senneh tribes would rise and assist him. When the cavalry unit from Kermanshah arrived he withdrew to Nowsud. He then spread the rumor that he was sending for cannon, rifles and ammunition. Furthermore, that there were no Iranian troops;

---

434. FO 248/1382, tel. Cowan/Kermanshah to Tehran, 26/08/1926.

435. The British blamed Iran for the insecure situation on the border, because of: "i. The countenance given to Shaykh Mahmud, the facilities given him for supplying himself in Persia and the failure to make any attempt to remove him from the frontier. ii. The release of the Pizhdar Agas in spite of the most urgent representations of the Iraq Government. This unfriendly act was aggravated by the acceptance of their ransom by from Shaykh Mahmud, thus putting them under a permanent obligation to this rebel leader. It eventually recoiled on the Persians themselves in the shape of the Shardast disaster." IOR/R/15/1/382, 'File 23/15, 19 I (D 89) Mesopotamia - General', Dobbs, Baghdad to Clive, London 16/12/1926, p. 2.

436. FO 248/1382, Fraser, Mil. Attache to Legation 25/08/1926. The reference to Khorasan concerns the rebellion near the Russian border by Lahak Khan, see Kaveh Bayat, *Qiyam-e nafarjam*. Tehran: Parvin, 1375. In Azerbaijan, there was a rebellion by the soldiers of the Salmas garrison, who plundered Maku and Khoy. In addition, there were rebellious Kurdish tribes that caused much turmoil and insecurity.

the Kermanshah garrison consisted merely of 500 men, Senneh and Hamadan. Moreover, the soldiers were all afraid and would surrender when attacked by his forces. Taj al-Din, a cousin of Esma`il Agha of Shikak (Simko) came to interview Salar al-Dowleh in Shaykh Mahmud's house and came to Zurab. The Special Services Officer sent his son Mohammad Amin Beg to welcome him.[437] Unfortunately, nothing is known what was discussed there, although it is clear that no assistance or a simultaneous rising was promised. On 10 September 1926, Abdol-Ghani al-Mandalawi received a letter from Salar al-Dowleh saying that he had engaged Iranian forces a few times and had defeated them. He was in contact with the Pizhdar tribes who promised to renew their actions in winter, and therefore, he asked to expedite his request for rifles and ammunition. To improve their chance of success, Salar al-Dowleh, Shaykh Mahmud and Ja`far Soltan wrote five letters to the Northern Kurds asking to join their attacks on Iranian troops.[438]

Reza Shah was angry about Salar al-Dowleh's rebellion, and believed that he had come with outside help. However, he was probably angrier about the unreliability of his troops of the Western Division given their bad performance against the Kurds and Salar al-Dowleh's force. According to the British, "they are unfit to take to the field against the enemy. There are rumors of panicky retirements and of surrenders to the enemy without fighting. Reinforcements have reached Senneh and more are underway from Tehran."[439] Salar al-Dowleh was still at Nowsud on 29 August 1926. However, thereafter things looked bad for him, because Iranian reinforcements defeated Ja`far Soltan of the Avroman and Salar al-Dowleh at Nowsud, who retreated to Halabja, while being pursued by Iranian troops. Baghdad had given orders to the Administrive Inspectors to arrest him.[440] The Iraqi Halabja garrison was especially warned to watch out for border crossings by Persian troops and to arrest Salar al-Dowleh if he entered Iraq.[441] While the rebellion died down, the rebels were quarreling among themselves. They returned captured men

---

437. FO248/1382, Spec. Services Officer Soleymaniyeh to Air HQ, 14/09/1926.

438. FO 248/1382, Baghdad 11/09/1926; AIR 23/391, secret, CDC to Advisor Min. of Interior, 14/09/1926.

439. FO 416/79, Intel. Summary No. 17 ending August 21, 1926.

440. FO 248/1382, Secr. High Commissioner Iraq to advisor Min Interior, 03/09/1926; FO 248/1382, Tel. High Commissioner Baghdad to Minister/Tehran, 03/09/1926.

441. FO 248/1382, High Commissioner to Admin. Inspector Sulaimaniyeh, 03/09/1926.

and machines guns to the Iranian authorities, presumably a token of goodwill and hoping for a pardon.[442] Iranian lorry drivers arriving in Baghdad told Iraqi agents that the prince was captured by the Iranian government after his defeat; another report was that Shaykh Mahmud had handed him over.[443] Neither report was true.

GENERAL BELIEF IN IRAN THAT SALAR AL-DOWLEH WAS A BRITISH STOOGE

At the end of August 1926, the British Minister went to the Minister of Foreign Affairs, Moshaver al-Mamalek Ansari's house and told him that the High Commissioner of Iraq had informed him that Ja`far Soltan and Salar al-Dowleh had been defeated by Iranian forces and were in retreat. The British Legation hoped that Iranian forces would not cross the border. Ansari said that something needed to be done about Salar al-Dowleh's going to one country and then fleeing again. The Minister then asked Ansari whether he believed that Great Britain was involved with the prince's rebellion. He said that he did not believe that the British were actively involved, but he implied that the Iraqi government should have stopped Salar al-Dowleh from entering Iran.[444] Not everybody in government believed that the prince's rebellion was engineered by the British. In his Memoirs, General Hasan Arfa rather matter of factually writes that Salar al-Dowleh had "managed to slip into Iran with a few armed followers. He had been seen at the frontier by a detachment of Iraqi police under the command of a British officer, but having no orders they did not interfere with him, merely reporting the matter to headquarters in Baghdad."[445]

The suspicion about British involvement with Salar al-Dowleh's role in the Kurdish rebellion did not remain restricted to the government of Iran, but was of course discussed in the Iranian press. A long editorial in the *Shafaq-e Sorkh* bluntly stated that Salar al-Dowleh was but Great

---

442. FO 248/1382, Tel. Cowan Kermanshah to Minister/Tehran, 03/09/1926.
443. AIR 23/391, secret, CDC to Advisor Min. of Interior, 13/10/1926.
444. FO 248/1382, Memo Legation Tehran, ca. end August 1926. Wilson 1932, pp. 158-59 agreed with Ansari. He wrote: "The Persian Government, not without reason, complained that the `Iraq Government showed negligence in failing to arrest the pretender, of whose intentions they had been made aware."
445. Arfa 1964, p. 202.

Britain's puppet,[446] and so did other Tehran newspapers. Therefore, the High Commissioner in Baghdad asked the British Legation in Tehran whether Britain should publish the fact that it warned the Iranian government?[447] The High Commissioner in Baghdad wanted to publish his warnings to Tehran and Syria about Salar al-Dowleh trying to flee in disguise from Beirut, as "this will I think convince everyone of genuine[-ness] of Iraq desire to prevent Salar al-Dowleh's entry into Persia."[448] His Tehran colleague did not agree, because it would not make a difference. The High Commissioner in Baghdad accepted that argument; he himself observed that this kind of finger pointing did not remain limited to Iran, because "The impression that Great Britain is supporting Salar al-Dawlah is so prevalent throughout the Near East."[449] What did not help either that there was an article in the Turkish press, from a Russian source, stating that Great Britain was supporting the Kurdish insurgents.[450] Indeed, for Russia the whole affair was a great opportunity to fan anti-British sentiments. On 9 September 1926, the *Pravda* reported that "Salar al-Dowleh heads Kurdish rebellion. Sardaresht [sic; Sardasht] occupied by Kurds; Persian troops suffered great losses; English and Anglo-Indian officers are commanding the Kurds together with feudals."[451] According to the TASS news agency, the *Pravda* reported on 10 September 1926 that Salar al-Dowleh had entered Iran accompanied by two British military advisers. It was expected that the British "will in the future continue finance and develop the movement of the Kurd feudals." On 13 September 1926, the *Pravda*-TASS reported a rumor that Kurdish forces had driven back government forces to Sowj Bulagh. However, rumors from Tehran had it that Salar al-Dowleh, who headed the rebellion, has fled, while the British were arming the Khuzestan tribes and that attacks from Iraq in that province had become more frequent.[452] Needless to say that this was pure agit-prop that the Persian public wanted to believe.

---

446. FO 248/1382, *Shafaq-e Sorkh* editorial 16 August 1926; see Appendix VII for the full text.
447. FO 248/1382, Tel. High Commissioner to Minister/Tehran. 24/08/1926.
448. FO 248/1382, Tel. High Commissioner Baghdad to Tehran 31/08/1926.
449. FO 248/1382, High Commissioner Baghdad to Cairo, 30/10/1926.
450. FO 248/1382, Constantinople to Chamberlain, 15/09/1926.
451. FO 248/1382, Pravda 09/09/1926.
452. FO 248/1382, Pravda 10 September 1926 (TASS); Pravda 13 September 1926 (TASS).

The Russians also used the Salar al-Dowleh episode in their negotiations with Timurtash and argued that Great Britain was behind Salar al-Dowleh's rebellion with the objective to terrify Reza Khan into an anti-Soviet attitude, according to the *Pravda*. The British ambassador in Moscow asked his colleague in Tehran: "Can you supply info that I can give Persian colleague to be used against Russians."[453] Tehran advised his colleague in Moscow that it was best to say: "Iraqi govt warned this Legation on 10/07 as well as French that Salar al-Dowleh was thinking of escaping; after they found that he had left French forgot to alert Iraq; then Iraqis ordered officials not allow any help from Iraqi side to Salar al-Dowleh; and that Salar al-Dowleh's failure shows he had no outside support."[454] According to the British ambassador in Moscow, the fact that Timurtash had negotiated a draft treaty, but that its signing was delayed until after the end of Salar al-Dowleh's rebellion, showed that the Iranians were nervous about the rebel-prince's activities.[455]

Meanwhile, Ja`far Soltan reported from Halabja on 15 September 1926 that Torab Ali Khan with a few thousand Kalhors was waiting to help and that the Vali of Posht-e Kuh also had promised help. The delay in action was due to the fact that they wanted to wait for Taj al-Din, a cousin of Simko. Ja`far Soltan reported that Salar al-Dowleh wanted him to go through Avroman and Marivan to Shaykh Mahmud, but he was unwilling to communicate with Shaykh Mahmud without British permission and therefore, asked for orders. The High Commissioner ordered that no reply should be sent. Also, that no Iraqi or British official should be in contact with Ja`far Soltan or with any Iranian concerning matters pertaining to the government of Iran. The Iraqi government had ordered its personnel in same vein and had forbidden Avroman and Marivan tribesmen in Iraq to help Salar al-Dowleh or tribal members on the Iranian side of the border.[456]

From Soleymaniyeh two written messages arrived from Salar al-Dowleh stating that he "can do nothing without approval of the British Government" and that he postponed his invasion to negotiate with the British authorities. Likewise, on 5 September 1926, in a letter

---

453. FO 371/11434, Moscow to Tehran, 01/09/1926.
454. FO 371/11434, Nicholson to Moscow 07/09/1926.
455. FO 371/11434, Tel. Moscow to FO, 30/09/1926.
456. FO 248/1382, Tel. High Commissioner Baghdad to Minister/Tehran, 21/09/1926.

to Captain Gowan, the administrative inspector of Soleymaniyeh, 37 chiefs and 37 village chiefs asked the British authorities for instructions and offered to attack Shaykh Mahmud and Khan Dizli. The High Commissioner commented, "They don't mention name of Salar al-Dowleh but are fishing for our attitude towards him." Furthermore, that "in May 16 and July 10, 1925 I strongly dissuaded Salar al-Dowleh to interfere with Persia and also dissuading Jafar Soltan and other chiefs (27/07/1925) from joining him. PG took no action or thanked us." He further informed the British Legation in Tehran about the letter of the 37 chiefs as well as about his reply.[457]

Meanwhile, the government of Iran remained convinced that the British were behind the Salar al-Dowleh rebellion. The British Legation in Tehran, wrote that "The message by Sir H. Dobbs disavowing Salar al-Dowleh does not change that; we only did that because Salar al-Dowleh has served our purpose. Shall we show them correspondence of HI Com; they will see that there was contact with Salar al-Dowleh, but they believe that anyway." The British were in a catch-22 situation. The British Legation further opined: "We should stop this silly rebellion, but by convincing tribes to do so convinces PG that we are behind it. Same holds for letter from tribal chiefs asking us for instructions!"[458] London instructed the High Commissioner to reply to the chiefs that he could not enter into relations with Iranian subjects or tribes that concerned the friendly relations with the government of Iran and not at all to encourage disloyalty to that government.[459] Following these instructions, H. Dobbs, the High Commissioner replied that since the problem was an Iranian affair he could not provide any assistance. If the Iraqi government wanted any action to be taken against Shaykh Mahmud it would ask Iran for assistance not individuals or tribes.[460] The High Commissioner also wrote to the British Minister in Tehran asking him to inform the Iranian government that "although Iraqi law does not allow extradition in case of political and military offenses Salar

---

457. FO 248/1382, Gowan to High Commissioner 05/09/1926; Idem, High Commissioner Baghdad to Minister/Tehran, 11/09/1926; Idem, Tel. High Commissioner Baghdad to Tehran 26/09/1926.

458. FO 248/1382, Memo to Minister/Tehran, 12?/09/1926.

459. FO 248/1382, Tel. Chamberlain to Minister/Tehran, 17/09/1926.

460. FO 248/1382, Dobbs to Mahmud Khan, 21/09/1926. See also text letter in French 28/09/1926 by Legation Tehran.

al-Dowleh will not be allowed to remain in Iraq if he returns apart for a short while to leave the country."461

SALAR AL DOWLEH'S CAPTURE

Dobbs wrote London that Gowan believed that Salar al-Dowleh could easily evade capture in disguise. He proposed sending a message to Ja`far Soltan that he could only atone for his past actions by ensuring that Salar al-Dowleh was handed over to Halabja. Ja`far Soltan had to be promised that Salar al-Dowleh would be given honorable treatment otherwise he would not cooperate.462 In case this plan did not work the High Commissioner wanted to know whether the French might be able supply him with the route taken by Salar al-Dowleh in May 1926, in case he wanted to use the same route on his return. So far the British surmised, without proof, that Salar al-Dowleh had gone from Nisibin to a place near Mosul, then on a raft on Tigris he had descended to Tikrit.463

Around mid-October 1926, Salar al-Dowleh sent a message from Nowsud that he wanted come to Baghdad. The High Commissioner issued orders to all officers not to reply and to arrest him if he came to Iraq. "Unless the Persian Government wants me to communicate with him I will not, for if I tell him to come to Baghdad I cannot arrest him. Do you agree?" he asked London.464 At the end of October 1926, it was reported that Salar al-Dowleh had left Avroman country in disguise and had entered Iraq. He was said either to go to Azerbaijan (Simko) or Syria.465 Hajj Ali Akbar Tabrizi, agent for Salar al-Dowleh was detained at Halabja, having arrived from Persia.466 It was also reported that the SU was supplying Salar with arms and ammunition to distribute among the various tribes in neighborhood of Kermanshah with the objective to start

---

461. FO 248/1382, Tel. High Commissioner Baghdad to Tehran, 29/09/1926.
462. FO 248/1382, Tel. High Commissioner to Minister/Tehran, 16/10/1926.
463. FO 248/1382, Tel. High Commissioner B to Minister/Tehran, 18/09/1926.
464. FO 248/1382, Tel. High Commissioner to Minister, 23/10/1926.
465. FO 248/1382, Tel. High Commissioner to Minister, 30/10/1926.
466. AIR 23/391, secret, CDC to Advisor Min. of Interior, 26/10/1926. [he had letters with him for various persons among whom Ja`far Soltan, al-Mandalawi, see AIR 23/391, secret, CDC to Advisor Min. of Interior, 27/10/1926).

insurrection against Reza Shah.⁴⁶⁷ However, that was the kind of news of which agents knew that their paymasters liked to hear, for there was no shred of evidence for this.

All Iraqi officials and friendly chiefs were warned to guard escape routes day and night. To facilitate his identification a description of Salar al-Dowleh was obtained and distributed.

> Description received from a Persian source:
> Height: middle, squarely built
> Complexion: fair
> Face: Broad
> Eyes: Black and large
> Moustace: Black and cut
> Hair: Black, slightly mixed with grey
> Age: 40 years
> Speech: lisps and stammers.⁴⁶⁸

By that time, the cooperation of all friendly chiefs in the district (*liwa*) had been ensured and all roads were watched. At dusk on 27 October there was news that Salar al-Dowleh was in Alaja (a village of Shaykh Ma'ruf, a Barzinja sayyed and father-in-law of the district chief (*motasarref*) of Erbil). Ali Tharwat Beg, the chief of police with inspector Majid Efendi and a police messenger (*chaous*) and some mounted policemen went to Alaja. But neither Shaykh Ma'ruf nor Salar al-Dowleh were there. However, they learnt that a party had arrived in the village of Akhura of Shaykh Taher, a son of Shaykh Ma'ruf. The police went there and arrived at 6 p.m. But Salar al-Dowleh had received information of their approach and had left and so had all guests and the Shaykh. The Alaja-Akhura districts was then cordoned off. Then Shaykh Ma'ruf returned to his village coming from Bitwin. He sent a letter to his son Taher with a letter to the *motassaref* with information that led to the prince's arrest. Once Salar al-Dowleh had recuperated from the shock of arrest he told Captain Gowan that he was the Shah and had been working hard for Iran the last 20 years and he would do so till the end of his life. However, he was willing to execute the orders of the High

---

467. AIR 23/391, Extract report dated 27/10/26 from Spec. Services Officer Diwaniyyah.

468. AIR 23/391, note undated f. 83; see also: AIR 23/391, secret, CDC to Advisor Min. of Interior, 31/10/1926.

Commissioner. The prince was kept imprisoned in the motassaref's house. Gowan wrote: "This morning I had a long conversation with Salar al-Dowleh. His aim in life was to bring progress to Persia and counter Russian grip. Reza Khan was unable to do so, and that many influential Persians in Tehran were paving the way for Russian takeover. He said he had not much choice but to use the Kurds although he had not much confidence in them. He had not much income to support himself and family and his allowance was small. He was loyal to Great Britain, asked not to be treated as common criminal, gave word not to escape and asked that his guards wear civic dress."[469] The prince also gave the British a letter to his son Majid Soltan. However, the British Chargé d'Affaires in Tehran replied that because the Minister of Foreign Affairs "would be almost certain to take offense at the passage where Salar recommends his son to put his affairs in the hands of the British Legation and to trust in God and the Legation alone." He could not be the channel of such communication and returned the letter. "Suggest that he take out the offensive language and try again."[470]

According to Salar al-Dowleh, he was one and a half year imprisoned in Iraq, where he was kept in a small damp and humid room, where day and night a lamp was lit above his head, and, as a result his eyesight had become weaker. From the text it is not clear whether the prince referred to the situation in 1926, or to another period. Nowhere else in the sources there is mention of him being imprisoned in such a dank place, and this story most likely is another Salari self-serving phantasy.[471]

CONTINUED SUSPICION ABOUT BRITISH INVOLVEMENT

Despite Salar al-Dowleh's arrest the government of Iran's suspicions concerning British support for Salar al-Dowleh were not abated and perhaps even were reinforced by Major Bentick's meeting with Salar

---

469. FO 248/1382, Admin. Insp. Soleymaniyeh to Adv. Ministry of Interior 01/11/1926; "Salar was then arrested by Ahmad Efendi, the motassaref and Ali Tharwat Beg, Cmdnt of Police; can you suggest to PersGovt sent a token of appreciation to them?" FO 248/1382, High Commissioner Baghdad to Clive, Tehran 05/11/1926. FO 248/1382, Baghdad, 08/11/1926. Salar al-Dowleh was arrested in a village Motka, dressed as a Kurd, stays in house motassrif. AIR 23/391, secret, CDC to Advisor Min. of Interior,01/10/1926.
470. FO 248/1382, Clive/ Tehran to High Commissioner Baghdad, 19/11/1926. For the text of this letter, see Appedix X.
471. Enayat 1340, p. 317.

al-Dowleh on 21 September 1926.[472] On 19 September, Major Bentick, commander 1st Iraqi Infantry of the Iraqi Army, was in Halabja, where the deputy-district chief (*qaemaqam*) told him that Salar al-Dowleh was at Nowsud, 3 km within the Iranian border. If he wanted he would be able to meet him at Tahwilah 1.5 km this side of the border. On 21 September with one nco, three soldiers, one interpreter and a sais he went to Tahwilah to verify whether the information was correct and see Salar al-Dowleh for himself. The *qaemaqam* of Halabja had his own escort and a few policemen with him. Given the strength of his force, Bentinck was unable to arrest him. Bentinck told Salar al-Dowleh that their meeting was unauthorized and personal. Salar al-Dowleh said that he was going to Kermanshah and then to Tabriz to raise an army, unless prevented by the British government. Bentick tried to persuade him to meet with the Administrative Inspector of Soleymaniyeh at Tahwilah or go to Baghdad; he then agreed to do so. Bentick then informed his commander that he could arrange such as meeting on 23 September and asked for a speedy reply.[473] Major Bentinck was immediately severely reprimanded. His commander wrote that this meeting was a great embarrassment. He had to inform Salar al-Dowleh that no meeting with the Administrative Inspector would take place and was ordered: "You are forbidden to have any contact with Salar al-Dowleh; send report why you did not arrest him."[474] Also, London was informed immediately that Bentinck had been so stupid to meet with Salar al-Dowleh in Iraqi territory.[475] London replied "to inform MFA in Tehran and to tell that Bentick is been removed; HMG regrets and is displeased about this; avoid use of word 'apology'."[476] The British Minister in Tehran did so, explaining that "The reason for this unthinking action was that he wanted to identify Salar al-Dowleh to facilitate his arrest." However, the High Commissioner in Baghdad feared that Salar al-Dowleh explained this meeting as British support for his activities as did the government of Iran.[477]

---

472. FO 248/1382, High Commissioner Baghdad to Amery, 21/10/1926.

473. FO 248/1382, Bentinck to CO, Baghdad 22/09/1926; FO 248/1382, Major Bentinck to Air HQ, Baghdad, 21/09/1926; FO 248/1382, Bentinck to Air HQ, 23/09/1926.

474. FO 248/1382, Air HQ to Bentinck, 22/09/1926.

475. FO 248/1382, Baghdad to Amery, London 21/10/1926.

476. FO 248/1382, Tel. Chamberlain to Minister, 07/10/1926.

477. FO 248/1382, Tel. High Commissioner Baghdad to Minister, 04/10/1926.

WHERE TO SEND SALAR AL-DOWLEH?

After Salar al-Dowleh's arrest the problem arose what to do with him? The High Commissioner in Baghdad proposed to ask the Consul-General in Beirut if he wanted to either deport him to Europe or keep him in Syria under strict surveillance.[478] Salar al-Dowleh himself suggested that he be sent to India.[479] Given Iranian interest to have Salar al-Dowleh extradited the High Commissioner in Baghdad informed Tehran that art. 4 of the Provisional Agreement prevented such action. Moreover, Salar al-Dowleh said that he would commit suicide if were to be handed over to Iran.[480] Baghdad finally decided that the best solution seemed to be to send Salar al-Dowleh to India; in that case his wife and children in Beirut also needed to be sent.[481]

However, the government of India did not want Salar al-Dowleh, and only after pressure from London and with great reluctance it allowed him to come, but on conditions.[482] Delhi accepted to receive Salar al-Dowleh in India, provided he accepted certain conditions and that he would be under surveillance. "If he does not respect these conditions he will be deported, probably Iraq. India will not pay for him and if PG payment are not regular he will not be kept in India, even for a short

---

478. FO 248/1382, Tel. High Commissioner to Minister, 01/11/1926.
479. FO 248/1382, Tel. High Commissioner to Minister, 02/11/1926.
480. FO 248/1382, High Commissioner to Minister/Tehran and Col. Off., 03/11/1926.
481. FO 248/1382, Tel. High Commissioner to Minister/Tehran and Col. Off. 07/11/1926.
482. FO 248/1382, Secretary of State India to viceroy, 12/11/1926.

period. Also, you need to get commitment from PG re this and cost of travel, also of wife and children, to India and their maintenance and surveillance in India. PG should make payment in advance."[483] On 23 November 1926, Sir A. Chamberlain informed Clive in Tehran of the conditions for the government of India's acceptance of the prince:

> 1. he will place himself under charge of Govt. official on arrival in India and proceed to place directed.
> 2. he will reside in place and area instructed and house approved by Government.
> 3. he will not leave prescribed area except on conditions fixed by Gvt. whose sanction he must first obtain form any journey.
> 4. he will submit to such police surveillance as Govt. consider necessary to ensure observance of conditions of residence. It might also be necessary to impose restrictions as to visitors and correspondence and to take steps to prevent him getting into debt.
>
> Estimated cost of surveillance is rupees 7.500 per annum which may be regarded as maximum.
>
> Colonial Office suggest that as Iraq Govt. would not presumably in any circumstances desire him to return to Iraq, he might be informed that if he attempts to escape or to infringe conditions P.G. will be invited to cease payment of his pension and he will be liable to be deported to Persia.
>
> I have expressed my concurrence in this suggestion.[484]

However, before the move could take place some financial problems had to be resolved. Salar al-Dowleh had £1,000 debt in Beirut, a family (one Swiss wife and three children under the age of 12) and could not leave unless this debt was paid. Moreover, he also had a debt of 45,000 francs in Lausanne, and all this would take time. Finally, the cost to transport the prince and his family to India via Baghdad amounted to

---

483. FO 248/1382, Chamberlain to Legation Tehran. 18/11/1926.
484. FO 248/1382, Chamberlain to Minister/Tehran, 23/11/1926; FO 248/1382, Vice-Roy to Secr. State India, 19/11/1926

£200, and it had to be decided who would pay for that.[485] On 20 November 1926, Clive, the British Minister in Tehran, officially informed the Iranian foreign minister, Ali Qoli Khan Ansari, of this offer.[486] The High Commissioner suggested to London that if Salar al-Dowleh did not accept these conditions, "we can tell him that Iraq will deport him to Persia under the Residency Law, the only legal action Iraq can make (art 10 (c)."[487]

On 30 November 1926 the government of Iran replied. It stated that in 1924 Salar al-Dowleh had taken advantage of problems in Khuzestan to make problems; he promised that would never do it again if allowed to stay in Syria. He reneged on this promise. Given his untrustworthiness, Tehran argued, it would be best to send him to Iran where he would be given an appropriate residence and means of living.[488] On 16 December 1926, Balfour, the British chargé d'affaires, had an interview with Reza Shah. The latter, who had obtained letters from Salar al-Dowleh sent to Kurds, was convinced from their contents that the British were behind Salar al-Dowleh's attempt. His arrest was merely a ruse to cover up his failure.[489] Therefore, it was no surprise that during the audience Reza Shah said that Salar al-Dowleh was a 'son of a dog' (*pedar-e sag*) and that India was only suggested, because the choice was between that and Syria, and Salar al-Dowleh had already fled from there. But the Indian option was expensive, therefore it would be better to send him to Iran, where he would receive amnesty and financial assistance. The Shah would instruct his Ministry of Foreign Affairs to write a note "offering a firm offer of pardon and future pecuniary assistance to Salar al-Dowleh if he would come to Tehran." This was followed by a discussion with the Ministry of Foreign Affairs on 22 December 1926.[490] London reacted that it would support the Shah's offer if it was just.[491] The Foreign Office informed the British Minister in Tehran that Bentinck had not only been removed from his job, but he also had been dismissed from Iraqi service

---

485. FO 248/1382, Tel. High Commissioner, Baghdad to Minister, 26/11/1926.
486. FO 248/1382, Clive to MFA, 20/11/1926 + Persian letter.
487. FO 248/1382, Baghdad to Minister, 22/11/1926; FO 248/1382, Tel. High Commissioner Baghdad to Legation Tehran, 22/11/1926.
488. FO 248/1382, MFA to Legation, 8 Azar 1305 - 30/11/1926.
489. FO 248/1283, Police Abstract of Intelligence no. 49, 04/12/1926 (according to a letter from Shaykh Mohammad al-Khalisi informing Baghdad).
490. FO 248/1382, Resume of conversation with Shah, 16/12/1926.
491. Followed up in letter FO 248/1382, Clive to Chamberlain 16/12/1926.

and been sent back to his regiment in Great Britain. He had to tell Reza Shah if this was useful.[492]

Meanwhile, the prolonged stay of Salar al-Dowleh became embarrassing to the Iraqi government, because there was no suitable place for him in Iraq to be kept. Moreover, his health was suffering and therefore, the High Commissioner asked Clive in Tehran whether the government of Iran could not make a quick decision? "Otherwise, release may have to be considered."[493] Therefore, Salar al-Dowleh was allowed to exercise in the streets of Baghdad with plains clothes escort. People in Baghdad, not only in Iran, were afraid of the mercurial and irresponsible behavior of the prince. Therefore, "Local inhabitants [were] unwilling to offer money required as bail for fear of being implicated in any trouble in which Salar caused or will cause."[494] Meanwhile, London wanted pressure to be put on Salar al-Dowleh by informing him that if he would not accept India as residence he should be told he may be deported to Iran under the 1923 Residency Law.[495] In 1927, pursuing Reza Shah's offer, Timurtash instructed the Iranian consul-general in Baghdad to meet with Salar al-Dowleh and to invite him to come to Iran, promising him a pardon and an income. Salar al-Dowleh replied that all matters should be addressed to the British and that he should not seek direct contact with him.[496] As I noted above, Salar al-Dowleh absolutely did not want to go to Iran and as he was detained by the British, of course, all correspondence had to go through them, as they did not trust him at all. Not only Iran as a place of exile did not work out, neither did that of India. From the available sources it is not clear why the India option was abandoned. It may be have been the result of the Iranian government's decision to pay Salar al-Dowleh a pension of 18,000 Rupees to be paid in two installments in the months of *Farvardin* (21 March-20 April) and *Mehr* (21 September-20 October) rather than upfront as the government of India had demanded.[497]

---

492. FO 248/1382, FO to Clive, Tehran. 07/12/1926.
493. FO 248/1382, Tel. High Commissioner to Minister, 17/12/26; Clive to MFA, 21/12/1926, with above message.
494. AIR 23/391, Extract Report dated 17/01/1927 Spec. Services Officer Baghdad.
495. FO 248/1382, FO to Col. Office, 26/11/1926.
496. Adhari 1378, p. 47 (docs. 193-94); see also FO 248/1083, Précis d'une communication adressée par S.A. Abol Fath Mirza à S.E. le Haut Commissaire de S.M.B. à Baghdad 28/09/1926.
497. Adhari 1378, p. 47 (docs. 195-99).

Residence in Haifa (1926-34)

Whatever the reason may have been to abandon India as a place of exile, it was decided to send Salar al-Dowleh to Haifa as long as the Iranian Government paid him Rs1,500/month. The prince gave a written understanding that he would not leave Haifa without the permission of the British authorities and refrain from intriguing against the Iranian government.[498]

> Copy (in translation) of undertaking given by Abul Fath Mirza (Salar-ed-Dowleh)[499]
>
> In His Name (Name of God)
>
> I hereby give His Excellency the High Commissioner my word of honour that I shall leave here for Beirut and from Beirut, if God the Almighty wishes, I shall go to Haifa (situated in Palestine) and that I shall not leave the latter place as long as the honourable British Government have not given me permission to do so.
> (signed) Salar-ed-Dowleh,
> Qajar
> Baghdad 21.6.1927

---

498. FO 371/13063. Memo 01/03/1928. Formalized in letter of FO 371/13063, 09/03/28; IOR/R/20/A/3722; File 1309; Typed undated note, probably dated 22/06/1934.

499. CO 732/60/11, enclosure no. 2 in Tehran despatch no. 427 of the 6th September, 1933.

I also give my word that I shall not take any action in any way against the Persian Government.
Dated 21.6.1927
(signed) Salar-ed-Dowleh

On 3 May 1927, Salar al-Dowleh was received by the High Commissioner, with the result that Salar al-Dowleh was allowed to travel from Baghdad to Beirut to fetch his wife and children. Gossip in Baghdad had it that this renewed British interest in the prince was because "he might be of considerable use to the British Government in the event of a rupture with Persia."[500] From Beirut the British authorities saw to it that on 15 July Salar al-Dowleh and family left for Haifa. There he was to reside in Karadah and live on a monthly allowance of 200 Turkish pounds, paid by the government of Iran from the income of the prince's property. The Consul-General in Beirut wrote "I have succeeded in getting off his multifarious impediments and am slowly dealing with his debts."[501] It was the British understanding that the Iranian government had promised only to pay his pension for a period of six months, which ended in November 1927. However, the December tranche of 1,500 rupees was paid into the IBP, which indicated that the Iranian government apparently intended to continue to pay. And indeed, it did, be it that there was a 3-months delay in payment. However, the ambassador in Tehran explained that "To Persians the present rate of payment is considered prompt, payment in advance would be unprecedented."[502] However, it was not good enough for Salar al-Dowleh, because he was not happy in Haifa.[503] On 16 February 1928 Salar al-Dowleh wrote a letter to Chamberlain complaining that his Iranian pension was inadequate, he summarized events in Iran since 1919, commented on Russo-Iranian anti-British activities, affirmed his pro-British attitude and suggested that he should come to London to discuss his policy observations in person or be given his liberty. One of Chamberlain's advisers commented that "the writer of this long screed is an irresponsible creature whose

---

500. AIR 23/391, Extract Spec. Serv. Officer's report, 02/06/1927.
501. AIR 23/391, Extract Spec. Serv. Officer's report, 21/06/1927; Idem, no. 77, CG/Beirut to HC/Baghdad, 21/07/1927.
502. FO 371/13063, Tehran-London, 09/07/1928.
503. FO 371/13063 Sistan diary; Clive to Lord Flumer/Palestine High Commissioner, 10/01/1928.

hobby it is to organize revolutions against the Persian Government. From the letter it is clear that he still yearns for another go at revolution. My advise is not to give a reply at all."[504] Because he did not get a reply to his earlier letter Salar al-Dowleh again wrote a letter (in French) complaining that "he is now pensioner for 16 months and he wanted to leave."[505] He stated that his affairs demanded his presence in Europe. The Foreign Office understood that his pension was often in arrears and his financial position was desperate. However, the FO took the position that it had try to get Salar al-Dowleh accept to stay if the pension would be regularly paid, for example through payments via the Ottoman Bank in Haifa. "If he wants to leave for property and other reasons, let us know, so we may inform Persian Government and see if they in that case want to continue to pay."[506] The Colonial Secretary Amery opined that if the pension was not paid on time there was no obligation to hold him in Haifa, but the Foreign Secretary disagreed, who instructed Clive to arrange for more regular payment of the prince's pension. This had the required result.[507]

In May 1929, Salar al-Dowleh wrote a letter to the Secretary of State Colonial Offices in which he threatened to raise a rebellion in Iran, unless the British government contacted the Iranian government about the return of his estates. London therefore, ordered that steps be taken so that he could not leave Palestine to which end the border authorities in Palestine, Trans Jordan and Iraq were warned to prevent a recurrence of the 1926 events. London also asked the French authorities to warn the border authorities in Syria. London did not want to upset the government in Tehan while discussions between the two sides were taking place.[508] Baghdad replied that steps were taken but that the border was long and porous. At the same time, the presence of the prince in the border area would be most embarrassing given "the nationalist feelings among the

---

504. FO 371/13063, img 9337 Memo 01/03/1928. Formalized in a letter, see FO 371/13063, 09/03/1928.
505. FO 371/13063, Salar al-Dowleh to Secretary FO.
506. FO 371/13063, Internal Memorandun, 12/11/1928; Idem, FO to Clive/Tehran, 17/11/1928.
507. FO 371/13063, Col. Office to FO, 23/08/1928; Idem, FO (Luke) to Amery, 22/10/1928; Idem, FO to Clive/Tehran 17/11/1928; Idem, Tel. Clive to FO, 07/12/1928.
508. AIR 23/391, Tel. SoS Colonies to High Commissioner/Baghdad, 16/05/1929.

Kurdish tribes in Iraq and the still unsuppressed insurrection of Kurdish tribes in the neighbourhood of Sauj Bulagh."[509]

The text of Salar al-Dowleh's May 1929 letter gave rise to suspicion that he was engaged in unspecified activities that were incompatible with his parole. The District Commissioner Northern District issued him a warning. In his reply of 16 June 1929, the prince denied that he had done anything untoward. London believed that the prince's profession of good faith and absence of any intention to break his parole or leave Palestine to raise rebellion in Iran, seemed sincere. However, it also observed that in his letter there was an indication that, "material discomfort and humiliation may in the end weaken his resolutions" as his suggestion that his properties had to be restored, his allowance increased and its payment punctual, implied a kind of threat. In a letter of 7 October 1929, the prince provided a list of his properties, but London concluded that given the tone of earlier correspondence on the subject the government of Iran did not seem inclined to give in on this point.[510] The High Commissioner of Palestine agreed that Iranian government would not restore any of the prince's properties, while concerning the insufficiency of the allowance he commented, "the prince might reasonably be expected to have realised by now the necessity of circumscribing his expenditure to the measure of his allowance."[511] In October 1929 it was reported in Tehran that the prince had escaped, but Clive told Timurtash that this news was erroneous. In December 1929, Salar al-Dowleh again complained that his pension was insufficient. However, the British government was not prepared to intervene on his behalf with Tehran, neither on the matter of the pension nor on his confiscated properties.[512] Because Salar al-Dowleh had to support 17 dependents in Haifa he was in difficult, if not in critical, financial straits. Therefore, in early 1931 the prince had written to the Nizam of Hyderabad, then one of the richest men in the world and a Moslem ruler, asking for financial assistance. Sadr al-Maham of the Nizam's government's political department asked the government of India to be provided with information concerning Salar

---

509. AIR 23/391, Tel. High Commissioner/Baghdad to SoS Colonies, 18/05/1929.

510. IOR/L/PS/12/3492, Coll. 28/86 Prince Salar-ed-Dowleh, letter to Passfield, Secretary of State for the Colonies, 23/10/1929.

511. IOR/L/PS/12/3492, Coll. 28/86 Prince Salar-ed-Dowleh, Chancellor, High Commissioner Palestine to CO, 11/1929.

512. IOR/L/PS/12/3492, Coll. 28/86 Prince Salar-ed-Dowleh, draft letter. 13/12/1929.

al-Dowleh's pecuniary circumstances.[513] I have not been able to establish whether he received any financial assistance from the Nizam, which seems unlikely given Salar al-Dowleh's worsening financial situation.

Apart from financial problems, his one-tracked mindedness and sense of privilege drove him on 10 October 1932 to contact Mr. Binah, the administrative officer of the Northern District, who had to keep an eye on him. In a long conversation he repeated the woes, ills, evils, and wrongs he had to suffer during his life, even as recently as 1925 and 1926 when the British had not supported his rebellion, which led to his imprisonment in Baghdad and exile to Haifa. He further tried to explain the many memos he had sent to the High Commissioner and the Foreign Office explaining that the new regime in Iran was anti-British and guided by Russia and Germany with the objective to end British influence in Iran. The cancellation of the oil concession was but the first step and no surprise to him. Britain was now reviled in Iran- if only they had listened to him, but no, they exiled him to Haifa. He had been ignored, received his allowance irregularly, and if not for the personal interest Mr. Binah took in his situation he would have been forgotten completely. Now was the time for Britain to use the influence of the Qajar family, i.e. him to rehabilitate British prestige in Iran. He could have easily clubbed together with enemies of Great Britain, who were willing to help getting him the throne, but "he took the oath on the thumb of his grandfather to remain loyal to the British and he will keep his oath until the last day of his life." Mr. Binah added that the prince wanted an interview with the High Commissioner to explain all this in more detail. In 1929 the prince had such a talk with the Officer Administrating the Government. Mr. Binah suspected that the prince was in contact with people in Iran through Syria. Also, the princess, his wife, occasionally went to Damascus and Beirut and he suspected that these trips were made for no other than political reasons. He had known the prince since 1927 and offered his opinion that "he does not strike me as being the type of man qualified to be "the Ruler of a state", which is his ambition." Mr. Binah

---

513. IOR/L/PS/12/3492, Coll. 28/86 Prince Salar-ed-Dowleh, Resident Hyderabad to FO government of India, Simla. 18/05/1931; Idem, Sadr al-Maham to Resident, Hyderabad, 12/05/1931 (At that time, the prince was living in Bait Galim, Haifa, Palestine).

added that the prince "speaks Persian, Turkish, Arabic (not much) and very poor French. Expresses himself with difficulty."[514]

Pursuant to this meeting, the Inspector Northern District asked the chief secretary of the High Commissioner: "Do you want me to see the man, and if yes, what am I to say?[515] The reply was resoundingly negative. The High Commissioner informed the Inspector Northern District that he only needed the see the prince in relation to his remittances. Moreover, if he met the prince "neither you nor your officers may say anything concerning Persia or Persian politics, and you and your officers must refuse to listen to anything concerning Persia or Persian politics."[516]

---

514. CO 732/60/11, secret, District Commissioner. My conversation of 10/12/32 with Prince Salar Ed-Dowleh Qadjar [Mr. Binah, administrative officer]

515. CO 732/60/11, secret, District Commissioner to Chief Secretary/Jerusalem, 19/12/1932.

516. CO 732/60/11, secret, Acting Chief Secretary to Inspector Northern District, 09/01/1933.

Iran Stops Payment of Salar al-Dowleh's Pension (June 1933)

In June 1933, the government of Iran informed the British government that it would cease to pay Salar al-Dowleh's allowance as of 21 September 1933. It seems that this allowance was until then paid from the Shah's account and it seemed he did not care any longer what the prince did.[517] The Inspector Northern District asked the High Commissioner, since the payment of the allowance was stopped, "What dispositions you propose to take with regard to the future."[518] The High Commissioner of Palestine commented that no allowance had been paid to the prince since March 1933 and since then he had been living on charity. He opined that the Iranian government had to be informed that if arrears were not sent immediately and regular payment in future guaranteed he was not prepared to accept the current arrangements under which the prince lived in Haifa. In short, this default payment freed prince form his parole.[519] The Secretary of State (SoS) of of the Colonial Office reacted that if the allowance was not paid then the prince was no longer under any obligation to the British or Palestine government as to his movements or actions. Nevertheless, the Foreign Office wanted to avoid a situation in which Great Britain would be presumed to have any

---

517. IOR/L/PS/12/3492, Coll. 28/86 Prince Salar-ed-Dowleh, Tel. no. 135, Mallet, Tehran to FO, 23/06/1933.
518. CO 732/60/11, District Comm's Office/Haifa to Salar. 22/-9/1933.
519. CO 732/60/11, HC Palestine to SoS Colonies, 15/06/1933.

responsibility for the prince towards the Iranian government.[520] London decided to inform Tehran that unless the allowance was paid the prince was free from parole. The government in Tehran replied that "difficulties had arisen about the payment" and that in the future no payments would be made. "In order, however, that he may not suffer from lack of notice, allowance for current half year has been paid from special credits."[521] On 20 June 1933, the government of Iran remitted Rs. 9,000 in last payment. The Tehran Legation informed London of the end of payment and that the FO understood that the prince was absolved from his parole as of 21 September 1933 and was under no obligation to Great Britain or the Palestine Government as to his movements.[522] In reaction, on 21 August 1933, London instructed its representative in Tehran to inform the Iranian Government that the FO understood that the prince's parole held until final day of payment and that Great Britain "have ever had any responsibility towards Persian Government for Prince Salar al-Dowleh will be absolved from parole by end payment and that Government of Palestine cannot assume any responsibility for payment or his debts."[523] At that time, the prince had no other income than the Iranian allowance and was in debt to local tradesmen for an amount of £P 600. The Palestine government did not want to take any responsibility for his upkeep or his debts and wanted to expel him.[524] From its side London also made it clear that it "cannot make under any circumstance make financial provision either for the Prince's maintenance or for the payment of his debts. HMS's Government and the Palestine Government have been careful in avoiding incurring any responsibility, financial or other, vis-a-vis either the Persian Government of the Prince himself" and we will not change this position.[525]

---

520. IOR/L/PS/10/1196, File 4010/1926, FO to Mallet, Tehran. Draft tel. 08/1933.

521. CO 732/60/11, Tel. no. 134. Tehran to London, 23/06/1933.

522. CO 732/60/11, Mallet/Tehran to FO, 06/09/1933; CO 732/60/11, secret. FO to SoS 03/07/1933 ("propose to keep prince to his parole until payment runs out").

523. CO 732/60/11, Draft Tel. FO to Tehran (Mallet) August 1933.

524. "Indeed if payment stops, not our responsibility; he has 600 debts, and I may have to deport him." Tel. no. 138, High Commissioner Palestine to CO. 15/07/1933; CO 732/60/11, Tel. HC Palestine to SoS, 15/07/1933.

525. CO 732/60/11, FO to SoS, 04/09/1933.

The money question being resolved, or so it was believed, the Foreign Office had to find a solution as to what to do with the prince. The Foreign Office informed the Colonial Office that it considered it unfitting and undesirable to hand the prince over to Iran. Also, before the prince would be deported from Palestine he would need a travel document with a visa for the country where he would be deported to. The best option was that the prince himself voluntarily tried to obtain a visa for a country that would have him. France seemed a good option given many Qajar family members were living there, who might assist him and obtain a visa for him. It was suggested to approach the French consul in Jerusalem about this matter.[526] The Legation in Tehran reported that the Head of the English section of the Ministry of Foreign Affairs in Tehran gave as his personal opinion that Salar al-Dowleh would be allowed to return to Iran. It would be best that he applied for a passport at the nearest Iranian Consulate. However, there was no guarantee that he would not be arrested on arrival. If the prince wanted to take this option the Legation made it clear that it did not want to be an intermediary, because he had sons and brothers in Tehran.[527]

Although London believed that the money question had been resolved, this was not Salar al-Dowleh's opinion. He wrote a long letter to the Inspector Northern District, his most immediate contact in the government of Palestine. In this letter, he claimed compensation for mental suffering due to his imprisonment in Baghdad in 1926-27 and his forced abstention from intervention in Iranian politics and his enforced 'negative life' in Haifa for the last six years. Also, compensation for material losses, "because he is only fit to earn a living by ruling, his enforced inactivity at Haifa has deprived him and his family of their means of livelihood!" The prince further claimed compensation for the loss of his pension, which he maintained was from the British government. Because he did not consider the Iranian government as legal the prince concluded that Great Britain had to shoulder his financial responsibilities. The High Commissioner sent the letter to London and asked

---

526. IOR/L/PS/10/1196, File 4010/1926, Warner, FO to Under-Secretary, CO. 17/08/1933; CO 732/60/11, FO to HC Palestine, 17/08/1933.
527. CO 732/60/11, Tel. no. 206, Tehran to FO, 16/09/1933.

what to reply and begged not to be involved in the matter.[528] Therefore, the High Commissioner replied to Salar al-Dowleh that he regretted his difficulties, but that he was too busy to receive him.[529] On 11 December 1933, Salar al-Dowleh wrote the High Commissioner, "because I have no money I cannot go anywhere, not even leave Palestine." If the British government paid his allowance he at least would be able to leave Palestine.[530] He added a letter sent by the lawyer of his landlord ordering him to pay the last 6 months rent or else face legal action.[531] Given his financial situation, the prince asked London for help to enable him to move.[532] One month later, Salar al-Dowleh sent a telegram asking for a reply to his letter of 11 December as his financial situation was insupportable.[533] London informed the High Commissioner to inform the prince that he would get reply on 22 January 1934, but meanwhile to tell him that he was under no further obligation to Great Britain or the Palestine Government.[534]

The High Commissioner who wanted to get rid of Salar al-Dowleh tried to speed up the decision-making process in London. On 3 February 1934, he informed the Colonial Office that the prince was completely destitute; his debts amounted to £P400 in Haifa. He was willing to go to Alexandria, but his creditors wouldn't allow him to leave without paying. Given that he had no advance notice of cancellation of his allowance the British government might pay the debt and his travel expenses on condition that he left Palestine immediately. Otherwise "he will become a charge on public funds here."[535] The Foreign Office reacted that the High Commissioner had earlier taken the position not to assume any financial responsibility and that this would remain the British government's the

---

528. For the text of this letter, see Appendix XI; CO 732/60/11, internal memo High Commissioner's office, 14/11/19 33, where one of the authors S.I. James notes, "I notice somewhere in the earlier correspondence that the Price is described as a person who is so eccentric as to be almost mad."). FO suggested to M/Tehran to give the Iranian government Salar's letter of 03/10/1933 to the High Commissioner and possibly SoS CO's reply of 03/01/1934. CO 732/65/9, FO to Hoare/Tehran, 29/03/1934.

529. CO 732/65/9, priv. secr. HC to prince, 27/11/1933.

530. Salar al-Dowleh to HC, Jerusalem, 11/12/1933 (was fowarded to SoS CO on 31/12/1933).

531. CO 732/65/9, Agranst and Halevy/Haifa to Salar, 22/11/1933.

532. CO 732/65/9, 11/12/1933.

533. CO 732/65/9, undated (14/01/1934).

534. CO 732/65/9, FO to SoS CO, personal letter, 16/01/1934.

535. CO 732/65/9, Tel. no. 33, HC Palestine to SoS 03/02/1934.

position. Salar al-Dowleh's case had to be treated as that of "an ordinary alien bankrupt."[536] London suggested that Salar al-Dowleh should seek assistance from his Qajar relatives. The British government was unable to do anything for him, the more so, because in the Persian press there was an ongoing campaign that indicated that Reza Shah suspected that Great Britain showed undue sympathy to exiled Qajar family members. Although the prince's willingness to go to Alexandria showed that he had friends there, London was not sure whether the Egyptian government wanted to be burdened with a large destitute family.[537]

On 26 February 1934, the High Commissioner informed the prince that the British government (in a confidential letter of 12/01/1934) could not assume any financial or other responsibility, because his arrest and detention in Iraq were the result of his attempts to use Iraq, for which Great Britain had Mandate responsibility, as a base for a rebellion against the government of Iran with which Great Britain had diplomatic relations. The arrangements of his stay in Palestine did not mean that Great Britain accepted any responsibility vis a vis the Iranian Government. The British government only acted as intermediary to transmit the Iranian government's conditions on which it would pay his debts, travel expenses and a monthly allowance of Rs. 1500. Moreover, the prince knew that the British government only acted as intermediary to pass on this payment. The British government informed the Iranian Government that, as of 21 September 1933, Salar al-Dowleh was absolved from his guarantee given to the government of Iran. The agreement between the Iranian government and the prince having been terminated meant that the British government had no further concern with the prince's affairs; he could go where he wanted, but the British government could not assume any financial responsibility.[538] That same day, the High Commissioner informed London that he had informed the prince about its position concerning his status and financial claim. At that time, the prince had been turned out of his house and was living in a flat that had been put at his disposal by a Moslem notable of Haifa. The prince wanted

---

536. CO 732/65/9, SoS CO to FO, 07/02/1934; CO 732/65/9, FO to SoS CO, 15/02/1934. Text of this letter wired to HC. CO 732/65/9, Draft Tel. no. 58, Confi. FO to HC Palestine. 20/02/1934.

537. CO 732/65/9, FO to SoS CO, 27/02/1934; Idem, draft tel. SoS CO to HC Palestine, 02/03/1934.

538. CO 732/65/9, Chief Secretary, HC to Salar, 26/02/1934; CO 732/65/9, FO to SoS, 02/01/1934.

to go to Alexandria so that his daughters might be raised in a Moslem country and environs. He had been forced to pawn his wife's last jewelry to get money to pay for food. The High Commissioner added that it would be difficult to get him to live in Europe.[539]

Salar al-Dowleh with his son Mohammad Reza in Alexandria, Egypt.

539. CO 732/65/9, HC to FO, 26/02/1934.

Residence in Alexandria (1936-59)

Faced with London's final and firm position Salar al-Dowleh informed the High Commissioner that he would leave for Alexandria on 18 March. He left per SS Helouan.[540] Apparently, he had received financial assistance from family members, although he still was believed to be in great financial difficulties.[541] By that time the British government did not want to have anything to do anymore with Salar al-Dowleh and the Foreign Office issued a circular note to its representations abroad that "Neither he nor his family should be granted a visa for any territory under British control without reference to this department."[542]

This was not the end of Salar al-Dowleh endeavors to get British attention. On 5 March 1936, the Iranian Chargé d'Affaires approached the British Resident in Cairo drawing his attention to an article about Salar al-Dowleh in the newspaper *al-Ahram*, which report suggested that Great Britain had some connection with the prince's claim to the throne. The Resident said: "we washed our hands off him a long time ago and never had anything to do with any of his rebellions."[543]

In May 1939 Salar al-Dowleh came to London and via a letter, dated 19/05/39, sent by Messrs. Lattey & Dawe, he approached the Foreign Office asking to speak with a senior member. London's reaction was

---

540. CO 732/65/9, Salar to HC, 17/03/1934.
541. IOR/R/20/A/3722; File 1309, Typed undated note, probably 22/06/1934.
542. IOR/R/20/A/3722; File 1309, Spencer, Passport Control Department, FO 20/05/1935.
543. FO 141/606/15, Memo 05/03/1936. See Appendix XII.

that he undoubtedly wanted to discuss his financial claims, which once again had been rejected as recent as in April 1937. Furthermore, in July 1937, Messrs. Catzeflis & Lattey of Alexandria, who were connected with Messrs. Lattey & Dawe, sent the Foreign Office an appeal on behalf of his son who had to go to the hospital because of an accident. The Foreign Office replied that the British government had nothing to add to its previous correspondence on the matter. Now also, it decided that it served no useful purpose to receive him and on 2 June 1939, a letter to that effect was sent.[544] Because in 1935 the Foreign Office had instructed its representations abroad not give Salar al-Dowleh a visa the fact that he was in Great Britain raised the question "why was the prince given a visa in contravention of the May 1935 circular." It appeared that not all Consular offices might have received the circular, while they received so many of that type of circular that if they thought that it probably was unimportant for their jurisdiction it was filed and forgotten. Despite all this, the Foreign Office decided to ask the Consul-General in Alexandria why the visa was given.[545]

At the beginning of January 1946, the Foreign Office received a letter from Salar al-Dowleh, via Mr. W.D. Roberts, drawing the Secretary of State's attention to the weak state of the crumbling Persian Empire. He wrote that Azerbaijan was already lost, that the other Northern provinces would follow suit; Isfahan was threatened and if this continued after another year nothing would remain of the Persian Empire. "It will be subjected to slavery to another power." It was decided to show neither interest nor to give a reply. Mr. Roberts was a lawyer, who recently had approached Mr. Fitzmaurice of the FO about Salar al-Dowleh's claim. Mr. Roberts was told that the British government had only been an intermediary for the Iranian government, which stopped payment of the prince's allowance and, therefore, he should address them.[546] This seems to have been Salar al-Dowleh's last attempt to contact the British government.

---

544. FO 371/ 3706, Internal FO memo 23/05/1939; FO 371/ 3706, FO to Lattey & Dawe, 02/06/1939.

545. FO 371/ 3706, handwritten note on Internal FO memo 23/05/1939 and note of 30/09/1939.

546. FO 371/5475, Salar/Alexandria to Bevin/London, 05/01/1946; FO 371/5475, Memo SoS 14/02/1946.

Salar al-Dowleh spent the remainder of his days in Alexandria. Here he lived until April-May 1959 when at the age of 80 he died.[547] In that city he lived in an apartment on the second floor of a three-storey building with his Swiss wife, with whom he spoke in French or in Ottoman Turkish; their children did not know Persian. When Hasan Enayat visited him in 1955 he met an unchanged man, who still used the royal 'We', who commanded (*farmudim; amr midehim*), issued rescripts (*dastkhatt kardim*), told people to obey him immediately (*fowri eta`at konid*), and other similar language. Salar al-Dowleh hardly had any recent knowledge of Iran and was not aware of the major changes in the country since he had left it in 1926. He did not know any of the politicians (except for Qavam al-Saltaneh and Mossadeq) and even had forgotten about his children, except for his oldest son. Enayat whose visit was arranged by one of Salar al-Dowleh's daughters does not mention how often she saw her father.[548] According to his grandson, Salar al-Dowleh indeed had little contact with his children, apart from the occasional exchange of letters.

---

547. Bamdad 1347, vol. 1, p. 50 (Ordibehesht 1338).
548. Enayat 1340, pp. 317-18.

Assessment

From the above emerges a picture of Salar al-Dowleh that is not very flattering, but that is how people perceived and experienced him through his behavior. On the positive side his skill as a chess player are mentioned and also that he prayed five times a day (which did not make him necessarily a good Moslem), while his handwriting was not bad, and, according to Litten he had a dreamy nature and beautiful eyes.[549] However, these possibly positive qualities did not outweigh the negative ones. His record shows that he was neither a good administrator nor a good politician or a military tactician. Sykes called him the "stormy petrel of Persian politics," as well as "a restless, if cowardly adventurer" and that he had been "destructive to life and property."[550] From an early age on Salar al-Dowleh showed that he was a selfish, willful and inconsiderate person. He felt that he was entitled to privilege, high position and wealth and he was not afraid to say so. After his father had become Shah on 1 May 1896, he displayed those character traits rather publicly and loudly. He could not stand his father's brother-in-law and favorite, Abdol-Hoseyn Mirza Farmanfarma, the Minister of War. On one occasion, later in 1896, the 15-year old Salar al-Dowleh shouted in the palace for everybody to hear: "This *pedar-sukhteh* [son of a burnt father], this dog Farmanfarma, has grabbed everything from my stupid daddy, including the War Ministry. I, Salar od-Dowleh, and not that rogue, that stinking Farmanfarma, should be Minister of War."[551]

---

549. Enayat 1340, p. 318; Litten 1925, p. 229.
550. Sykes 1969, vol. 2, pp. 430-31.
551. Kazemzadeh 1968, p. 189. His older brother Sjo`a` al-Saltaneh displayed similar character traits, see Eyn al-Saltaneh 1377, vol. 2, pp. 1052-53.

Despite his youthful claim that he could do better he failed in all his endeavors. The prince was dismissed from all of his posts of governor, because of his misbehavior such as rape, exactions, even murder, and utter lack of empathy for or interest in the welfare of the people over whom he had been placed. The management style of his governorship of Khuzestan-Lorestan 1901-04 was described by Lorimer as "youthful, willful, and imprudent," which is rather positive compared with the rather disturbing reasons that led to his dismissal from that function.[552]

There is no doubt that Salar al-Dowleh could be charming and seemingly sympathetic for the welfare of his subjects, be it that also in those cases he tended to overdo things. For Salar al-Dowleh certainly had a sense for theater and grand-standing, and, if it did not cost him much and gained him political coin, he was very much in favor of making a grand gesture. For example, in October 1902, Salar al-Dowleh took positive action in the case of the murder of three Jewish peddlers from Borujerd by some inhabitants of Deh-Kordeh on 18 August 1902. Initially, government officials and religious leaders wanted to protect the killers, because, according to a fatwah by the local *mojtahed*, only a payment not exceeding 40 *tumans* sufficed in case of the killing of an unbeliever, while a death sentence was excluded. Therefore, the director of the *Alliance Israelite School* of Hamadan, wrote a letter to Salar al-Dowleh explaining the matter and asking for justice. The prince invited the director to Borujerd and received him respectfully, stood up when he entered, asked him to sit and offered him a cigarette. Salar al-Dowleh said that hearing the news of the murder of the three Jews had brought tears to his eyes; he had fasted for three days and for two weeks he had not suffered to have music played in his presence. He promised a firm, objective judicial process and invited the director to be present at the proceedings. The entire visit lasted 6 hours. The director stayed in a house in the Jewish quarter, to which Mo'taman al-Mamalek, governor of Borujerd paid a visit, the first time that a governor entered the house of a Jew in Borujerd. As a result, the streets and roofs were filled with people. During his visit the governor said that his visit was a sign that the Shah did not make a difference between his subjects based on religion, and that the killers

---

552. Lorimer 1915, vol. 1, p. 1737.

would be found and sentenced. Salar al-Dowleh sent the director a *shal-e termeh* and gave him an escort of 10 *savars* for his return trip to Hamadan.[553]

However, in general, the prince was an uncaring and rapacious governor and a murderous, destructive, plundering rebel, who did not care for the harm and misery he inflicted on his country and his countrymen, thinking only about himself, his position and wealth. Ehtesham al-Dowleh wrote that "to describe the deeds and savagery of Salar al-Dowleh and Sho`a` al-Saltaneh, two beloved lights of the eye of Mozaffar al-Din Shah, would require several tomes." He even went further, writing that "the killing of Salar al-Dowleh was and is obligatory for each human being."[554] The prince's tenure of office in Lorestan was described as follows: "the policy of every governor is to pit tribe against tribe, utilizing the services of one to coerce the other, such a policy is only temporarily successful, it ends by impoverishing the district and embittering tribal relations. Only coercion by an independent force can ensure permanent results." Salar al-Dowleh, who was governor-general of Lorestan in 1904 and 1906, "is responsible to a large extent for the prevailing anarchy. His ideas of government were limited to inciting one tribe to plunder another. ... By his short-sighted policy he encouraged Lur chiefs to harbor hitherto unimagined pretensions, and showed them plainly that the power to make and unmake Governors was in their hands," as his successors found out at their cost.[555]

If this was the verdict about his impact on a province when he was its governor it is obvious that the results were significantly more negative when he raised the banner of rebellion, which he did many times. In fact, one may call Salar al-Dowleh a serial rebel and looter, for "he led a life of a brigand, fomenting local troubles and blackmailing the rich."[556] His repeated rebellious behavior also kept the government apparatus unnecessarily occupied with his misdeeds, during a time when its limited resources, with foreign borrowed money, could have been used for better purposes.[557] Moreover, apart from the killing, plundering and the kidnapping of women, in the aftermath of his failed campaigns he left

---

553. Anonymous 1902, pp. 54-58. That he did not lack social skills, see Eyn al-Saltaneh 1377, vol. 2, pp. 1075, 1089.
554. Ehtesham al-Saltaneh 1366, pp. 597-98, 607.
555. IOR/L/MIL/17/15/10/5, Military Report on (S.-W) Persia, vol. 5, Luristan, p. 10.
556. Sykes 1969, vol. 2, p. 430.
557. Sharif Kashani 1362, vol. 3, pp. 786-87, 839.

starving peasants. Dr. Blanche Wilson-Stead, an American missionary based in Kermanshah, who knew the district well and organized relief work in the Malayer district in 1912 with the help of funds ($500 or 6,985 qrans) from the American Red Cross, writes:

> The ravages of the forces of the Salar ed dowleh who camped in the Malayir district for several weeks, the raids of the wild Lur tribes who had entered the region under the Salar's colors, but whose presence was ostensibly plunder and not war, the return of part of these forces of the Salar after his defeat at Sahveh [sic], followed by the presence of the Bakhtiaris, nothing remained to the poor inhabitants of the region either in the way of food stuffs or property which they might sell to secure food. A mild winter made the suffering less than it would ordinarily have been, but as time went on and what little had been available became less and less, the suffering began to be more and more. An agent from the government arriving toward the end of the winter, gave some hope of assistance from that direction, but as time dragged on nothing definite resulted.[558]

Also, as a serial rebel Salar al-Dowleh was a failure, because he did not have a program (apart from killing, plundering and looting) that supporters might believe in. In fact, his rebellion had no other cause than himself. Salar al-Dowleh told each audience what it wanted to hear, so that he passed himself off as a constitutionalist, nationalist, royalist, anti-Russian, pro-Russian, anti-British, pro-British, Islamist and anything else. However, he was not for anything or anybody but himself. As Litten rightly pointed out: "As seems to be the case with most non-ruling pretenders to the throne, he loved above all to talk about how easy it was to rule over these people, how good a people they were, how easy it would be to make them happy, [...] and how pleased they would be

---

558. RG 91-1-12, Report on Relief Work in the Malayir District Conducted During the Spring of 1912. Dr. Stead wrote to Mr. Russel, the American Minister in Tehran who raised the money for her. She started food distribution of 30 April, i.e. one *gerdeh* or flat round loaf of bread per adult and a half loaf for children, but only for women and children; only old and disabled men were included. She reached 1,500 people per day. Later she also received 400 *tumans* from Sardar-e As'ad and 200 *tumans* from Dr. Mody of Tehran, In this way she was able to extend aid until the time had arrived to thresh barley. Nevertheless, quite a number of people starved to death.

when he, for example, had been born not as the third son but as the heir-apparent."[559] Despite the lofty ideas and ideals that Salar al-Dowleh peddled to whomever was willing to listen, his activities were exclusively aimed to satisfy his own egotistical fantasies. In trying to realize those fantasies Salar al-Dowleh's activities were very destructive to the life and property of many people in Persia; they harmed his country and its people and served no other purpose than his own mania. Therefore, this faux king gave his contemporaries, whether authorities, notables, or the common people, the shivers, because of his unpredictable, mercurial and above all destructive behavior.[560] His most loyal followers were the conservative olama and landowners, because he promised them the restoration of their rights to unbridled domination of their flocks and securization of their large revenues. His tribal following was mostly attracted by the promise of plunder as that fit their way of life, which was mostly divorced from the rest of society and followed its own rules.

But even in fighting for his own cause he was very impractical, out of his league, and unable to lead by example. Sykes characterized his behavior as cowardly, which is understandable. Salar al-Dowleh always led from behind and never risked his own life, although his actions led to the death and misery of many of his countrymen. He always choose a location behind the lines to await the result of the fight or battle, so that, in case of victory, he could assume command and receive the adulations of success, but in case of defeat, the waiting place selected allowed him ample time and opportunity to flee to safety, as is clear from the above. The newspaper *Shafaq-e Sorkh* stressed Salar a-Dowleh's impractical nature as did some of his partisans. In 1926, for example, Ja`far Soltan reported that Salar al-Dowleh's advisers had told him that logistically his large force could not remain in the field for long and could not take Senneh or Kermanshah, but he insisted on trying to do that anyway, believing himself a second Napoleon. He actually sat 14 days outside Senneh hoping that the tribes would rise and assist him, which did not

---

559. Litten 1925, pp. 229-30.

560. According to Eyn al-Saltaneh 1377, vol. 5, p. 3495, Salar al-Dowleh only wanted to gather lots of money to live in comfort and leisure in Europe. According to one of the prince's supporters, Yaman al-Dowleh, during their time in Lorestan he was totally obsessed with the idea of becoming Shah. Eyn al-Saltaneh 1378, vol. 7, p. 5599.

happen and a cavalry force from Kermanshah arrived he had to withdraw precipitously to Nowsad.[561]

The general opinion seems to have been that Salar al-Dowleh had psychiatric problems. In 1926 the *Shafaq-e Sorkh* writes: "We all know Salar al-Dowleh and we are sure that that this poor fellow had never a sound scheme, that is to say that he is not sane and is not sound of mind."[562] Kasravi called him *saboksar* (stupid), *nadani* (ignorant), and *sabokmaghz* (crack-brained), while Malekzadeh called him an inexperienced and ambitious youth (*javani-ye kham va jah-talab*).[563] At the end of 1912 the Tehran newspapers called him mad (*divaneh*) and stupid (*safih*), as did Shuster,[564] while the British had a similar opinion. According to Churchill, the Oriental secretary in Tehran, Salar al-Dowleh "is mentally imbalanced," and he "is not really responsible for his actions,"[565] while, in general, the British thought him to be mad. Even in his old age he had a high opinion of his smarts (*zerangi*). In 1955, he told Hasan Enayat that when his brother Sho`a` al-Saltaneh was governor of Fars, Qavam al-Molk and many others rose up against him. Mozaffar al-Din Shah asked Salar al-Dowleh, who then was governor of Kurdistan to assist his brother in putting down the uprising. Although Salar al-Dowleh had prepared measures to do so, he, before leaving, claimed to have sent a telegram to Qavam al-Molk with the following line from Ferdowsi's *Shahnameh*, spoken by the hero Rostam:

If your reply is not to my liking/I will face Afrasiyab with my mace striking

اگر جز به کام من آید جواب   من و گرز و میدان افراسیاب

The result of the reception of this threatening text was that the troublemakers allegedly immediately surrendered.[566] The story, as usual, is

---

561. FO 248/1382, Spec. Services Officer, Soleymaniyeh to Air HQ, 14/09/1926. Salar al-Dowleh tested his horses to see whether they would be able to carry him to safety. When Adel al-Mamalek asked him whether a Yamut horse would be able to carry him through the mountains, he replied in the affirmative and that he had tested that horse. Eyn al-Saltaneh 1378, vol. 6, p p. 4372-73.

562. FO 248/1382, *Shafaq-e Sorkh* editorial 16 August 1926 (see Appendix VII).

563. Kasravi 1319, vol. 1, p. 117; vol. 2, p. 119; Malekzadeh, vol. 3, p. 33.

564. Eyn al-Saltaneh 1377, vol. 5, pp. 3433, 3792 ; Shuster. p. xxiv (madcap prince).

565. FO 248/1181, McDouall/Hamadan to Tehran, 23/05/1917; Churchill 1909, p. 95.

566. Enayat 1340, p. 317.

self-serving, because there was no uprising in Fars at that time and as governor of far away Kurdistan, there was not much that Salar al-Dowleh could have done. The facts are that Sho`a` al-Saltaneh, Mozaffar al-Din Shah's second and favorite son, arrived in June 1904 in Shiraz to assume his post as governor of Fars and began a very oppressive and unscrupulous rule. On 30 September 1905 he left to Europe via Tehran, "probably feeling that he had created so much hostility towards himself in the minds of the people of Fars that there inevitably be an upheaval against him if he remained longer." On his way to Europe, he was accompanied by his enemy Qavam al-Molk as far as the capital. Thus, there was no rebellion, but a widespread movement in the province to prevent his return and in December 1905 Eqbal al-Dowleh replaced him.[567]

But worse than being described as mad and unhinged, many Iranians believed him to be a tool of foreigners and that he even had a British passport.[568] Eyn al-Saltaneh wrote that British policy in 1907 was different from that in 1911; then they handed him over to the government, now Great Britain did nothing as it was to its advantage.[569] The conspiracy believer Khan Malek Sasani, who saw the British hidden hand everywhere, worked in Istanbul at the Iranian Consulate as of 1918. He relates how Salar al-Dowleh, presumably in late 1919, came to the Iranian embassy in Istanbul to get an Iranian passport. At that time, according to Khan Malek Sasani, the prince only had a British passport. However, that seems unlikely given that the prince had lived since October 1914 in Turkey and he would have had Turkish and Russian papers. On 30 December 1918 Salar al-Dowleh was arrested by the British, then sent to Baghdad where he stayed for some three months, and then he was exiled to Switzerland via Istanbul. I doubt that he was given a British passport, given British disgust with the prince. The British authorities also were opposed to Salar al-Dowleh's return to Iran and it is unlikely that they would have facilitated his return by getting him an Iranian passport or given him a British one, although the British government may have given him or obtained a restricted travel document for him.[570] The British had

---

567. Administration Report 1905-06. p. 25.
568. Bamdad 1347, vol. 1, p. 50; FO 248/1382, *Shafaq-e Sorkh* editorial 16 August 1926.
569. Eyn al-Saltaneh 1377, vol. 5, p. 3495.
570. Sasani 1352, p. 99; Idem 1345, p. 23. That, as far as I know, there is no document in the British archives that confirms that Salar al-Dowleh had a British

no sympathy or even use for Salar al-Dowleh, as is clear from their contacts with him and their estimation of him throughout his career. As the British Minister in Tehran wrote in 1917, "Salar can go to perdition,"[571] and that British attitude did not change. However, any politically correct Iranian historian has to go out of his/her way to emphasize that Salar al-Dowleh was a British tool and that he was used by that perfidious nation to harm Iranian and promote British interests.

Salar al-Dowleh's actions were only possible, because of the political chaos in Iran and the political weakness of its central government, which allowed all kinds of local warlords to rise up in the various parts of the country, between 1907 and 1921. In this situation of *moluk-e tavayef* he had a broader appeal than the other rebels, because he was a prince, and, after the abdication of his brother Mohammad Ali Shah, he had a claim to the throne. As noted above, he failed in all his endeavors due to his ineptitude and inability to provide leadership to the reactionary conservative propertied class. This lack of ability was reinforced by the fact that he believed that by just showing up the grateful people of Iran would embrace and fight for his cause, i.e. give him the throne. However, Salar al-Dowleh was widely feared by the populace and his so-called supporters were mainly interested in the opportunity to plunder rather than fight for a cause or a rather uninspiring man. Finally, Russia and Great Britain mostly remained neutral, but at important moments these two powers financially and politically intervened to support the central government to thwart Salar al-Dowleh's actions. In short, Salar al-Dowleh was self-centered and narcissistic and was until his dying day convinced that he was superior to his fellow men. When in 1956, Hasan Enayat visited him in Alexandria he still spoke about himself as the royal 'We,' who did not say things, but 'commanded' (*farmudim*).

---

passport, is, of course, for believers in the British hidden hand proof that he had one.
571. FO 248/1181, McDouall/Hamadan to Tehran 18/04/1917.

Appendix 1

Salar al-Dowleh's wives and children

	Name wives		Name children
1.	Khanom Fatemeh Forugh al-Saltaneh, also Nur al-Dowleh[h]	`Aqdi	Nur al-Dowleh (d)
2.	Khanom Monir al-Dowleh	`Aqdi	Qamar al-Dowleh (d); Soltan Majid Mirza
3.	Khanom Malekeh Qods al-Dowleh	`Aqdi	Mohammad Reza Mirza
4.	Khanom Farah al-Saltaneh	`Aqdi	Maryam Shekuh-e A`zam (d)
5.	Khanom ?	`Aqdi/sigheh?	Mo`azzez al-Dowleh (d)
6.	Helen Khanom Banu-ye Mo`azzam	`Aqdi	Naser al-Din Mirza; Farah (d), Monizheh (d), Nahid (d)
7.	Khanom Agha Ziba	`Aqdi/sigheh?	No children
8.	Khanom Shams al-Saltaneh	Sigheh	No children
9.	Khanom Veqar al-Saltaneh	Sigheh	No children

Source: Davood Ghajar-Mozaffari, son of Mohammad Reza Mirza (letter 19/08/2017).

The dates of the deaths and/or divorce of the `aqdi wives are not known, but it is clear that Salar al-Dowleh could not have had more than four `aqdi wives at the same time. Of two wives (nos. 4 and 7) the marital status is not known and of one (no. 5) the name is unknown. Khanom Malekeh was the daughter of Gholam Reza Amir-e Jang, the Vali of Posht-e Kuh. Farah al-Saltaneh was of the Kermanshah `Emad al-Dowleh family and the niece (baradarzadeh) of Monir al-Dowleh, wife no. 2. Khanom Agha Ziba was the daughter of the Lur chief Nazar Ali Khan Amra'i of the Esfandiyari Balvand lineage, of the Dilfan tribe.[1] Helen Khanom (I have not been able to find her family name) was a Swiss woman from Neuchatel, whom Salar al-Dowheh probably married in 1914, because in 1926 her oldest child was not yet 12 years old. She was the only wife living with him in Alexandria.

It would appear that the prince had many other wives and/or sighehs, whose names are as yet unknown. For example, in 1904, in Arabistan he married the daughter of an Arab chief.[2] Also, the daughter of Ali Mardan Khan of the Beyrawands was "one of Salar-ul-Dauleh's many fiancees."[3] Just prior to his defeat on 27 September 1911, the prince married a daughter of Seyf al-Dowleh.[4] While in Gilan, in April 1912, Salar al-Dowleh married a daughter of Da'ud Khan Kalhor, which was "said to be the 10th matrimonial alliance of the prince during this campaign."[5] Also, fleeing from his Astarabad-Gilan failure the prince arrived in Garrus where he raised some support among the Jaf and married at least one local girl.[6]

Dehkhoda in his satyrical journal Sur-e Esrafil suggests that Salar al-Dowleh had or intended to have a sexual relationship with a boy. "Later I found out that Salar al-Dowleh had summoned the coffee shop lad Ahmad Qahvechi to Arabistan, and Mirza Hasan's son had sent the students to Shah Abd al-Azim to turn him back. ... How could a boy who was the object of a feud between Salar al-Dowleh and Mirza Hasan's son ever be mine?"[7]

---

1. Administration Report 1906-07, p. 33.
2. Churchil, p. 95; Litten 1925, p. 229.
3. IOR/L/MIL/17/15/51, Who's Who in Mesopotamia, General Staff, India (Serial no. 22), p. 19.
4. Eyn al-Saltaneh 1377, vol. 5, p. 3543.
5. IOR/L/PS/10/212, File 211/1912 'Turkish Arabia Summaries', p. 7.
6. Eyn al-Saltaneh 1377, vol. 5, p. 3900.
7. Dehkhoda 2016, p. 102 (Sur-e Esrafil 1, no. 6, p. 7).

Appendix II

LETTERS SALAR AL-DOWLEH TO BRITISH KING AND BRITISH MINISTER IN TEHRAN (20/06/1920)

To H.I.M. My Uncle, the King-Emperor

In view of the friendship existing between the two Governments it became expedient that I should present myself at Y.M.'s Consulate and to offer my thanks for the everlasting hopes which the said Consulate inspires with me.

I always pray to the Providence for Y.M.'s prosperity and good health and I appeal on this occasion to Y.M.'s graciousness and benevolence for the protection of my honour, position and family.

Sd. Salar ud Dawleh
Abul Fath, Kajar

To H.M.'s Minister

I am leaving Persia and my requests are as follows.

1. My property should be protected and any claim against me should be settled with the knowledge of the British Legation.

2. The property and person of my people should be safe (Kafi ud Dawleh at Garrus, Samsam ul-Mamalek in Irak have property. Their property should be safe).

3. Nazar Ali Khan Amra'i is my father-in-law and is hereditary chief of Tarhan. He and his posterity should continue to be chiefs. The Persian Government should promise not to oppress him or his people and they should be safe.

4. I request the British Government to promise me with a document that myself and my people should be always under the British protection.

My accounts with people should be settled. Last year when I was appointed Governor of Kermanshah, Borujerd and Lorestan I honoured and paid as a present to the Governement a sum of Tomans 55,000. The Ain ud Dawlah obtained from the Amir Afkham, deputy Governor of Kermanshah, a bond promising to pay me Tomans 36,000 a year at the rate of 3,000 Tomans a month.[1] He paid me only Tomans 8,000 in 17 months. The balance should be recovered from him with interest and paid to me. I paid Tomans 600 to the Government for the Shaykh Smaili tribe which was taken from by the Jalal ud Dawleh. This money should be returned to me. My salary Tomans 30,000 should be given to my children. I cannot live as a beggar in a foreign country. The Government should pay my debts so that my property may remain for me. In 1319 I bought some property in Kermanshah but by misrepresentations made by the Ekbal ud Dawleh the property was confiscated. In 1318 H. when the late Shah was in Europe the case was tried in the Court by H.M.'s order and it was settled in my favour. The decision was also signed by Mohammad Ali Shah when regent. The different governors of Kermanshah such as Ala ud Dawleh and Moayad ud Dawleh and olama have also given their decision in my favour. The property should be returned to me and damages paid. The consul can make inquiries into that case. My people such as Mirza Hussein Khan Nezam and Heshmat Nezam who was looking after my affairs should not be molested.

I hope you will soon get these matters settled so that I may leave this country as soon as possible.

Sd. Abul Fath Kajar

Source: FO 248/907, Enclosure to Haworth to Legation, 20/06/1907 (also includes the incomplete Persian version of which the last page is missing).

---

1. Sepehr 1368, part 2, p. 312 (Amir Afkham has to pay 30,000 *tumans*/year to Salar al-Dowleh)

Appendix III

Salar al-Dowleh's letter to British Consul in Kermanshah 26 March 1911

Enclosure in Consul McDouall's dispatch No. 26 dated March 14 [1911]
Translation of letter from Salar-ed-Doweh to H.M. Consul

Yesterday with M. Nicolsky, Russian Consul, you stated the contents of a telegram from Tehran. Although I gave the necessary answer verbally at the time, yet I write this summary, which you will agree to telegraph. First, you stated that H.M. Mohammed Ali Shah, the natural and glorious King, has agreed to leave Persia. Although order to this effect has not been issued to me, yet it is necessary for me to write. After I had undergone for four years every kind of adversity and trouble and loss and imprisonment and exile from my fatherland, having spent two and a half years in Europe in great straits, I constantly stated my case to the Persian government and received no reply. They did not even pay me what was due as arranged through the Russian Government. To settle the business I went to London and stayed at the Persian Legation, and stated my case to the late Regent Azad-el-Mulk. He replied, "What is necessary for your case in Europe will be arranged." They did nothing. This is a small matter; they have confiscated all my property without reason; as all my estates are pledged to the Banque d'Escompte for 150,000 tomans and interest borrowed through Arbab Jamshid, and my receipt is there. The estates which my Royal father bequeathed me they have seized. They have given Eshratabad on lease, and confiscated Mardabad, and have not given me what was due to me. They have also seized the revenues of my purchased estates; my family were in such straits that they had to sell their house furniture to live. This is concealed from no one. A telegram came from Sattar Khan and Bagir Khan that it is necessary that you come to Persia to end the disorders, and plainly called me in this language: "The people approve your coming, and will esteem it a favour." I came to Resht, and they imprisoned me for two days; however much I implored them to take me to Tehran in that state, and let me remain there two days, and after making arrangements for my family I would leave Persia, [they did not agree.]

[After my return from Persia I promised His Majesty Mohammed Ali Shah] and I swore to him that as long as His Majesty wished for the rights of his ancestors I would not fail in his service to spend my last breath. Provided that Mohammed Ali Shah is in Persia, I have no opinion of my own whatever. I and the three million people of these provinces will not fail in carrying out his desires to the last drop of our blood. What is said to me must be said to him; I am only in reference to him an unworthy subject. But if H.M. Mohammed Ali Shah is willing to give up his personal rights my promises to him are void, and I consider myself entitled to the rights of my forefathers. Your statement that with regard to me the Persian government had proposed to the two Legations that a sum of six thousand tomans for myself and a like sum for my family be granted, that I should sell the graves of my ancestors for this price, and that the confiscation of my estates should be annulled. Under the circumstances, I write this reply, that all the world may know that I have no personal spite, and undertook this trouble to put an end to the confusion and disorder of the last four years, which has been caused by the incapability of the Persian government. Firstly, if the remaining one of seven Kings is to become a beggar, he will earn more than this. Secondly, when in Europe this was my charge to my friends there: "if I die in Europe, take my body and bury [me] in the soil of my beloved native land." Far be it that I should be alive from this soil. As before stated, if Mohammed Ali Shah does not want his rights, I consider myself entitled to take them; but to-day, for certain reasons, I put aside the taking of the rights of my forefathers to show all the world the last scene in this sad drama. Therefore, that I be not suspected of causing the continuance of this civil war and destruction of a six thousand year old state and the desolation of Persia, I will cease from war and obey, provided that the Persian Government accept the undermentioned conditions through the Ministers of the two Powers.

The countries in my possession as below be under my rule, and the sovereignty of the King of the Kajar dynasty for this time being (Azerbaijan, Kurdistan and Garus, the mines of Upper and Lower Tarem), which by concession of Muzaffir-ed-Din Shah were granted to Amanianz the Christian, and by zeal of the Foreign Office and Atabeg Azam transferred to me with the villages of (Azeriad and Anguran) situated in Zinjan, where I have property (Hamadan, Kermanshah and neighbourhood, Kangawar and Assadabad, Burujird, Luristan and Arabistan, the three districts of Kamara, Gulpaigan, Khunsar, the thee districts of Malayir, Sultanabad Irak). The above districts, which were and are in my possession, are my home, and all my wives are the children of the chiefs of these countries, and my estates are situated in them. Some of these countries are necessary for the preservation of order in the others. It is known generally to all the world, and to Great Britain in particular, that Persia is powerless to preserve order in these countries, especially in Burujird, Luristan, and Kermanshah; no one but myself has the power to hold these countries and collect the revenue and repel the criminal. If accepted, I will promise to agree to the order of the King of Persia as far as they do not interfere with the order of the country in my occupation. After this agreement has been made and the expenses of the amount of troops that I can raise for the protection of these countries, and the expenses of civil government paid, I will pay the remainder of the revenue [and other receipts] into the King's Treasury in two installments yearly. [Orders to me to be issued only by His Majesty.] The damage which has been done to me in these four years and to my dependants, and the persons who caused this damage to me and took my property to be handed to me, according to a list which I will give, by the Persian Government. No official of the Persian Government is to come to these countries unless with my concurrence and agreement. They shall give no orders unless in a matter which concerns me personally. In all matters, civil and military, without any exception of these countries, I am personally answerable to His Majesty. From the date of the signature of this agreement, if Persia makes any agreement with any European Power whatever concerning these countries it must be with my knowledge and consent; otherwise the people of these countries will have the right of acceptance or refusal; in the event of refusal by the people of these countries they will not be responsible for any loss or damage to that Power. For the repair of the damage of these four years, the restoration of what has been ruined, and for making guardhouses on the highways and roads and organising a gendarmerie, and repair government buildings in these countries which are all laid to waste, and for assistance to the *rayats* of the estates which are ruined – perhaps to-day there is no vestige of them - the Government of Persia after approval must give the money either from the Treasury or by borrowing on terms approved by Persia from the two Powers. Whenever money is required it is to be arranged as above. I will buy what arms are necessary and sufficient for protection of these countries, because to-day the Government arms do not exist, and countries cannot be held by the arms of the tribes, and revenue will not be collected, and order and peace will not be arranged, and things will remain as they are. With the consent of the two Powers teachers for agriculture, commerce, colleges and army will be engaged from abroad, and I myself will summon them and make arrangements with them; this is my personal business and wish, and after it will be reported to the King. I will be satisfied when an agreement is signed and guaranteed by the two Powers. Should the Persian Government at any time by a trick stretch out its hand and cause disorder to the people of these countries, the Powers to be judges. Should these conditions of mine be accepted I undertake to render obedience to my King, Sultan Ahmed Shah. Further, should he require service from me temporarily in any other place I am ready to carry it out - obedience to the King is imperative. After signature of the agreement the Persian Government to give me without delay official permission with full powers to treat with Turkey regarding the land from Baneh to Katr, which without the cognisance of the Persian government, to obtain the evacuation of that district. Should the Government of Persia not accept this agreement the two Powers, with that kindness and generosity to Persia that they have always shown just as at the time when Mohammed Ali and myself came to Persia they decided to be neutral, and informed the Persian Government officially of this, at this time when I am ready with all my power to recover my rights being neutral, I and this honourable people will be content.

All this is, provided that Mohammed Ali Shah is not in Persia and has resigned his rights, otherwise I am only one of his subjects faithful to His Majesty, and have no opinion of my own. I beg that a reply in affirmative or negative may be obtained from the Persian Government without delay or procrastination because that Amir Jang and all the chiefs of these countries are ready to move with their forces, and I myself on the fifth of the next month (25th March), if these conditions are not accepted, will be obliged to move and send an army and finish my business if war is to continue.

Signed. Salar ed-Dowleh

Source: IOR/L/PS/20/261/7, 'Persia. No 1 (1913). Further correspondence respecting the affairs of Persia', pp. 16-18 (encl. no. 2 in no. 23); see also FO 248/1053 (has a copy of the Persian text).

Appendix IV

Petition of the bastis to British Consul, Kermanshah 26 September 1912

Petition of *bastis* 26 September 1912. Source: FO 248/1053.

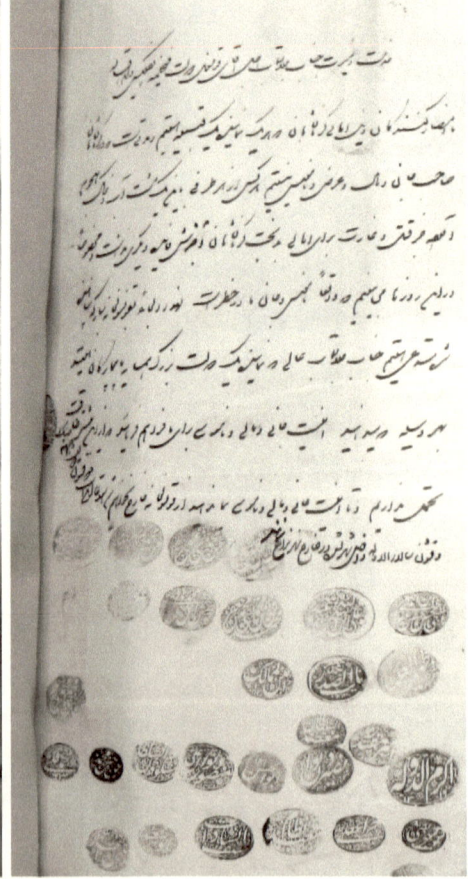

Annex V

Salar al-Dowleh's debts in Switzerland, 1925

Lausanne	
M. Foujallaz	15,000
lent by him	
Gauranteed by M. Foujallaz	
1922 interest 7%	22.000
Dr. Mich. Beurnier	5,000
Ecole Lemania	1,170
Dr. Dentiste Breuleux	1,800
Geneva	
M. Ed. Quartier La Tente	
21.22.23 interest 7%	17,000
Neuchatel	
Jacque Montmollin	700
M. Nicolet prof	
since 1924 interest	12,000
Total	84,670
Plus interest over 3 years from	
17,000 and 22,000	10,590
Total	95,260

Source: FO 684/2/25/29, Translation letter Salar al-Dowleh to Mr. Smart, Consul, Damascus, 06/01/1925, enclosure; also on a handwritten note.

Appendix VI

Salar al-Dowleh's letter to his wife Helen, 3 September 1925

Resumé of a letter dated 14 Safar or 3 September 1925 addressed to Dear Helen.

Writer states that this is the seventh day that he is in Persian territory.

Tell Z if he is there, if not you know. Sarem-Eyalat arrived at Auroman (Kurdistan) 4 days after my departure with 400 mounted men from Kalhur and others. The 2nd G (General) of Persia sent the director of Finance of Kurdistan to where I was, with these conditions: increase my salary and payment of what was deducted since 1921 and the debts, restitution of half the number of villages. You will tell him that I had reasons to wait. My destiny was like that. Now it is better because all Kalhur are with me. I have only little things to wait for. I will send you money shortly. I understand your situation, God is my witness that only your love pushed me here, otherwise I would have abandoned this infernal attempt. But your love and the idea of saving you from this damned situation has given me force to resist all difficulties and they are many. Up to now I have succeeded. Before receiving your 1st letter I had a place: it was slow but sure, but since I understood that because of De Berguer and the girls you need money, I have changed it in order to come to your assistance as soon as possible. In-shah-allah you will receive the money within a few days. What is surprising that my sons of Tehran do not think of me: insensibility is the motto of our family. Happily I have sons who love me and for whom I work. I have only received one letter from Touran since 4 months. I cannot give you the address. As soon as (Dieu/God ?) indicates the future, I will write to you.

Since yesterday evening I could not find the time to write you. I slept well last night and had abundant food. After (receiving) news today I think I will return afresh to Kurdistan (with Ja`far Sultan). This evening I shall be at 7 hours distance. Everywhere there is effervescence against the General of Persia. I receive letters that they are ready to assist me. Naturally I encourage (it, him?) You will hear shortly that I will conquer all Kurdistan, Karmanshah. Kisses to you and to dear Mistinguel and Ferrouke.

My Darling,

I hasten to give you this news. Two days ago several mounted men of my troop by error on the frontier had a skirmish. The Police thought they were robbers.

If my name is mentioned in the newspapers do not be alarmed. Thanks to D.T.P. (God? [*Dieu Tout-puissant*]) I am in good health, and I am going to our home, where I had been, three months ago.

If Z is there, tell him that the letter in Turkish that he wrote to him, has caused many mishaps to me because he wrote things that he might not to have mentioned. The person to whom it was addressed read it, then ... you should understand. Despite everything thanks to God I have arranged (matters). I will give you good news shortly.

Thousands of kisses to my dear children and to you. I hope Monsieur Guisi makes everything in his power so that you may be, In-sha-allah, tranquil.

Your devoted husband

Source: AIR 23/391, fol. 49a-c.

These two unsigned letters, written in French, were intercepted. They were delivered to a tribesman to give to Farakh Khanum Afandiya of Salahiya, Arnous no. 27, Damascus. The man said the letters were from Salar al-Dowleh who was with the Zargosh section of the Bani Wais near Qizil-Robat. One was dated 14 Safar = 1 September, the other, though undated, mentions a skirmish, which, according to a police report, occurred on 9 September, thus, as the letter states it was written two days before that event, it must have been written on 7 September. AIR 23/391, secret, CDC to Advisor Min. of Interior, 21/09/1925.

Appendix VII

Extracted from The Shafaghi Sorkh, 16 August 1926.

The following article has been published in today's issue:

SALARED DOWLEH IN KURDISTAN
NEW ROLE PLAYED BY THE BRITISH GOVERNMENT

There has been a rumour during the last few days in the city to the effect that Salared Dowleh has come to Kurdistan and has commenced committing actions which used to be taken by him several times previously. Although this news has not yet been confirmed by the official sources but the news which reached to us has been from a reliable source and later reports confirm it.

Granting that Salared Dowleh has come to Kurdistan and that he has gathered a gang of villains round himself and began to create disturbances in that region which may prolong for a fortnight or a month. What important effect this will have? Undoubtedly the matter itself is of no importance, because we all know Salared Dowleh and we are sure that this poor fellow had never a sound scheme, that is to say that he is not sane and is not of a sound mind. He has never taken advantage of his action except that he has always incurred heavy substantial losses on the Persian Government.

There is, however, a point which is worthy of consideration. As Modarres said: "Salared Dowleh is a puppet." This incapable prince during the whole period of his life has been recognizsed as the instrument for the execution of the foreign policy. When the foreigners wanted to create fresh difficulties for the Persian Government they have mobilized this prince and sent him to the simpleton tribes of Luristan and Kurdistan.

One may remember the participation of Salared Doweh in the recent crisis in Khuzistan. Salared Dowleh in that time had asked permission from the Persian Government to return to Persia, he even arrived at Baghdad, but his arrival coincided with the outbreak of disturbances in Khuzistan, on hearing this news the said prince immediately hurried to join the rebels. After the annihilation of the insurgents the prince habitually fled and took his residence at Syria. Now he has appeared in Kurdistan. Who sent him to Kurdistan? Via which route he has come there? Which policy is working in the Turkish and Persian Kurdistan? The above three questions are worthy of contemplation.

We wrote some time ago about the mutinies committed in Salamas [sic] and Marava Tappeh [sic] and in accordance with some evidence we said that the mutinies were instigated by some elements and this saying caused the vexation of the Moscow radio-telegraph agency. Now if the Reuter permit us to express our views and if it would not publish news expressing the discontent of the political circles in London from The Shafagh (as Moscow wireless did) we should disclose the facts and say that the instigation of the foreigners is being noticed in this matter. If we add to this news the intrigues and instigations made among the tribes of Khuzistan and the tribes of Baluchistan and Doust Mohammad Khan, more light is cast on the question.

We were of the opinion that the British Government have given up the old and rotten policies which are unadvisable at this time which the Bolshevik Russians are in neighbourhood of Persia. We thought that after those wrong politics which were played by the British Government in Persia and which resulted in public hatred made a bar for the progress of the British political and economic policies and despite of heavy expenses which they used to afford they always were facing an irritated and nervous nation, the British Government have relinquished that kind of policy and have adopted in the last few years a quiet policy. We are very sorry that we notice things in these days which are contrary to our realization.

The British Government think that they can make grounds for the establishment of an independent Kurdish Government. by sending Salared Dowleh in Kurdistan and causing disturbances in that region and so to make a buffer State between themselves and the Soviet Russia now that Mosul is annexed to Iraq and the Soviet Russia has become more close to Iraq. Or the British Government has the intention of making a poor and feeble Persia by causing disturbances to be created in different parts of the country which compels the Persian Government to dispatch troops to the places and to suffer great losses. These are all dreams. The adherence to such policies entails in detriments which is directly to the loss of the British Government and will make the Persian Government to approach the rival.

We are not very much optimistic to the attitude of the British Government in Persia. The British Government wishes to see a poor, feeble, crippled, indigent and unprosperous Persia in the East and they commit various illegal actions with this end in view.

We have not still forgotten the action of the British Government. at the Geneva Conference concerning the Persian Gulf, and we hope that the Britishers may not think that the Public opinion in Persia could not realize the severe blow which they were going to give to the independence and integrity of Persia.

The question of prohibition of the cultivation of opium which was ardently persisted by the British representatives and which is still insisted by them is not from the point of view of human welfare. If the British Government were fond for the welfare of mankind they would never doomed three hundred and seventy million inhabitants of India to slavery. As one of the merchants of Bushire said the Britishers want to make Persia indigent by their new economic policy.

The freedom of the export of the coins, which was reported in the previous issue, is another role devised for the economic ruination of Persia.

In the southern ports which are officially under the supremacy of the British Government all sorts of facilities are made for smuggling, in another word the same restrictions which are made in north by the Russians are set on foot by the British in the South.

What is the intention of our Government against these conspiracies? Is the only remedy to cross the river Jajrood and to open Mazandran road?

We hope that if the Council of Ministers and the Ministry of Foreign Affairs do not consider these important affairs the Ministry of War may not neglect to study the question completely.

Source: 248/1382, file 437, Prince Salar ed Dowleh.

Appendix VIII

Report of the contents Salar al-Dowleh's captured bag, 12 September 1926

At the request made by the S.H.O. we attended at the office of the Administrative Council and after examining the Khurj belonging to Salar al Dawlah, we found the articles mentioned in the attached list. Besides this, when the Khurj was brought before us by the S.H.O. we noticed that there was a hole in it. On inquiring of Salar al Dawlah's servant as to whether there was any hole in the Khurj, his reply was in the negative.

Sd/ Acting Qaimmaqam Mandali
Peace Judge Mandali
Mudir Mal
Katib Tahrirat
Member of the Administrative Council
S.H.O. Mandali

Dated 12.9.1926

List showing the articles belonging to Salar al Dawlah.

No.	Nature
1	Winter drawer
1	Short overcoat
1	Persian flag
1	Stockings
1	Towel white
4	Shirts
4	Drawers, made of cloth
1	Head dress
1	Slipper
1	Soap
1	Big handkerchief
1	Cone of sugar
1	Bag containing 20 bottles of medicine
1	Towel
1	Bottle of perfume
1	Bag containing 7 surgical instruments
1	Bag containing thread and buttons
1	Piece of wool
1	Small tin containing 7 pieces of paste
1	Bag containing 80 photos
1	Shaving brush
1	Bottle of water
1	Box containing shaving plates
1	Compass
1	Bag containing thread & other sewing articles
1	Bag containing buttons, small key, etc.
1	Box containing medicines
1	Small bottle containing medicine
1	Thread
1	Shaving soap
1	Koran
1	Bottle containing red medicine.

Source: FO 248/1382

Appendix IX

Letter from an Egyptian Air Officer to Salar al-Dowleh
20 October 1926

Secret.
No. S.O. 2628 The Residency
Baghdad, the 30th October, 1926.

Sir,

1. have the honour to transmit to you herewith copies of translations of a letter and enclosure which I have received from Khair al Din Labadidi, who gives his address as House No. 38 Fajjalah Street, Cairo.

2. I should be grateful if you would take such means as you may think fit to inform Khair al Din Effendi that as His Britannic Majesty's Government is at peace with Persia and regards with the strongest disapproval the present activities of Salar al Daula I cannot consent to be the medium of correspondence of any kind between him and Salar.

3. The impression that Great Britain is supporting Salar al Daulah is so prevalent throughout the Near East that I should be glad if you would use this opportunity to convince at least one misguided and misinformed person that far from wishing in any way to help Salar al Daulah my instructions from His Britannic Majesty's Government are that I am to persuade the `Iraq Government to use all its resources to capture Salar should he enter `Iraq.

I have the honour to be,
Sir,
Your most obedient servant,

Sd. B.H. Bowdillon
Ag. High Commissioner for `Iraq.

Enclosure 1.

To:

H.E. the High Commissioner,
Baghdad.

I beg to bring to your kind notice that when Salar al Dawlah, the uncle of Ahmad Shah, was in Damascus he requested the Staff Officer Zakariyah Beg to form a group of technical officers and make an agreement with them to join Sardar [sic] al Dawlah for the purpose of leading the revolutionary movement against Riza Khan who has forced the right of that noble family. Being an Air Officer I agreed with him and I was told by Zakariyah Beg and the Sardar [sic] that they shall acquire from the British Government an aeroplane in accordance with the agreement made for the supply of material to the Sardar [sic]. Since then I left Syria for Egypt where I received letters from my friends intimating that the Sardar [sic] had left me a message in Syria asking me to join him. I heard that the Persian revolution has now started, and as I am under obligation to the Sardar [sic] I request that the attached letter may kindly be sent to him enclosed in your despatch, because I do not know other means except Your Excellency's medium.

If any reply sent in by the Sardar [sic] please have it forwarded to me on the following address:

Khairul-Din Al Lababidi
c/o Monsieur Levy, House no. 33,
Fajjalah Street,
Egypt.

Dated 20/10/1926.
Sd. Khairul-Din-Lababidi,
Air Officer

His Britannic Mahesty's High Commissioner
for Egypt,
Cairo.

Enclosure 2.

To:
H.E. Sardar [sic] al Dowlah (He intends to address Salar ud Dowlah, translator).

I have been informed of the national rising against the Government of Reza Khan the transgressor on the Royal Family and on your legitimate rights. When Your Excellency was in Damascus I was called by Zakariyah Beg, the staff officer and asked me to accompany him and join you in the revolution. I agreed to the suggestion as you were informed by Yahya Kadhim Beg and Zakariyah Beg who communicated to me your salaams. The latters [sic] mentioned to me that the British Government is prepared to help you and it would therefore be possible for you to take an aeroplane from that Government which will be used by me for the purpose of flying over the Persian countries over which revolutionary proclamations in your name would be thrown.

I left Damascus when the Syria troubles broke out[1] and in which I participated, but unfortunately there was no aeroplane with which I could carry out my duty and I had therefore to lead rebels and fight the French severely.

As the French have deputied Monsieur Bonsau as a new High Commissioner who agreed with the nationalists to work for the maintenance of peace and give them their rights, I left for Egypt where I received letters from Damascus intimating your departure for burning the fire of revolution in Persia, and suggesting that it is necessary for me

---

1. On August 23, 1925 Sultan Pasha al-Atrash officially declared revolution against France.

to communicate Your Excelleny as I promised in the name of military honour to Zakariyah Beg. It would be a great honour to me to participate in this sacred fighting in order to recover Your Excellency's rights from Reza Khan. As I did not know how to send this letter to you, I sent it through the British High Commissioner in `Iraq who was requested to arrange for its despatch to you as I understand you are in harmony with the British Government. I shall not reveal this secret to the detriment of your honour. I am awaiting for your reply which should be sent to Egypt and arrange for my travelling expenses and for facilities to be extended to me to join you. First of all please arrange that the British Government may detail one light and small aeroplane of the Godron type which will be of great use for dropping leaflets on the Persian provinces and other important things of which great success can be derived. I am awaiting your reply and instruction.

Sd. Khairul-Din Lababidi

Air Commandant.

Dated 20.9.1926.

Address.

House of Monsieur Levy No. 33, Fajjalah Street,

Egypt.

Source: FO 248/1382, Baghdad to Cairo, 30/10/1926.

Appendix X

Salar al-Dowleh's letter to his son Majid
8 November 1926

Translation.

Baghdad, November 8th 1926

My dear son Majid,

Thanks to God I am well. You should not be anxious on my account. I am glad to say that I have made two great victories in Persia. It was only by God's wish that they may remain (useless?). I am not disappointed from the mercy of God. I entrust all of you to the powerful and merciful God. I have accepted and am bearing all these troubles and calamities for the sake of releasing you from (illegible) ...

Please enquire after the health of your mothers. I hope your brother is all right. Kiss your sisters and brother. …. You better refer all your affairs to the British Legation i.e. to ask them to assure your tranquility. You should entrust your affairs first to God and then to them.

Please let me know at once the good news of your health. You should know how much I am anxious on account of your destitute conditions and hardships (illegible).

My dear Majid, it is your duty to look after the family and respect the dignity of your family above everything.

Write to me as soon as possible of your conditions till a further address (?) and send your letter according to the following address through the horourable Legation:

C/O Director General of the Police of Baghdad.

I kiss your eyes.

Your father.
Source: FO 248/1382.

ANNEX XI
SALAR AL-DOWLEH'S LETTER TO GOUVERNEUR-GENENERAL DU DISTRICT DU NORD, HAIFA 3 NOVEMBER 1933

Haifa, le 3 Octobre, 1933.

Excellence,

J'ai l'honneur de porter à votre connaissance que l'ai reçu la lettre que vous avez voulu m'envoyer en date du 22 September, concernant la décision prise par le Gouvernement Rébél de Téheran au sujet de la somme allouée à moi et pour laquelle je vous avais déjà envoyé un accusé de reception en date du 29 Sept. et promis de vous en répondre sous peu.

Je m'empresse maintenant, Excellence de formuler ces quelques observations que je vous prie bien vouloir faire porter à la connaissance des Gouvernement de la Palestine et de Londres.

Le Gouvernement de Sa Majesté Britannique se rappelle sans doute que c'était par son ordre par l'intermediaire des les autorités Britaniques de L'Irak pendant l'année de 1926-1927 pour une durée de neuf mois environ et j'ai été privé ainsi de ma liberté personnelle durant tout ce temps. Il est vrai que j'avais passé la moitié de ce temps en prison et suis resté l'autre moitié conformement à sa demande à Bagdad.

Pendant cette longue et triste periode le Representant de Sa Majesté Britanique me posait chaque jour d'autre conditions qui ont eu pour fin mon consentement forcé de séjourner à Bagdad pour un temps indéterminé, me demandant à donner un engagement par écrit par lequel je devais m'abstenir de toute intervention dans les affaires de la Perse. Je préferais alors comme lieu de séjour Palestine ceci pour question de santé de ma famille, ce qui me fut accordé. Le Gouvernement de S.M. Britanique m'alloua une pension de 1500 Roupies par mois que je n'ai pas discuté.

Vous comprenez/

Source: CO 732/60/11

-2-

　　　　　Vous comprenez Excellence de ce que je viens de dire, que c'est le Gouvernement de S.M. Britanique lui même qui m'avait forcé de cesser toutes interventions dans les affaires de la Perse et m'obligea à mener une vie tout à fait negative, durant toute cette longue periode.

　　　　　Mais il est impossible par conséquent de ne pas considérer le Gouvernement de S.M. Britanique comme responsable de pourvoir à mon existence étant donné que c'était lui même qui m'avait forcé à subir cette vie negative que je mène depuis six ans. Si le Gouvernement de S.M. Britanique ne veut plus continuer dorénavant le payment de la somme qu'il me versait autrefois, cela ne devra aucunement affecter ma position vis-a-vis du Gouvernement de la Grande Bretagne, car c'est avec ce Gouvernement et NON avec d'autre c.a.d. le Gouvernement Rèbel usurpateur de Téhéran, que j'avai réglé ma situation financière.

　　　　　J'ignore d'ailleur completement que le Gouvernement Rèbel Persan ait pris un engagement vis-a-vis de moi, car je n'ai jamai consideré ce gouvernement COME LEGAL et LEGITIME et ne peu par conséquent avoir aucune rélation avec lui.

　　　　　Mais si le Gouvernement de S.M. Britanique voudrait maintenant cesser soudainement tout payment à moi à l'avenir il a parfaitement le droit de le faire. Mais m'ayant causé par ma détention d'abord dans sa prison en Irak ensuite ma détention forcée à Haifa, pendant plus de six ans, j'ai le droit de lui demander réparation des domages causés à moi. Le Gouvernement de S.M. Britanique est donc responsable pour cette réparation des domages causés logiquement - legalement et enfin humainement.

　　　　　　　　　　　　　Logiquement/

-3-

Logiquement : parceque ce sont les autorités de S.M. Britanique en Irak qui m'ont également arreté d'abord et exilé ensuite et non les autorités du Gouvernement Persan.

Legalement : parceque c'est lui qui m'a empêché la continuation de mes actions militaires et politiques contre le regime actuel existant en Perse et m'a forcé de donner un engagement formel de m'abstenir de toutes sortes d'intervention dans mon pays ce qui m'a fait perdre le grand prestige et l'influence que j'avais sur la majorité de la population Persane qui m'a soutenu honnetement et fidèlement pendant une longue periode 22 ans. Ces faits ne sont poins inconnus au Gouverement de S.M. Britanique; qui savait parfaitement jusqu'a quel dégré mes compatriotes et mes amis se sacritiaient âme et corps pour ma cause.

Le Gouvernement de S.M. est enfin humainement responsable parceque couper soudainement les moyens de vivre de toute une famille occupant dans la vie sociale un rang comme le mien c'est porter, vertablement un coup terrible à cette famille, particulièrement je suis un Prince qui ne connait d'autre metier que celui de régner et qui est absolument uncapable de trouver une occupation qui puisse pouvoir aux besoin d'une grande famille comme la mienne.

Et maintenant pour toutes les raisons je me permets Excellence de formuler ici les demandes que je trouve raisonable et que je vous prie de bien vouloir porter à la connaissance des Gouvernements de la Palestine et de Londres :

I./

Annex XII

al-Ahram article about Salar al-Dowleh, 1936

AL-AHRAM - 9.2.35.

A PERSON CLAIMING THE THRONE OF PERSIA IS IN ALEXANDRIA.

It is known that Prince Salar ed Dawlat Qajar claimed the throne after the abdication of Ahmad Shah, the last King of the Qajar dynasty, but he failed ~~in facing Rida~~ to stand [against Reza] Khan, the present Shah's ~~rebellion~~ [when the latter made his rebellion]. Finally he was deported to Astrabad and all his properties were confiscated by the Persian Government. Afterwards he was allowed to go to Iraq, then to Europe. He left for Lausanne where he remained. He possessed nothing for his living.

The English, being aware of what had happened to him asked the Persian Government to provide a salary for the Prince sufficient for his expenses in Europe. The Persian Government gave him a salary of £ 100 which he used to depend upon for his living. Some years afterwards he left for Palestine and then to Egypt. He now stays at Ibrahmieh, Alexandria with his family. The Persian Government stopped his salary as from last November. One of the Prince's sons started to help him but the Persian Government decided not to send money out of Persia except for commercial business.

The Prince is now compelled to continue his endeavours through the British Government in order to obtain his material rights.

It is expected that his case will end in a good resolution.

The Prince is a man of high and good character.

FO 141/606/15, text al-Ahram
FO 141/606/15, 2626 Ahram Arabic article

AL AHRAM
5th Feb. 1936.

المطالب بعرش ايران فى الاسكندرية

البرنس سالار الدولة قاجار

الاسكندرية فى ٤ فبراير — لمراسل الاهرام الخاص — يعلم الواقفون على شئون ايران السياسية ان البرنس سالار الدولة من آل قاجار — اسرة الشاه السابق — كان قد تقدم على اثر خلع احمد شاه آخر حكام تلك الاسرة للمطالبة بالعرش اذ كان احق اعضائها بالارتقاء اليه بعده

وقد هب فى ذاك الوقت لمقاومة ثورة رضا خان (الان جلالة شاه ايران) ولكن مسعاه فشل

وكانت النتيجة ان اعتقل البرنس سالار الدولة وهو عم الشاه السابق وسجن فى استراباد وصادرت الحكومة الايرانية الجديدة امواله وممتلكاته . ثم اذن له بالخروج من البلاد فذهب الى العراق وبعد ان اعتقل فيها اجيز له السفر الى اوربا فسافر الى لوزان بسويسرا واقام فيها وهو لا يملك شيئا ولما رأى الانجليز ، وكانت عيونهم تراقبه ، ماحل به بسببهم طلبوا من الحكومة الايرانية تعيين للامير راتبا يكفى لمعيشته فى اوربا فعينت له الحكومة راتبا قدره مائة جنيه فى الشهر فاخذ يعول على هذا المورد الوحيد . وبعد ان

اقام فى لوزان بضع سنوات انتقل الى فلسطين مفضلا ان تكون اقامته فى بلد شرقى ، فظلت الحكومة الايرانية تمده بتلك المساعدة

ثم انتقل الى مصر ونزل فى الابراهيمية برمل الاسكندرية ومعه اسرته فانتقل راتبه الى هنا ايضا . وظلت الحال على هذا المنوال الى نوفمبر الماضى فانعكس الامر

ذلك ان حكومة طهران قطعت راتب الامير دفعة واحدة . فتقدم احد ابنائه فى ايران لمعونته ولكن ذلك لم يغل ايضا لان الحكومة قررت لاسباب اقتصادية وطبية منع اصدار المال من البلاد فلم يعد يؤذن بارسال شئ منه لاحد الا من طريق المعاملة التجارية والتبادل

وقد اضطر سمو البرنس سالار الدولة الى استئناف السعى عن طريق انجلترا للحصول على شئ من حقه المادى .

ولا يبعد ان يؤدى السعى الى حل مشكلة سموه باتفاق خاص

ولا يزال الامير مقيما فى الابراهيمية بالرمل الى الآن وسيظل فى ضيافة مصر مدة من الزمن وهو على جانب كبير من الوقار ورقى الاخلاق وعلو النفس

BIBLIOGRAPHY

ARCHIVES

NATIONAL ARCHIVES, KEW GARDENS, LONDON, UK

AIR 20/511 Case re rebel Prince Salar-ed Dowlah [1919]
AIR 23/391 Salar Ud Dowlah: reports [1925-29]
CO 730/112/4, Salar ed Dowleh: various arrangements for his residence and payment of his debts [1926-27]
CO 732/60/11, Prince Salar Ed-Dowleh Qadjar: non-payment of allowance from Persian Government
CO 732/65/9; Prince Salar-ed-Doleh: H.M. Government can offer no financial assistance because of his political activities [1923-35]
FO 141/606/15 Kadjar, Salar ed Dowlat (al-Ahram article)
FO 248/907 Kermanshah
FO 248/1031 idem
FO 248/1053 idem
FO 248/1073 idem
FO 248/1112 idem
FO 248/1181 idem
FO 248/1382 idem
FO 371/11401
FO 371/11434
FO 371/13063
FO 371/23265/3706, Affairs of Prince Salar ad Dowlat Qajar. Code 34 file 3706 [1939]
FO 371/45489, Prince Salar el Daolat Kadjar. Code 34 File 667

FO 371/52751
FO 416/79 Foreign Office: Confidential Print Persia (Iran)
FO 684/2/25/29, H.H. Salar-ud-Dowleh [1925]
FO 800/70 Foreign Office

BRITISH LIBRARY/INDIA OFFICE, LONDON, UK.

IOR/L/PS/10/209, File 52/1912 Pt 1 'Persia Diaries', Meshed Consular Diary.
IOR/L/PS/10/210, File 52/1912, Pt 2,"Persia Diaries," Meshed Consular Diary.
IOR/L/PS/10/211, File 52/1912 Pt 3 'Persia Diaries', Intelligence Summary.
IOR/L/PS/10/212, File 211/1912, 'Turkish Arabia Summaries'.
IOR/L/PS/10/1196, File 4010/1926 Persia: Prince Salar-ed-Dowleh; future residence
IOR/L/PS/11/40, file P 4899/1912 Persia: terms offered to Salar-ed-Dowleh; the Regent in Paris; Tehran affairs; the Cabinet
IOR/L/PS/11/46, P 664/1913 Persia: future of Salar-ud-Dowleh
IOR/L/PS/11/48, file P 971/1913 Persia: Salar-ed-Dowleh at Resht; strike and disbandment of gendarmes at Bushire; threatened attack on Bunder-Abbas
IOR/L/PS/11/60, P 2972/1913 Persia: escape of Salar-ed-Dowleh
IOR/L/PS/11/78, file P 2075/1914 Persia: Salar-ed-Dowleh; threatened return to Persia; 23 May 1914-27 May 1914
IOR/L/PS/11/81, file P 3059/1914 Persia: rumoured disturbances at Shustar and Dizful, and appearance of Salar-ed-Dowleh at Bahrein
IOR/L/PS/11/82, file P 3492/1914 Persia: return to Persia from France of Salar-es-Sultaneh; Kermanshah affairs
IOR/L/PS/11/82, P 3699/1914 Persia: movements of Salar-ed-Dowle
IOR/L/PS/11/84, P 4167/1914 Persia: Salar-ed-Dowleh's movements
IOR/L/PS/11/84, file P 4382/1914 Persia: affairs at Kermanshah; reported presence of Salar-ed-Dowleh on the frontier; 3 Nov 1914-10 Nov 1914
IOR/L/PS/11/85, file P 4570/1914 Persia: proposals for new cabinet; Salar-ed-Dowleh's movements
IOR/L/PS/12/3492, Coll 28/86 Prince Salar-ed-Dowleh
IOR/L/PS/18/C144, 'Extracts from Annual Persia Reports, 1906, 1909, 1910, 1911, 1912, 1913 regarding loans, and complete reports for 1908 & 1913'.
IOR/L/PS/10/478, File 3516/1914 Pt 1, German War: Persian attitude towards Turkey,'
IOR/R/15/1/382, 'File 23/15, 19 I (D 89) Mesopotamia - General'.
IOR/L/PS/18/C221, 'British Relations with Khazal, Shaykh of Mohammerah,'.
IOR/L/PS/20/211, 'Summary of Principal Events in 1907.
IOR/L/PS/20/223, 'Who's who in Persia. Calcutta: General Staff, India, 1916'.
IOR/L/PS/20/227, 'Biographical Notices of Persian Statesmen and Notables, September 1909'.

IOR/L/PS/20/261/4, 'Persia. No 3 (1912). Further correspondence respecting the affairs of Persia.'
IOR/L/PS/20/261/5, 'Persia. No 4 (1912) Further correspondence respecting the affairs of Persia'.
IOR/L/PS/20/261/6, 'Persia. No 5 (1912). Further correspondence respecting the affairs of Persia.'
IOR/L/PS/20/261/7, 'Persia. No 1 (1913). Further correspondence respecting the affairs of Persia'.
IOR/L/MIL/17/15/10/5, Military Report on (S.-W) Persia, vol. 5, Luristan.
IOR/L/MIL/17/15/11/3, Who's who in Persia?
IOR/R/20/A/3722; File 1309 Prohibition against the entry of Prince Salar-Ed-Dowleh into territory under British control [1935]
Presbyterian Historical Society, Philadelphia (USA). RG 91-1-12, Report on Relief Work in the Malayir District Conducted During the Spring of 1912.

BOOKS AND ARTICLES

Adhari, Reza 1378/1999. *Dar takapu-ye taj o takht (asnad-e Abu'l-Fath Mirza Salar al-Dowleh)*, Tehran.

Adinehvand, Mas`ud; Yegani, Meysam Reza'i; and Sepahvand, Esma`il 1395/2016. "Owza-ye siyasi-ejtema`i-ye manteqeh-ye Tarhan dar dowreh-ye Qajar," *Pazhuheshnameh-ye Tarikhha-ye Mahalli-ye Iran* 4/1, pp. 142- 56.

Administration Report = *Administration Report on the Persian Gulf Political Residency for the year (1873 to 1940)* in Government of India. *The Persian Gulf Administration Reports 1873-1947*, 10 vols., Gerrards Cross, Archives Editions, 1986.

Afshar, Iraj ed. 1362/1983. *Asnad-e Mashrutiyat* 4 vols. Tehran, Ferdowsi.

___ 1367/1988. "Asnad-e jang ba Salar al-Dowleh," in Idem, *Namvareh-ye Doktor Mahmud Afshar* 22 vols. Tehran: Bonyad-e Mahmud Afshar, vol. 4, pp. 2000-21.

Afzal al-Molk, Gholam Hoseyn 1361/1982. *Afzal al-Tavarikh*. eds. Mansureh Ettehadiyyeh and Sirus Sa`dvandiyan. Tehran: Tarikh-e Now.

Anonymous 1902, "Israeliten Persiens," *Bericht der Alliance Israelite Universelle vom 1 und 2. Semester*. Paris, pp. 47-67.

___, 1913. *The New Hazell Annual and Almanack*, vol. 28, p. 305.

Arfa, Hassan 1964. *Under Five Shahs*. London: John Murray.

Bakhtiyari, Sardar Zafar 1362/1983. *Yaddashtha va Khaterat-e Sardar Zafar Bakhtiyari*. Tehran: Yasavoli.

Bamdad, Mehdi 1347/1968. *Tarikh-e Rejal-e Iran qorun-e 12-13-14*. 6 vols. Tehran: Zavvar.

Bashiri, Ahmad 1367/1988. *Ketab-e Naranji*. 3 vols. Tehran: Nur.

Basri, Ali 1335/1956. *Yaddahstha-ye Reza Shah dar zaman-e ra'is al-vozara'i*. Tehran.

Bast, O. 1377/1998. "Salar al-Dowleh va diplomasi-ye Iran va Aleman dar ava'el-e jang-e jahan-e avval." *Tarikh-e mo`aser-e Iran*, vol. 2/7, pp. 35-52.

___ 1997, *Les Allemands en Perse pendant la premiere guerre mondiale*. Leuven: Peeters.

___, 2002. Olivier Bast, *La Perse et la Grande Guerre*, Tehran: IFRI.

Browne, E.G. 1966. *The Persian Revolution of 1905-1909*. London: Cass.

Chamanara, Daryush 1384/2005. "Mashrutiyat va mowze`-e Gholam Reza Khan Vali-ye Posht-e Kuh (Eylam)," *Payam-e Baharestan* 51, pp. 95-98.

Churchill, George P. 1909. *Biographical Notices of Persian Statesmen and Notables*. Calcutta.

Colby, Frank Moore and Churchill, Allen Leon eds. *New International Yearbook: A Compendium of the World's Progress for the Year 1913*. New York: Dodd, Mead and Co., 1914.

Daftar-Rava'i, Naser 1363/1984. *Khaterat va asnad-e [...]*. eds. Iraj Afshar and Behzad Razzaqi. Tehran: Ferdowsi.

Dehkhoda, Ali Akbar 2016. *Charand-o Parand. Revolutionary Satire from Iran, 1907-1909*. translated by Janet Afary and John R. Perry. New Haven: Yale UP.

Destree, Annete 1976. *Les fonctionnaires belges au service de la Perse 1898-1915*. Tehran-Luik: Brill.

Divsalari, Yahya 1364/1985. "Akharanin talash-e Salar al-Dowleh," *Armaghan* 36, pp. 162-64.

Dowlatabadi, Ali Mohammad 1362/1983. *Khaterat-e Sayyed Ali Mohammad Dowlatabadi*. Tehran: Attar - Ferdowsi.

Dowlatabadi, Yahya 1330-31/1950-51. *Hayat-e Yahya*, 4 vols. Tehran.

Ehtesham al-Saltenah 1366. *Khaterat [...]*. ed. Sayyed Mohammad Mehdi Musavi. Tehran: Zavvar.

Enayat, Hasan 1340/1961. "Salar al-Dowleh," *Yaghma* 14/7, pp. 312-19.

Ettehadiyeh, Mansureh and Sa`vandiyan, Sirus eds. 1366/1987. *Gozideh'i az majmu`eh-ye asnad-e `Abdol-Hoseyn Mirza Farmanfarma 1325-1340 h.q.* 2 vols. Tehran.

Farid al-Molk Hamadani, Mirza Mohammad `Ali Khan 1354/1975. *Khaterat-e Farid*. Tehran: Zavvar.

Farmanfarma'iyan, Hafez 1341/1962. "Nameh-ye Salar al-Dowleh beh Farmanfarma," *Yaghma* 11/15, pp. 500-03.

Farmanfarma'iyan, Mehrmah 1382/2003. *Zendeginameh-ye Abdol-Hoseyn Mirza Farmanfarma*. 2 vols. Tehran: Tus.

Floor, Willem 1973. "The police in Qajar Iran," *ZDMG*, vol. 123, pp. 293-315.

___ 1998. *A Fiscal History of Iran in the Safavid and Qajar Period*. New York: Bibliotheca Persica.

___ 2018. *Kermanshah: Its People and Politics*. Washington DC: Mage Publishers.

Fortescue, Capt. L. S. 1920, *Military Report on Tehran and Some Provinces in N.W. Persia*. Tehran, in: FO 248/1300.

Grothe, Hugo 1910. *Wanderungen in Persien*. Berlin: Algemeiner Verein f. Deutsche Literatur.

Hashimi, Fatemeh 1389/2010. Peyamad-e shuresh-e Salar al-Dowleh dar velayat-e Thalatheh," *Payam-e Baharestan* vol. 2/8, pp. 602-38.

Jurabchi, Hajj Mohhammad Taqi 1363/1984. *Harfi az hazaran kandar `ebarat amad*. eds. Mansureh Ettehadiyyeh, Sirus Sa`dvandiyan. Tehran: Tarikh-e Iran.

Kariman, Zahra 1380/2001. "`Esyan-e Salar al-Dowleh dar salha-ye 1329 ta 1331 az negah-e asnad," *Tarikh-e mo`aser-e Iran*, vol 5/18, pp. 195-260

Kasravi, Ahmad 1319-21/1940-42. *Tarikh-e Mashruteh-ye Iran*. 3 vols. Tehran: Taban.

___ 1350/1971. *Tarikh-e Hejdeh Saleh-ye Azerbaijan*. Tehran: Amir Kabir.

Kazembeyki, Mohammad Ali 2003. *Society, Politics and Economics in Mazandaran, Iran, 1848-1914*. London: Routledge.

Kazemzadeh, Firuz 1968. *Russia and Britain in Persia 1864-1914*. New Haven: Yale UP.

Lorimer, J. G. 1908-15. *Gazetteer of the Persian Gulf, Oman, and Central Arabia*, 2 vols., Calcutta.

Mafi, Hashem Mohit 1363/1984. *Moqaddamat-e Mashrutiyat*. 2 vols. ed. Majid Tafarashi.Tehran: Elmi-Ferdowsi

Malekzadeh, Mehdi 1328-33/1949-54. *Tarikh-e Enqelab-e Mashruyiyat-e Iran*. 7 vols. Tehran: Ebn Sina.

Mardukh, Shaykh Mohammad 1351/1972. *Tarikh-e Kord va Kordestan va Tavabe` ya Tarikh-e Mardukh*. 2 vols. in one. Tehran.

Me`zi, Fatemeh 1390/2011. "Abu'l-Fath Mirza Salar al-Dowleh," *Majalleh-ye Tarikh-e Mo`aser-e Iran* 60, pp. 155-90.

Mirza Saleh, GholamHoseyn ed. 1384/2005. *Mozakerat-e Majles-e Avval 1324-1326, towsi`eh-ye siyasi-ye Iran dar vartah-e siyasat-e beyn al-mellal*. Tehran: Mazyar.

Mo`aser, Hasan ed. 1348/1969. *Tarikh-e esteqrar-e mashrutiyat dar Iran*. Tehran: Ebn Sina.

Mo`ayyer al-Mamalek, Dust Ali Khan 1361/1982. *Vaqaye` al-Zaman (Khaterat-e Shekariyyeh)*. Tehran: Tarikh-e Iran.

Moberley F.J. 1987. *Operations in Persia, 1914-1919*. London: HMSO.

Mo`jezi, Mohammad Reza Valizadeh 1380/2001. *Tarikh-e Lorestan*. eds. Mohammad and Hoseyn Valizadeh. 2 vols. Tehran: Horufiyeh.

Mogith al-Saltaneh, Yusef 1362/1983. *Namehha-ye Yusef Moghith al-Saltaneh*. ed. Ma`sumeh Mafi. Tehran: Tarikh-e Iran.

Mo'men Abu'l-Fath 1384. "Marg-e Yaprim dar Jang-e 'Surcheh', *Mahnameh-ye andisheh va tarikh-e syasi-ye Iran-e mo`aser* vol. 4/31-32, pp. 59-66.

Moore, Arthur 1914. *The Orient Express*. London: Constable & Company Ltd.

Mo'tamadi, Amir Mas'ud 1347/1978. "Gha'eleh-ye Salar al-Dowleh," *Barrasiha-ye Tarikhi* 3/3-4, pp. 201-24.

Mostowfi, Abdollah 1324/1945, *Zendegani-ye Man*. 3 vols. Tehran: Zavvar.

Nazem al-Eslam Kermani 1346-49/1967-70. *Tarikh-e Bidari-ye Iraniyan*. 2 vols. and a *Moqaddameh* volume. Tehran: Bonyad-e Farhang-e Iran.

Nezam-Mafi, Ma'sumeh; Mansureh Ettehadiyeh (Nezam Mafi); Sa'vandiyan, Sirus and Ram Pisheh, Hamid eds. 1361/1982. *Khaterat va Asnad-e Hoseyn Qoli Khan Nezam al-Saltaneh Mafi*. 3 parts in 2 vols. Tehran: Tarikh-e Iran.

Parvin, Nader 1385/2006. "Shuresh-e Salar al-Dowleh va Naqsh-e Il-e Kalhor," *Faslnameh-ye Motale1at-e Tarikhi* 15, pp. 42-79.

Political Diaries = *Political Diaries of the Persian Gulf* 1904-1947, 17 vols. n.p. Archive Editions, 1990.

Qasemi, Abu'l-Fazl 1372, "Abu'l-Fath Qajar Salar al-Dowleh," *Ayandeh* 19/1372, nos. 1-2, pp. 70-71.

Qezelayagh, Hoseyn Qoli 1349/1970, "Salar al-Dowleh va Amir-e A'zam," *Yaghma* 23/6, pp. 357-60.

Ra'in, Esma'il 1347. *Faramushkhaneh va framasuneri dar Iran*. 2 vols. Tehran.

Ra'is-Niya, Rahim 1382/2003. *Iran va 'Othmani*. 2 vols. Tehran/Tabriz: Mabna/Serudeh.

Ruznameh-ye Tarbiyat 1377/1998. 3 vols. Tehran: Ketabkhaneh-e Melli.

Safa'i, Ebrahim 1344/1965, *Rahbaran-e Mashrutiyat*. 2 vols. Tehran: Sharq.

___ 1346/1967. *Asnad-e tarikhi-ye dowreh-ye Qajariyeh*. Tehran: Sharq.

___ 1348/1969. *Namehha-ye Tarikhi*, Tehran: Babak

Saki, Ali Mohammad 1343/1964. *Joghrafiya-ye Tarikhi va Tarikh-e Lorestan*. Khorammabad.

Sasani, Khan Malek 1352. *Dast-e penhan-e siyasat-e englis dar Iran*, Tehran: Babak.

Sayyah, Hajj 1346/1967. *Khaterat-e Hajj Sayyah ya Dowreh-ye Khowf va Vahshat*. eds. Hamid Sayyah and Seyfollah Golfar. Tehran: Ibn Sina.

Sepehr, Mirza Mohammad Taqi Lisan al-Molk 1337/1958 *Nasekh al-Tavarikh* 3 vols. ed. Jahangir Qa'em-Maqami. Tehran.

Shahedi, Mozaffar *Tarikh-e Bank-e Esteqrazi-ye Rusi dar Iran*. Tehran: Vezarat-e Omur-e Khareji, 1381.

Sharif Kashani, Mohammad Mehdi 1362/1983. *Vaqe'at-e ettefaqiyeh dar ruzgar*. 3 vols. Tehran: Tarikh-e Iran.

Sheybani, Mirza Ebrahim 1366/1987. *Montakhab al-Tavarikh*. Tehran: Elmi.

Shuster, Morgan W. 1968. *The Strangling of Persia*. New York: Greenwood Press.

Soltani, Mohammad Ali 1381/2002. *Joghrafiya-ye Tarikhi va Tarikh-e Mofassal-e Kermanshahan-e Bakhtaran*. 10 vols. Tehran.

___ 1386/2007, *Nahzat-e mashrutiyat dar Kermanshah: az arshiv- e Ayatollah Hajj Shaykh Mohammad Mahdi Kermanshahi (Feyz Mahdavi)*. Tehran: Mo'asseseh-ye Tahqiqat-e Olum-e Ensani.

Stead, F.M. 1908. "From Hamadan, Persia," *The Westminster*, vol. 33, 11 January, p. 18.

Sykes, Percy M. 1969. *A History of Persia*. 2 vols. London: Routledge.

Taj al-Saltaneh 1361/1982. *Khaterat-e Taj al-Saltaneh*. eds. Mansureh Ettehadiyeh and Sirus Sa`dvandiyan. Tehran: Tarikh-e Iran.

Uzhan Bakhtiyari, Abu'l-Fath 1344/1965. "Tarikh-e Bakhtiyari," *Vahid* 3, pp. 235-49.

Vahidniya, Seyfollah ed. 1362. *Khaterat-e Siyasi va Tarikhi*. Tehran: Ferdowsi.

Vakil al-Dowleh, Hoseyn Maqsudlu 1362/1983. *Mokhabarat-e Astarabad* 3 vols. eds. Iraj Afshar and Moh. Rasul Daryagasht . Tehran: Tarikh-e Iran.

Vaziri, Ali Asghar 1352/1973. "Mokhtasari az karha-ye Salar al-Dowleh va chand nameh-ye tarikhi," *Vahid* no. 32, pp. 49-67.

Wilson, Sir Arnold T. 1932. *Persia*. London: Ernest Benn.

Yaghma'i, Abdol-Karim Hekmat 1363/1984. *Jandaq va Qumes dar avakher-e dowreh-ye Qajar*. Tehran: Tarikh-e Now.

Index

A

Abbasabad 69
Abbas Ali 116, 118
Abbas Khan 28, 36, 40, 42, 64
Abbas Khan Chenari 28, 36, 40
Abdol-Ghani al-Mandalawi 138, 144
Abdollah Khan Farrash-bashi 1, 99
Abu'l-Hasan Khan 43
adliyeh 8, 26, 27
agha-bashi 113
Ahmad Qader 139
Ahmad Shah 115
Ahvaz 121, 122, 123, 124
airplane 129
Akbar Khan Mo`aven-e Lashkar 26
Akhund Khorasani 39, 42
Akhura 150
Alaja 150
Aleppo 117, 134
Ali Akbar Brothers 46
Ali Akbar Sanjabi 54
Ali Akbar Tabrizi 149
Alishtar 62
Ali Tharwat Beg 150
allowance 114, 122, 123, 124, 156, 158, 160, 163, 164
Amanollah Khan 40, 41, 54
Ament 78
Amin al-Soltan 15, 16, 17
Amir Afkham 11, 13, 16, 17, 18, 19, 36
Amir Akram 85
Amir al-Mamalek 26
Amir As`ad 73, 89, 107
Amir A`zam 57, 73, 74, 75, 76, 78, 79, 81, 83
Amir Heshmat 109
Amir Mofakhkham 28, 29, 35, 38, 56
Amir Mokarram 85
Amir Nezam Qaragozlu 57
Amir Saiyid 77
Anatolia 110
Anjoman-e Sa`adat 22
Aqa Habibollah 94, 97
Aqa Janbazi 26
Aqa Mahmud 26, 27, 42, 48
Aqa Mohammad Mehdi 11, 17, 42, 48, 54
Aqa Qoli Farrash-bashi 26
Aqa Rahim 26, 42, 48, 53, 54
Aqa Sayyed Hoseyn 20
Aqa Sayyed Reza Qomi 48
Aqa Vali 48
Arab military officers 137
Arbab Jamshid 101, 185
Ardabil 107
Arfa` al-Mamalek 102
Armenian fida'is 58
Armenian mojaheds 67
Armenians 22, 37, 61, 64, 65, 71, 72
Asaf al-Divan 92, 94
Asaf Divan 24

INDEX

Ashja' al-Molk 83
Ashraf 85
Ashraf al-Molk 3
Astarabad 23, 24, 73, 76, 77, 79, 80, 81, 82, 83, 84, 85, 86, 87, 96, 107, 114, 141, 182
asylum 21, 27, 41, 43, 71, 73
Ataba'i 75
a'tas 26
Avroman 98, 99, 128, 129, 130, 132, 138, 139, 140, 144, 147, 149
Avromans 24, 143
Azad al-Soltan 21, 28, 38, 39, 40
A'zam al-Dowleh 42, 43, 46, 49
Azud al-Dowleh 22

B

Bagh-e Shah 20, 37
Bahador al-Saltaneh Kordestani 24
Bahrain 105
Bahram Soltan 99
Bajlan 109
Bakhtiyaris 67, 72
Baku 90, 103, 114, 115, 116, 117
Bandar-e Gaz 79, 81, 82, 87, 93
Baneh 132, 142
Barforush 86, 87, 88
Basra 121, 131, 135
bast 9, 20, 43, 49, 93
Bawanur 128
Behbahani 7, 19
Beirut 123, 127, 137
Bentick 152
Bern 106, 107
Bestam 76
Beyrawands 10, 182
Biara 128
Binah, administrative officer 119, 161
Bisetun 47, 61
Bitwin 150
Bojnurd 78
Bolshevik 115, 131, 195
Borujerd 3, 5, 14, 15, 16, 25, 28, 29, 40, 46, 173

brothels 2, 75
Bursa 111

C

Caiffa 138
chaous 150
cheraghani 19, 25
Chia Sorkh 50, 71, 99, 109
coin
  Salar al-Dowleh 35
commission of justice 53
Constitutional flag 47
Cossacks 51, 57, 69, 73, 74, 82, 83, 87, 89, 90, 94, 95, 96, 97, 100, 103, 115, 122
crown lands 2, 3, 4

D

Damascus 123, 125, 128, 134
Damghan 74, 75, 76
Dashti Kolah 82
Da'ud Khan Kalhor 16, 18, 26, 38, 47, 53, 54, 56, 57, 60, 94, 182
de Bacheracht 106
debt in Switzerland 124
Delfan 10, 14
Delgosha 27, 38, 101
Derow 90
description of Salar 150
Dezful 4
Dilwar 105
Dirakwands 28
Divandarreh 94, 97, 98
divan-khaneh 2
Diziaish 128
Dobbs, High Commissioner Baghdad 140
Do Dangeh 74
Durdi Khan 78

E

education 1
Ehtesham al-Dowleh 39, 41, 52, 174

Ehtesham al-Mamalek 59
Ehtesham al-Saltaneh 108, 109
electric fan 116
Emad al-Ra`aya 43
Enver Pasha 108
Enzeli 22, 33, 77, 82, 90, 114, 116
Eqbal al-Dowleh 178
Esharizur 128
Eshratabad 9, 11, 20, 120, 123, 185
Esma`il Khan Amir Mo'ed 77
Esma`il Osmanov 116, 117
Ettela al-Dowleh 50
extradition to India? 153
Eyn al-Dowleh 4, 7, 10, 36, 41, 90, 94, 96
E`zam al-Molk 85
Ezra 128

F

Fakhim al-Dowleh 43
family size Salar 124
Farid al-Molk 53
Farid al-Saltaneh 139
Farmandari-e koll-e Khuzestan 52
Farmanfarma 47, 51, 53, 57, 60, 61, 62, 63, 64, 69, 93, 95, 99, 100, 101, 172
Farrokh Khan 26, 41, 42, 43, 44, 47, 54
Farrokh Khan Ilkhani 26, 41
Fatah Beg 99, 109
Fath-e Lashkar 18
fathnamehs 19
Fendereski Turkmen 113
Firuzkuh 88
flight to Iraq, 1925 127
Freemasons 22, 104, 126
French 17, 126, 127, 129, 134, 137, 138, 140, 147, 148, 149, 159, 162, 165, 171, 193, 201
Fumen 90

G

Garrus 6, 7, 25, 31, 72, 94, 97, 182
gazmeh 26
Gholam Hoseyn Bakhtiyari 34
Gilan
  Kalhor country 53, 55
  province 76, 79
Goklan 78, 81
Golpeygan 6, 35
Gowan 148, 149, 150
Grant Duff 106
Guklan 78
Gumush Tepeh 24, 75, 115
Gurans 54, 62, 98

H

Habib Tajer 24
Haifa 157
Hajj Hasan Kalantar 26
Hajjilar 78
Hajji YakLag Torkman Ataba'i 74
Hajj Mo`tamad 24
Hajj Sharif Khan Mo`tamadi 26
Halabja 128, 130, 132, 133, 139, 144, 147, 149, 152
Hamadan 6, 10, 12, 13, 15, 17, 25, 28, 29, 37, 38, 40, 42, 44, 45, 47, 51, 52, 54, 55, 56, 57, 68, 69, 72, 103, 108, 110, 111, 112, 113, 132, 144, 173, 187
Hartwig 23
Hasan Khan Mo`aven al-Molk 26
Hasan Mo`aven al-Ra`aya 95, 102
Hazar Jarib 74
hejab 8
Hessarak 72
Heydar Qoli Khan Mas`ud al-Soltan 75
Hinaidi 116
Hojjatollah Khan Kermanshahi 88
Hoseynabad 78
Hoseyn Homayun 115, 116, 118
Hoseyn Ra'uf Bey 110

I

IBP manager 45
Imam Jom`eh 2, 92
Incha 78
Istanbul 21, 107, 108, 109, 114, 115, 117, 178
Italian consul 134, 142
Ivanov 77, 81, 82, 83, 86

J

Jaf 23, 24, 28, 94, 98, 109, 112, 128, 182
Ja`fara'i 75, 81
Ja`far Qoli Bakhtiyari 34, 40
Ja`far Qoli Khan 89
Ja`far Soltan 132, 139, 142, 143, 144, 147, 149
Jahangir (bandit) 78
Jahangir Qalkhani 140
Javanrud 129, 140
Jews, murdered 173
jihad 16, 17, 59
jiqeh 8, 35
jireh 34, 40, 77
jireh va `aliq 34
Judekis 10
Jular village 139

K

Kafshgiri 81
Kajur 73
kalantar 75
  of district 75
Kalantar Asad Khan 4
Kalbegis 94, 96, 97, 98
Kalhors 133, 147
Kamarian 69
Kangavar 17, 32, 43, 44, 49, 51, 59, 68
Karadah 158
Karaj 88
kargozar 28, 51, 53, 113
Karim Beg Jaf 139
Karim Fattah Beg Jaf 140
Karkandeh 77, 83
Kazem Khan Sanjabi 58, 60
Keller 139
Keri Khan 58, 59, 65, 72
Kersallidze 131
Khalkhal 90
Khamseh 2, 3, 13
Khaneqin 52, 110, 128, 131, 132, 133, 134, 139
Khezel 39
Khodabandlu 13
Khodadad Khan 12
Khorasan 107
Khorramabad 5, 11, 14, 18, 21, 41, 88
  Mazandaran 88
Khosrow Bakhtiyari 42
Khurmal 139
Khvajeh Nafas 73, 74, 76, 77, 78
Khvajehvand 73
Khvansar 6, 35
Kifri 128
Kilich Ishan 78
Kirai regiment 79
Kirkuk 112, 139
Koliya'i 48, 52, 112
Konya 113
Kord Mahalleh 75, 76, 82
Krasnovodsk 82, 115
Kuleh 96
Kurdish hizb 139

L

La`lchin 13
Leleux 78, 80, 86
Lezgis 75
libido 2
lifestyle 126
looting
  of bazaar 50

M

Madraseh-ye Mozaffari 1

Madraseh-ye Salariyeh 8
Mahdi Pahlavan Reza 43
Mahidasht 26, 47, 49
Mahmed Khan 93
Mahmoud Persan 105
Mahmudabad 73
Mahmud Khan Dizli 129, 132
Majid Effendi 129
Majid Soltan 151
Malayer 6, 13, 28, 35, 36, 41, 44, 111, 175
Malek al-Motakallemin 7, 9, 21
malek al-reqab 6
Malek Mohammad 53
Mandali 134
Manzileh 47
Maragheh 24, 57
Marivan 98, 130, 140, 147
Mashdi Hasan 54, 103
Mashhad 79
Mashhad-e Sar 87
Masuleh 90
mateshkeh-khaneh 75
Mazandaran 73, 77, 84, 85, 86, 87, 88, 90, 92, 94
Mehdi Shah 85, 97
Meyamey 78
Minorsky, Vladimir 112
Mir Mehdi Khan 97
Mir Panj Makzimi 57
Mirza Abu'l-Qasem Khan 13, 18
Mirza Ali Khan Qarasuran-bashi 45
Mirza Aqa Khan 82
Mirza Sa`dollah Khan Ilkhani 85
Mirza Yanz 65, 66, 72
Miyan-Band 95
Miyan Darband 70
Miyandoab 24, 60
Miyanj 57
Mo`azed al-Saltaneh 28
Mody, Dr. 175
Mohammad Ali Genel 42
Mohammad Ali Khan Sartip 76
Mohammad Amin Effendi Eitonni 131
Mohammad Baqer Mirza 100, 102

Mohammad Geldi Khan 78
Mohammad Khan Asanlu 28
Mohammad Rashid Beg 129
Mohammad Reza Mirza 19, 108, 181
Mohammad Zakariya al-Idrisi 131, 135
Mohammerah 121, 123, 131, 210
Mohtasham al-Dowleh 28, 39
mojaheds 47, 48, 50, 57, 61, 62, 64, 65, 67, 72
Mojallal al-Saltaneh 42, 57, 61
Mokris 24
Molitor 27, 32, 34, 40, 43, 55, 64, 71
Moqtader al-Dowleh 112
Mosayeb Qoli Khan 62, 74, 76
Moshaver al-Mamalek 145
Moshir al-Divan 7
Moshir al-Mamalek Zanjani 3
Moshir Divan 24
Moshtari 106
Mostafa Chelebi 134
Mostowfi al-Mamalek 109
Mosul 112, 139, 149, 195
Mo'taman al-Mamalek 173
motavalli-bashi 79
Mo`tazed al-Dowleh 27, 36
Mo`tazed al-Mamalek 26
Movaththaq al-Dowleh 5
Mozaffar al-Mamalek Nuri Esfandiyari 88
mozhdeh 76
Mullah Sheikh Hasan 139
Mumiwands 11, 14

N

Naderi Guards infantry regiment 132
Na'eb-Sadr 48
Najaf 118
Nardin 78
Naser al-Din Shah 1
Nasir al-Molk Shirazi 7, 8
Nasir Bakhtiyari 40
Navvab Mohammad Hoseyn Khan 118

Nazar Ali Khan Amra'i 10, 11, 14, 37, 52, 61, 62, 182
Nazem al-Olama Malayeri 36
nazmiyeh 26, 27
Nehavand 10, 11, 12, 13, 15, 16, 18, 29, 41, 111
Ne`matabad 61
newspaper Ashkabad 86
newspaper Iran 1
newspaper Tarbiyat 8
New York Herald 22
Nezam al-Saltaneh 3, 4, 5, 6, 10, 21, 43, 111
Nilavar 100
Nisibin 138
Nizam of Hyderabad 160
Nobaran 31, 36
Nowkandeh 74, 83
Now-Shahr 88
Nowsud 132, 133, 140, 143, 144, 149, 152
Nur 1, 19, 73, 88, 181
Nur al-Dowleh 1, 19, 181

O

Odessa 22, 23, 107
offer of pardon, 1926 155
Olghi 75

P

Pasha Khan 12, 99
pedar-e sag 155
Peel 121, 123, 124
Pishdar Kurds 143
pishkar 8
Poona 115
poorly armed 37
Pravda 146
Prince Reuss 109

Q

Qader Mahmud 139
Qahar Khan 74, 82
Qahar Khan Salar-e Ashja` 74
Qalawands 28
Qalkhani 96
Qaratowreh district 95
qaravol 8
qaravol-khanehha 8
Qaria Chirmagh village 139
Qasr-e Shirin 54
Qavam al-Molk 178
Qazvin 25, 29, 47, 53, 57, 72, 115, 116, 139
Qom 73
Qonbad-e Qabus 74
Quchani Kurds 88

R

Rahman Khan
  beglerbegi 1
Ra'is al-Tojjar 95
ra'is-e qoshun 50
Ramiyan 78
rape 4
raqs-e chubi 8
Rashid al-Soltan 88
Rasht 77, 79, 80, 81, 82, 83, 88, 89, 90, 92, 97, 103
Rassam 33, 34
relief work 175
Reza Khan 21, 57, 60, 94, 103, 119, 120, 123, 126, 127, 133, 134, 135, 147, 151, 201, 202
Reza Khan Afshar 73
Reza Neyrizhi 140
Rokn al-Dowleh 26
Rokn al-Saltaneh 108
Rostam Beg 43
Rostam Khan 48
Rudsar 87, 88, 89
ruffians 26, 46, 48
Russian Bank 22, 38, 101

S

Sabline 90, 101
Sabzavar 78, 79, 80
Sa`d al-Dowleh 76

Sadeq al-Mamalek 100
Sadiq Akram 8, 10
Sadr al-Maham 160
Safar Khan Soltan 48
Sagwands 10
Sahneh 47, 51, 59, 60
Salah al-Din Kalay 88
Salar Arshad Kurdistani 58
Salar Bahador 88
Salar British stooge 178
Salar claims compensation 165
Salar financial claim, 1939, 1946 170
Salar goes to Alexandria 166
Salar Homayun 40, 43, 46
Salar is the Shah, 1926 150
Salar Mokram 47
Salar Moqtader 113
Salar Mozaffar 54, 93, 95, 99, 102, 103, 111
Salarnameh 19
Salar Rashid Kurdistani 48
Salar's companions, 1925 128
Salar threatens rebellion, 1929 159
Salar warned, 1929 160
Samsam al-Mamalek 54, 56, 58, 109
Sanandaj 8, 24, 64, 72
Sanjabi 28, 64, 67
Saqqez 43, 61, 132
Sardar Akram 28, 50, 55, 62
Sardar Bahador 37, 40
Sardar-e As'ad 175
Sardar Jang 25, 35, 38, 97
Sardar Mokarram 10
Sardar Mozaffar 28, 38, 44, 50, 59, 60
Sardar Rashid 130
Sardar Zafar 25, 28, 29, 35, 37, 38
Sardasht 143
Sardashtis 24
Sari 51, 84, 85, 87, 88
Saveh 36, 37, 38
Sayed Khalil Aqa 139
Sayyed Akbar Shah 95
Sayyed Habib, Malek al-Tojjar 38

Sayyed Mohammad Rowzeh-khvan 48
Sayyed Musa 113
Sazonof 107
Schönemann 110
Senneh 6, 25, 62, 64, 66, 92, 94, 96, 97, 98, 112, 132, 139, 140, 142, 143, 144, 176
Sepahdar 84, 88
Seyf al-Dowleh 16, 19, 36, 41, 182
shabnamehs 102
Shafaq-e Sorkh 145
Shah Abdol-Azim 7, 9
Shahrud 73, 74, 76, 78
Shahsavar 88
Shahseven 90
Shanin 143
Sharaf al-Molk Kurdistani 48
Sharafbeyni 99
Sharazor 128
Sharistanak 73
Shehab al-Saltaneh 57, 67
Shehab Nezam 48
Sheikh Ala al-Din 129, 139
Sheikh al-Eslam of Hersin 48
Sheikh Ali 129
Sheikh Ali Asghar 26
Sheikh Hosam al-Din 23, 130
Sheikh Khaz'al 121, 123, 126
Sheikh Mahmud 127, 128, 129, 132, 134, 139, 142, 143, 144, 145, 147, 148
Sheikh Ma'ruf 150
Sheikh Meydan 128, 140
Sheikh Mohdosman 130
Sheikh Said revolt 127
Sho'a' al-Saltaneh 23, 38, 174, 177, 178
Shoja' al-Dowleh 24, 37
Shoja' al-Saltaneh 87
shulooks 125
Sid sayyed 14
Sid Mehdi Khan 14
Simko 129, 131, 140, 144, 147, 149

Soane 54
Soleymaniyeh 111, 129
Soleyman Khan 94, 99
Soltanabad 25, 28, 29, 35, 36, 41, 57, 65, 113
Soltan al-Olama 92
Soltan Kirish Khan 133
Sowj Bulagh 143, 146
Sowjbulaghis 24
starving peasants 175
Surcheh 59
surveillance 101, 106, 137, 138, 140, 153, 154
SU supplying Salar with arms 149
Switzerland 101, 104, 105, 106, 107, 108, 114, 115, 116, 118, 119, 123, 124, 178, 191

T

Tabataba'i 7, 20
Tabriz 1, 15, 24, 33, 37, 39, 61, 90, 141, 152
Taj al-Din 144, 147
talar-e hokumat 2
Talesh 90, 92
Tawilah 129, 140
taxes 15, 22, 24, 26, 36, 41, 46, 74, 82, 86, 87, 98
Thalatheh 13, 19, 52
Thalatheh-Malayer 13
Tikrit 149
Tonakebunis 89
Torab Ali Khan 147
Tuna district 88
Turkish press 146
Tuyserkan 6, 111, 113

U

Ujaimi Pasha Sa`dun 127
undertaking by Salar, 1927 157
unreliability Iranian troops 144
Usanlu 73

V

Vakil al-Molk 24, 42, 94, 143
Vali of Posht-e Kuh 5, 10, 11, 15, 18, 27, 40, 61, 99, 109, 121, 147, 182
Vienna 23
Vilain 55
von Kardorff 109
von Oppenheim, Max 109
von Wangenheim 108
Vothuq al-Dowleh 90, 126

W

Waisseh 129
Walad Begi Jaf 99
Walajir 140
Wilson-Stead, Dr. Blanche 175

Y

Yamut 74, 76, 77, 81, 83, 115
Yamut horse 177
Yar Mohammad Khan 47, 48, 49, 50, 51, 57, 62, 63, 65, 66, 67, 69, 70, 71
Yeprim Khan 37, 47, 49, 58, 59, 65, 67

Z

Zabulinsky 98
Zabulowsky 100, 103
Zafar al-Soltan 12, 14, 18
Zahir al-Dowleh 13, 16, 17, 19
Zakharchinkov 103
Zanjan 2, 3, 25, 28, 36, 57, 90, 92, 94, 101
Zarand 36
Zargham al-Saltaneh 90, 91
Zaru Khans 130
Ziya al-Soltan 57, 67
Zoka al-Molk 124, 126
Zurab 144
Zürich 105, 106

www.ingramcontent.com/pod-product-compliance
Lightning Source LLC
Chambersburg PA
CBHW021944290426
44108CB00012B/953

In this section we will address these questions:

- How did giants of the faith see the Holy Spirit?
- Was there any speaking in tongues in the 1800 years before Pentecostalism emerged?
- How did the Pentecostal understanding come about?
- How did it spread through the world?

First, giants of the faith.

Since the Reformation, there have been many famous revivalists and faith giants: Wesley, Booth, Moody and others, who had wide and dramatic spiritual influence in their day. They would have read about the baptism in the Spirit in the Bible many times. Did they experience it? How did they understand it?

A fascinating journey, filled with intriguing stories and facts, much of which has rarely seen the light of day.